Globalisation, Educational Transformation and Societies in Transition

To our families

Globalisation, Educational Transformation and Societies in Transition

Edited by
Teame Mebrahtu
Michael Crossley
David Johnson

SYMPOSIUM
BOOKS

Symposium Books
PO Box 65 Wallingford, Oxford OX10 0YG, United Kingdom
www.symposium-books.co.uk

Published in the United Kingdom, 2000

ISBN 1 873927 78 9

© Symposium Books, 2000

Typeset in Melior by Symposium Books
Printed and bound in the United Kingdom by Biddles Ltd *www.biddles.co.uk*

Contents

Acknowledgements

The origins of this book stem from an international conference on the theme of Educational Reconstruction and Transformation. This was convened in 1998 by the Centre for International Studies in Education and Graduate School of Education at the University of Bristol, United Kingdom. Selected papers have since been reworked, updated and complemented by additionally commissioned chapters. Our thanks go to all involved in these activities, and especially to Pat O'Brien for support with conference organisation and initial word processing, and to all at Symposium Books in Oxford.

Foreword

We are interested in both how the international is nationalised and how the national is exported in different settings and epochs. (Hannerz & Löfgren, 1994, p. 199)

One paradoxical consequence of the process of globalisation, the awareness of the finitude and boundedness of the plane of humanity, is not to produce homogeneity but to familiarise us with greater diversity, the extensive range of local cultures. (Featherstone, 1993, p. 169)

Globalisation is a slippery concept. On the one hand we have analysts like Hannerz & Löfgren, who argue that through the process of globalisation, our lives are becoming more and more similar. On the other hand, there are those like Featherstone, who argue exactly the opposite; that what globalisation reveals is just how different we all are. In reality, the issue of globalisation is far too complex and multidimensional to be pinned down as either one of these two opposite poles. I suspect that both views are true in part; in some ways we are becoming more similar but at the same time as we are starting to recognise, understand and perhaps appreciate our differences. But the balance between these two states is in a constant state of flux – varying over time, from field to field and across different societies and cultures.

What globalisation is and the impact it is having is therefore hard to to pin down; yet none of us can deny its significance. Even in situations where Featherstone is correct and the result of globalisation is the realisation of just how different we are, it does not mean that globalisation is not a profoundly significant social force to be reckoned with. And nowhere is this more true today than in the field of education. As many of us are only too well aware, the speed with which educational ideas are simply transplanted from one country to another, often with little understanding of their impact on local needs, priorities and traditions, is, to say the least, disturbing. It is particularly disturbing where the transfer is from 'developed' societies to those that are in different stages of 'transition to development'.

To sound such a warning is not to adopt a 'cultural restorationist' point of view; it is not to put up the barriers and oppose all internationally driven change in principle. Rather, it is to argue that all of us with an interest in education, and as a matter of urgency, need to develop a far deeper understanding of the processes involved in globalisation. And this is why I particularly welcome this book. In it the editors have gathered together an impressive range of contributors who write from a wide variety of different points of view. They bring to their contributions experience from many different parts of the world and from different institutional settings. But what all of them have in common is a recognition of the importance of globalisation in educational policy and a desire to contribute to a deeper understanding of its origins and its impact, particularly on 'societies in transition'.

The breadth of this book is therefore impressive but so too is the fact that it is written with such a common purpose; these characteristics mark it out as unique within the field of education. As such, I believe that it makes a very important contribution to our understanding of the complex global forces that, as we face the new millennium, will come to shape the lives of us all.

John Furlong
University of Bristol

References

Featherstone, M. (1993) Global and Local Cultures, in J. Bird, B. Curtis, T. Putnam & L. Tickner (Eds) *Mapping the Futures: local cultures, global change*. London: Routledge.

Hannerz, U. & Löfgren, O. (1994) The Nation in the Global Village, *Cultural Studies*, 8, pp. 198–207.

INTRODUCTION

Educational Development and Social Transformation in a Global Economy

TEAME MEBRAHTU, MICHAEL CROSSLEY & DAVID JOHNSON

The closing decade of the twentieth century saw major social, political and economic transformations on a global level. These developments, combined with increasingly rapid and far-reaching advances in the nature and impact of information and communications technologies (ICTs), have had a powerful influence upon all societies and cultures worldwide. Amidst this intensification of globalisation, however, many communities are ever more forcefully acknowledging their distinctive characteristics and celebrating their cultural differences.

In this turbulent era, societies that have undergone particularly rapid political, economic and social change have a great deal in common – and their collective experience offers much from which we can learn at the outset of the twenty-first century. The analysis of such societies in transition and their efforts to transform educational policy and practice is a focus of this volume. This is especially timely as we move into the 'global century', as the pace of technological change continues to escalate, and as the importance of culture and identity (be it national, local or individual) is increasingly valued as an integral part of the development process. Economic and management imperatives have dominated attention in recent decades, but international agencies such as UNESCO (1998), and writers such as Mazrui (1990), are increasingly acknowledging that 'cultural forces' deserve greater attention if we are to understand and deal creatively with the impact of globalisation and 'go beyond macroeconomics to shape our collective destiny' (James Wolfensohm, cited in UNESCO, 1998).

9

While the term 'societies in transition' is often used in the literature to refer to former communist countries, in this volume we adopt a wider usage of this, and of the related concept of educational transformation. Like McLeish & Phillips (1998), we are concerned with countries that have experienced rapid transformation in their educational systems following political transition from authoritarian rule to democratic government. We are, however, also interested in the impact of the processes of globalisation and geopolitical change upon the ongoing transitions of post-colonial societies; and upon the implications of the analysis for related international agency policy and practice. The latter is strategically important because of the increased influence of international agendas upon educational development worldwide.

The contributors to the volume are drawn from a wide range of professional and academic backgrounds. Collectively, they represent national governments, international agencies, research bodies, policy-makers, researchers and practitioners. All have extensive first-hand experience of the issues and contexts that they deal with. Some report upon original field research, some present wide-ranging and theoretically informed analyses, two contributions represent politically inspired perspectives, and others reflect more directly upon professional and practical experience.

While most of the studies deal explicitly with the thematic concepts of globalisation, educational transformation and social transition, the specific national contexts considered in depth include Estonia, Poland, Germany, South Africa, Eritrea, Belize, Brazil, Hong Kong, Macau, Egypt, Nigeria and Ghana. The analyses generated include both insider and outsider perspectives on the multiple dimensions of the processes of educational development and social transformation in our rapidly globalising world. In broad scope, the collective work highlights the tensions between powerful international social and education agendas, and efforts to improve the quality and relevance of educational provision in vastly different sociocultural contexts. The ever-increasing speed of socio-political, economic and technological change has greatly intensified such tensions – making educational transformation ever more imperative, but problematic, in, and beyond, societies currently classified as 'in transition'.

Indeed, reflecting the postmodern critique of social science theorising (Øyen, 1990; Paulston, 1999), there is much in this volume to challenge such categorisations – and to emphasise the importance of increased context sensitivity in educational and social development – if we are to be more successful in promoting worthwhile and sustainable innovation and transformation in practice. Certainly, the arguments presented here challenge the uncritical international transfer of educational policy and practice. The volume also demonstrates the renewed pertinence of comparative and international research that recognises the dilemmas generated by global influences upon educational development at all levels. As Watson points out in his chapter, 'the comparativist's role has become both more important but also more difficult'.

Returning to the basic themes of the studies, McLeish's (1998) work, and that of the Oxford Group from which it is derived, provides a valuable conceptual framework upon which we, and the reader, are able to build. Firstly, McLeish argues that terms like 'educational change' and 'reform' do not capture the essence of the link between political, social and economic transition and the radical democratisation of education systems. However, educational systems do not change simply because there is a change in national government. Factors that spark both 'macro-level' and 'micro-level' transitions often consist of a complex interplay of global and local political, economic and social forces – including the influence of international development assistance agencies. The implications of such issues are evident in a number of chapters reviewed here – indicating the relevance of the Oxford model for analysis across a wider range of education systems and contexts than considered to date.

Complementing the themes we have raised, two wide-ranging and well-informed chapters dealing directly with globalisation, by Hallak and Watson, help to develop further theoretical perspectives that are useful in interpreting the subsequent studies. These contributions are followed by a group of chapters focused upon the dramatic transformations in eastern and central Europe, chapters attending to transition in a complex range of post-colonial contexts, and three development policy oriented studies that have major implications for international agencies involved in educational and social transformation.

The chapter by Hallak comprises three parts. Hallak regards the conclusions and recommendations of the Jomtien Conference on Education for All, and the Delors Commission on Education for the Twenty-first Century, as sources of inspiration for those who are concerned with the effects of globalisation on educational policies and reforms. In the first part, which deals with the characteristic features of globalisation and its consequences, this chapter defines 'globalisation' as an essentially economic phenomenon. It identifies and discusses key aspects of the six dimensions of globalisation affecting all societies everywhere. The first major feature of globalisation identified is the economic and financial dimension. This is seen to have spread so rapidly that all factors of production are now crossing national boundaries.

The second dimension seen to stimulate the pace of globalisation is the rapid expansion of scientific and technological innovation. The third is identified as the interdependence of globalisation's economic, technological, geopolitical and sociocultural dimensions, all of which blend – sometimes uneasily – with each other to weave a 'kind of technological web' over the planet.

Globalisation, Hallak goes on to argue, is supported by dominant socio-economic models and mass communication networks which are difficult to resist, and which are affecting seriously the organisation of human societies. This argument is well substantiated by focusing on three major consequences of globalisation. These include the erosion of the power of the nation state by regional entities like the European Union, by subnational entities and by transnational companies. The second consequence of globalisation is that it generates both cultural 'diversification' and simultaneous cultural 'standardisation'. The third is the segmentation and division of societies and the entire international community. This dichotomisation process is best highlighted by the emergence of three types of players described by Hallak as those who 'globalise', those who are 'globalised' and those who are 'left out by globalisation'. Combined together, these three consequences of the 'process' of globalisation are generating a reaction which Hallak portrays as 'social schizophrenia' and individual loneliness and sadness in an increasingly antagonistic, unjust and fragmented world.

Part two of the chapter dwells on the relationship between education and globalisation. This warns the reader to exercise modesty and humility when discussing the effects of globalisation on educational reforms and changes. This advice is proffered because of the varying assumptions people make about (a) the extent to which education systems are being shaped by globalisation and (b) the kind of policy reforms which need to be adopted to address the consequences of globalisation.

Part three, the longest and perhaps the most important part of the chapter, discusses five areas of concern for education policy-makers. These deal with the goals of education, the structure of the system, the educators, the assessment of outcomes and the role of government.

Educational goals are seen to be an area of great concern in the era of globalisation because the latter has contributed to the weakening of the nation and the family, and to the breaking up of societies by aggravating conflict between groups of different identities. Given this trend, educational institutions have the responsibility to 'rebuild' the social link; to engender equal participation in the development of societies through the teaching of universal values such as tolerance and human rights, and by promoting respect for others and for their cultures.

Teaching and certification are areas of concern because teachers need to be trained how to teach in a changing world, how to become brokers in the information society and how to provide society with an efficient and effective certification system. Hallak warns against the dangers of 'economism' and calls for the formulation and implementation of educational policies that reconcile local and global demands with those of the state and those of the new education protagonists (non-governmental organisations [NGOs], communities and the private sector).

Convinced of the significant role education will play in an increasingly global world, the chapter concludes by urging national and international decision-makers to mobilise greater resources for education, to enable it to achieve its aims in optimal conditions and to meet the challenges raised by globalisation.

Watson's chapter, entitled 'Globalisation, Educational Reform and Language Policy in Transitional Societies', is also subdivided into three major parts. Part one introduces the reader to definitions of key terms, and warns against the danger of categorising states into watertight compartments of 'developed' or 'developing', 'transitional' or 'transformational' in an era of rapid change. Whilst stressing that comparative analysis at a macro-level is bound to be superficial, this section also argues that it is possible to identify certain common features that link all societies, irrespective of their geographical location. These features, which contribute to the process of globalisation, include the rapidity of change, the weakening of the power of the nation state, and the increased impact of global economic frameworks. Moreover, on the grounds that the poor in all countries are the most severely affected, this analysis challenges Fukuyama's (1992) thesis which hails globalisation as benign and as a triumph of 'liberal democracy'.

Part two dwells on three key areas of reform and compares the impact of globalisation in different regions of the world. The first area of financial reform, which has been spearheaded by the multilateral organisations like the World Bank and the International Monetary Fund (IMF), is currently operating in different countries at different levels of transition. The significance of this is highlighted by comparing and contrasting the varied and at times opposing rationales behind moves towards 'greater decentralisation' and the 'financing of education locally'. The content of what should be taught, and how, is the second area of reform addressed. The message which comes across loud and clear is that different states – transitional or transformational – follow different curriculum reform routes for complex and at times contradictory reasons. The third area, which deals with the medium of instruction, is characterised by trends towards the rejection of the use of a language of oppression (e.g. Russian, Portuguese, Amharic or Afrikaans), the revival of national/ethnic languages (e.g. in the former Soviet Union) and the growing use of English as a global language.

The final part of this chapter identifies six consequences of the rapid process of globalisation which are likely to pose challenges for the future. These deal with issues of quality and quality control in education; inspection; the balance between the private and the public sector; ethnic nationalism; the impact of globalisation on the development of flexible teaching materials; and growing inequality between and within societies.

The major premise of Elsner's chapter is that five decades of communist rule have left a legacy of social, political, economic and educational problems in Poland as well as in other central and eastern European countries. The process of transition from the old highly controlled education system into a more democratic one, has, Elsner argues, proven difficult and at times painful.

Some of the characteristic features of the Polish education system in transition that are discussed include (a) the implementation of a new national curriculum; (b) the decentralisation of the administrative system; (c) the elimination of the state monopoly of schooling; and (d) the loosening of the uniform school structure. Elsner then goes on to compare and contrast trends in the new education system with Caldwell & Spinks's (1992) classification of 10 mega-trends in western European education systems, and examines the extent to which the latter are relevant to the Polish context.

Using a comparative analysis of these trends, the chapter contrasts the features of 'Homo Sovieticus' with those of 'Homo Europeacus'. Elsner then makes three major recommendations. One of these is that the new educational system, which is emerging from the ashes of the old communist model, should correspond to the modern needs of a democratic society. The second recommendation is that too much emphasis should not be placed on implementing western European solutions at the expense of ignoring characteristically Polish ones. The third, and perhaps the most practical, is that Poland must direct its attention to the future of the teaching profession and to the training and retraining of teachers if the educational reforms that are to be put in place are to be effectively implemented.

Streitwieser also focuses upon practitioners in his study of the attitudes of former East German teachers towards the 'West German system' that they have inherited. This is a unique study of a distinctive window of transitional time in its own right – and one that the author claims is most appropriate for an independent outsider to pursue.

The chapter by Märja & Jõgi outlines the historical and political circumstances underlying Estonia's transition to democracy and the consequent challenges for its education system. The five 'periods of political, ideological, cultural, technological and social changes' in Estonia discussed by Märja & Jõgi are interesting parallels to the models of transition developed by the Oxford research group (see McLeish & Phillips, 1998). This sets out six phases: a pre-phase, which is characterised by an anti-authoritarian climate, the threat to prevailing ideology and eventual ideological collapse; this is followed by a period of uncertainty (phase I), which leads to the seizure of power through national elections (phase II), and local elections (phase III). The adoption of educational legislation marks a period of 'macro-level transition' (phase IV), followed eventually by 'micro-level transition' or implementation of policy at the school level (phase V).

In the case of Estonia, Märja & Jõgi identify the mid-1970s to mid-1980s as a period characterised by economic and political stagnation, which posed a serious threat to the prevailing political ideology at the time. The mid-1980s to 1991, characterising the era of *glasnost* and *perestroika* in the Soviet Union, are seen as a period of national awakening and struggle for independence in Estonia. The democratic state emerged in 1991 and the period between 1991 and 1994 marked a time for rebuilding and transformation. The authors then go on to show how Estonia is responding to the challenge of translating democratic policy into meaningful gains for the Estonian population. They discuss the role of adult education and demonstrate the powerful influence of social movements in educational transformation.

There is no doubt that the processes of political transition are likely to spark periods of educational transition, or put another way, that the 'dynamic for educational change is politically controlled' (Salter & Trapper, 1981). This link between the politics of education and the transformation of the educational system is also illustrated by N'zimande & Mathieson in their chapter titled 'Educational Transformation in South Africa's Transition to Democracy'. The chapter argues that the ongoing process of educational transition needs to be understood in the context of the broader political, social and economic transformations both within South Africa itself as well as internationally. N'zimande & Mathieson outline the tensions and competing ideological positions within South Africa's first Government of National Unity and show how these impact on the nature of both macro-level (policy and legislation) and micro-level (implementation of educational policy) actions. The authors then outline some of the advances made by the African National Congress (ANC) in transforming the educational system, but also the constraints and dilemmas which riddle the process. The critical issues for N'zimande & Mathieson are autonomy versus the state, establishing the new democracy, education and nation-building, the state and the market, equity versus quality and elitism versus massification.

The chapter by Hailemariam provides the reader with an overview of the history, geography, demography, economy and the education system of the neophyte state, Eritrea. This highlights the transformation of Eritrea from a peripheral and dependent Ethiopian province into a fully-fledged and self-reliant nation – a process accompanied by political, economic, sociocultural and educational reconstruction. Hailemariam then discusses the nature of these challenges of educational reconstruction and transformation in independent Eritrea. These include the negative impact of the legacies of war and neglect; the problem of integrating theory and practice; the need to increase access as well as improve quality and equity; the need to share the financing of education between the Government and the local communities; the need to synchronise the roles of central and regional administrative bodies; and the need to produce well-trained Eritrean citizens who are also sensitive to their global responsibilities.

In the face of powerful global forces, small states such as Estonia, Eritrea and Belize are especially vulnerable to the influence of international agendas. Thompson & Crossley's critical analysis of the teacher education component of the Belize Primary Education Development Project demonstrates this; but also shows how increased local ownership led to significant modifications to externally-inspired project proposals. The Belizean successes and challenges documented here can serve as an example to other small states involved in development agency partnerships designed to promote sector-wide educational transformation.

The capacity of social movements to transform national policy in education, as identified earlier, is developed further by Groves & Johnson. The central concern of this chapter is to trace the response in Brazil, both legislative and in the provision of services, to the conditions of street and working children. The chapter begins by outlining a number of phases in Brazil's transition from military rule to democratic government. It shows how in each phase, the response to the education of street and working children, through legislation and educational provision, is a reflection of the prevailing ideological and political conditions. In a somewhat different conceptualisation of the Oxford model, Groves & Johnson show that the tensions between macro-level and micro-level educational transitions are present throughout a country's transformational process. The Oxford model is in danger of suggesting that educational transitions are linear outcomes of political transformations, whereas it is argued here that the tensions between macro-level and micro-level transition are recursive. Another crucial departure is the point that the progression from macro-level to micro-level is not simply an attempt to turn progressive policy into progressive practice over a period of time. A useful illustration of this point lies in the fact that between 1960 and 1970, when Brazil was ruled by a military regime, it consciously adopted conflicting macro- and micro-level policies and practices. The military government passed two major laws to protect the welfare of street children. However, the laws gave the military and police wide powers to intervene in the lives of children and adolescents in 'irregular' circumstances, and in practice, the policy criminalised the gatherings of street children, effectively repressing informal learning and recreational activities (Dewees & Klees, 1995).

The chapter by Bray provides a comparative analysis of globalisation, educational and colonial transition in Hong Kong and Macau. The analysis attends to the subtleties of the relationship between both global and local issues by showing 'how Hong Kong and Macau are similar but different from other parts of the world, and second, how they are similar but different from each other'. While the colonial transitions of Hong Kong and Macau are part of the global process of decolonisation, they have each followed different patterns – and challenged pre-existing models of decolonisation. As the author points out, 'The global forces of change have still been evident among the remnants [of empire] but have produced different patterns in different places and at different points in history'.

One powerful mechanism of influencing shifts in policy and interventions in practice is through donor-funded projects. Kiernan's chapter in this volume introduces the development assistance section and outlines the extent to which external donor agencies set the educational agenda in nations in transition. Kiernan argues that not only do donor agencies seek to influence the educational policy debate in many such contexts, but that they influence the political, ideological and economic basis of these countries. If we employ the Oxford model of transition discussed earlier, the legislative frameworks that are adopted in macro-level transitions are often imposed by external forces. Indeed, there are many other studies that highlight the strategies donor agencies employ to persuade countries to undergo political and economic transitions (see, for example, Jones, 1992; Watson, 1996). Most often this is achieved through the imposition of conditionalities. An interesting alternative view in this respect is that structural change and reform is also induced through micro-level change, often in the form of donor-assisted projects. In this way, micro-level transition can precede macro-level transitions.

Looking more carefully at the notion of micro-level transitions, it is clear that they are almost always extremely lengthy processes. Further, it is difficult to know when micro-level transition may be 'completed' as systems are dynamic and respond to change at local, national and global levels. Given that the global and national impetus on political and educational systems will always be present, the transitional process is, in some respects, always ongoing. The chapter by Smith, therefore, poses a fundamental question for development assistance agencies and for readers of this volume. This is: how do we measure when change has been successful? The implications of this question for the evaluation of educational transition are enormous. Smith argues that the concept of success is often contradictory. In one sense, it could mean that a project is achieving what it set out to do. Thus, a project's success may be measured against a very specific set of criteria. What is less clear is when success is measured in terms of 'favourable outcome'. Favourable outcome might mean a number of things, and depends in part on the ideological and geopolitical positions which underlie donor assistance strategies. According to Smith, the perspective on whether change is

17

seen as successful or unsuccessful is often that of the donor agency. This can undermine local priorities and our sense of where the transitional process is heading.

Allsop's final chapter reiterates concerns raised throughout the book relating to the need for greater local determination of internationally supported development assistance initiatives. He uses direct professional experience of educational projects in Egypt, Nigeria and Ghana to demonstrate how increased participation of local personnel is essential if international agencies are to improve the relevance and success of the development initiatives in which they are involved. This challenges the uncritical application of global models and the 'purveyors of recipe-like approaches', and draws attention to the importance of contextual and cultural factors in the processes of educational development and social transformation.

In conclusion, while the forces that combine to prompt educational transformations and transitions vary considerably from context to context, it is clear that global factors are playing an increasingly influential role everywhere. Comparative and international studies, as reported here, are especially helpful in revealing the complexities of such developments and the cross-cultural implications for policy and practice. If the quality and relevance of educational change is to be improved, and the translation of innovative policy into practice is to be more successful, transformations must also be effected throughout the professional cultures of those involved in the educational development process in the future.

With this in mind, many distinctive lessons can be learned from those systems and societies currently undergoing dramatic social, economic and political transformation; but persistent tensions between local and global agendas and priorities stand out most clearly in all cases. Dealing with these tensions requires both an awareness of global trends and a working understanding of local sociocultural and educational priorities. This is also true for a much broader range of post-colonial societies undergoing sustained change, as many of our contributors point out.

Recognition of this is invaluable in its own right, but it also helps point to ways in which the professional culture of development assistance itself can change. Some indicators are encouraging in this respect, including policy statements calling for participatory change strategies and new development partnerships. As we have shown, promising initiatives are also beginning to be visible, but this process is both a political and professional one that requires considerable cultural sensitivity, theoretical reconceptualisation, mutual respect and trust (Crossley, 1999). Translating such principles into general working practice, therefore, deserves increased bridge-building between agencies, paradigms and personnel, and sustained attention from all partners in a joint venture. It also demands further critical analysis of the very processes and dilemmas of globalisation that are considered here.

References

Caldwell, B. J. & Spinks, J. M. (1992) *Leading the Self-managing School*. London: Falmer Press.

Crossley, M. (1999) Reconceptualising Comparative and International Education, *Compare*, 29, pp. 249–267.

Dewees, A. & Klees, S. (1995) Social Movements and the Transformation of National Policy: street and working children in Brazil, *Comparative Education Review*, 39, pp. 76–100.

Fukuyama, F. (1992) *The End of History and the Last Man*. Harmondsworth: Penguin.

Jones, P. (1992) *World Bank Financing of Education*. London: Routledge.

Mazrui, A. A. (1990) *Cultural Forces in World Politics*. London: James Currie.

McLeish, E. A. (1998) Introduction: processes of educational transition in countries moving from authoritarian rule to democratic government, in E. A. McLeish & D. Phillips (Eds) *Processes of Transition in Education Systems*. Oxford: Symposium Books.

McLeish, E. A. & Phillips, D. (1998) (Eds) *Processes of Transition in Education Systems*. Oxford: Symposium Books.

Øyen, E. (Ed.) (1990) *Comparative Methodology. Theory and Practice in International Social Research*. London: Sage

Paulston, R. G. (1999) Mapping Comparative Education after Postmodernity, *Comparative Education Review*, 43, pp. 438–463.

Salter, B. & Trapper, T. (1981) *Education Politics and the State: the theory and practice of educational change*. London: Grant McIntyre.

UNESCO (1998) *Our Creative Diversity. Report of the World Commission on Culture and Development*. Paris: UNESCO.

Watson, K. (Ed.) (1996) World Bank's Education Sector Review: priorities and strategies for education, Special Issue of *International Journal of Educational Development*, 16.

Globalisation and its Impact on Education

JACQUES HALLAK

Introduction

Since the World Conference on Education for All (Jomtien, Thailand, 1990) and, more recently, International Commission on Education for the Twenty-first Century, chaired by Jacques Delors, there has emerged a rather broadly shared consensus on (i) the issues facing education systems today; (ii) the aims of education; and (iii) the policies offered to address the challenges to education.

For students of the development of education, the recommendations inspired by Jomtien are familiar: there is a need to address the issues of 'access', 'quality', 'relevance', 'equality', 'gender' and 'efficiency' of education. At the same time, it is suggested that policy-makers, planners, decision-makers, educators and managers should adopt a change in their approach to education; namely, from state and foreign agency concerns, to more 'ownership', 'participation', 'collaboration' and 'mobilisation' of all protagonists of education; from systems to institutions and schools; from input to resource allocation outcome criteria; from higher levels to basic education; from a teacher- to a learner-centred education; and from traditional systems of delivery with excessive attention paid to memorisation, to more active and participatory teaching–learning strategies.

More recently, the Delors Report (1996) to UNESCO, concluding the work of the International Commission, proposed a highly dense, rich and comprehensive agenda of aims which, by implication, should determine several features of education systems of the coming decades. They are: learning to be, learning to know, learning to do, and learning to live together.

Even if, during the Jomtien Conference and the deliberations of the Delors Commission, the globalisation phenomenon was not – prima facie

– the only and main concern of the participants, in both cases, a great deal of attention was paid to the effect of globalisation on the reform and reconstruction of education. Therefore, their conclusions and recommendations should be regarded as sources of inspiration for those who are concerned with the effects of globalisation on educational policies and reforms.

Part I. Main Features of Globalisation

Globalisation is a much talked-about term today and we cannot deny the fact that it is a phenomenon that is greatly affecting society. Globalisation is, in fact, a combination of the free exchange of goods, services and capital. It dates far back in history, with the development of international trade (the 'silk road', the '*villes-monde*' of the Middle Ages). During the second half of the nineteenth century, it was highlighted by the Industrial Revolution as a result of colonial exploitation. The continuous modernisation of the international exchange process during the twentieth century and its ratification through international agreements (the General Agreement on Tariffs and Trade [GATT] in 1947 for example) have maintained and given pace to an increasing globalisation of society. However, for the past few years, we have observed an acceleration in this trend, which is characterised by three essential factors. The first is the extent of the economic freedom, which is spreading worldwide; the second is the increase in technological innovation, especially in the communications field; and the third is the interdependence between these different dimensions. However, it is, above all, the consequences that these factors have on globalisation that makes it so influential in the organisation of our society.

1. The Three Dimensions of Globalisation

1.1 The economic and financial dimension

Globalisation is above all an economic phenomenon that is spreading worldwide. Firstly, it is spreading geographically; in the nineteenth century, global economic activity was focused mainly in developing countries [1] and on the edges of non-developed areas. Today, millions of Chinese, Russians, Indians, Italians and Guatemalans work in a globalised economy. However, it has only just begun: in nations where economic growth is strong, such as the Asian 'Tiger' countries, only a small percentage of the population contributes to national production. Secondly, the globalisation phenomenon is spreading qualitatively: at the beginning of the century, only goods, services and capital crossed borders. Today, all factors of production are being exchanged: technology, the norms and means of production, labour and, especially since deregulation, finance. This allows the economy to have a global economic space at its disposal today, in terms of the goods and services market, the employment market, the capital market, etc. This in turn urges those who control economic theories (and theorists), company strategies and even economic policies to take into account all aspects of this evolution in a global sense.

1.2 The scientific and technological dimension

The rapid expansion of scientific and technological innovation in the fields of communication, biotechnology and microelectronics stimulates the forces of globalisation. Technological innovation facilitates exchanges, speeding up production and allowing the sharing of ideas, goods and services worldwide.

Technological progress in the communications field has produced the most spectacular and visible feature of globalisation. Where it used to take days and weeks, cumbersome infrastructures and physical difficulties for images and messages to be transmitted around the world, it now only takes a fraction of a second. It is, of course, all about an integrated communications network, which affects the living standards, and the political and cultural conditions of all societies. The communication society has offered users multiple options in the form or volume of information. Users can access information at any time, choosing when it is convenient to exchange information and with whom. However, faced with this extent of choice, a tendency towards uniformity is developing. This move towards uniformity can be explained by the fact that – while expanding – the number of users remains a small minority of the world population, which is mainly located in one part of the world. Some people regard the development of uniformity through the language of communication – English – as a progression towards an improvement in human understanding and a global society. However, some observers believe that it does not make authenticity of expression easy, nor does it allow an equal capacity for communication among different linguistic groups.

1.3 The interdependence of the dimensions of globalisation

The main characteristic of globalisation is the interdependence of its different dimensions. Technological innovation has facilitated the increase in capital flow to such an extent that it has created a stock market which functions 24 hours a day by moving from place to place and increasing the volume of capital to such a point that it has weakened economic regions, affecting a large number of countries. The increase in economic flows concerning all the factors of production has led to a growing interdependence of companies. This is tending to lead to a globalised world, a global society that must continuously produce new forms of social organisation, and assure the production of new knowledge and expertise. This is imposed on all structures of society, which must constantly adapt if they want to keep up with global evolution. A kind of huge technological web is being woven over the planet, covering all aspects of human activity. For instance, at an economic level, new norms of organisation of economic activity are generated every time new models of production based on knowledge and innovation are discovered. Then at a social level, these discoveries in turn bring about new forms of social organisation and vigorously question its types of regulation.

2. The Consequences of Globalisation on Social Organisation

These globalisation characteristics seriously affect the organisation of human societies; thus, we have to rethink the needs of our societies in order to meet them better.

2.1 The geopolitical consequences

The increase in flows around the world presents what we can call the fluidity of boundaries. Borders are usually drawn to define the territories of a nation state. When borders lose their strength, the authorities of the nation state experience the erosion of their capacity for action. We all observe the gradual dislocation of governments' room for manoeuvre in terms of industrial, monetary and fiscal policy. Consequently, even national social policy seems to depend heavily on the world economic situation, global tendencies and market needs. Alongside this, and as a consequence, three levels of political organisation are developing. At the supra-national level, governments are transferring part of their sovereignty to regional entities (e.g. Association of Southeast Asian Nations [ASEAN], Commonwealth of Independent States [CIS], European Union [EU] Mercado Común del Sol [MERCOSUR] and Southern African Development Community [SADC]) that manage economic, social or political areas. At the infra-national level, states are rivalled by their own subnational entities through decentralisation measures. At the third or national level, states have to adjust to 'private concerns' of transnational companies. Multinational expansion of national companies in the industrial or financial sector has been necessary in order to increase the competitiveness of the national economy. At these three levels, civil society unavoidably emerges as a principal player in the definition of social organisation: the non-governmental organisations (NGOs) as partner and essential link for international organisations, associations at the heart of society that take charge of activities that meet the communities' needs.

2.2 The cultural dimension

From a cultural perspective, globalisation produces two contradictory phenomena: standardisation and diversification. Standardisation of eating habits, clothes and cultural products tends to produce growing similarities in the living conditions of societies. On the other hand, diversification strives to preserve the multiple facets of society by promoting access to the diverse features of world heritage. Moreover, faced with the wave of standardisation of lifestyles, communication, languages and cultures, which tends to even out idiosyncrasies of different population groups, there is resistance in the economic and political field, as in the cultural field, in an effort to preserve the identities and defend the rights of minorities. However, resistance is not always effective. Globalisation is supported by dominant models and mass communication networks that are difficult to resist. The struggle to preserve identities therefore tends to be aggressive and violent. The progress of globalisation seems to generate a reaction, which we could call social schizophrenia, and individual loneliness and sadness, in an increasingly antagonistic, unjust and fragmented world. Globalisation therefore tends to encourage the emergence of isolated societies that take refuge in traditional or local, regional, ethnic or religious groups and thus to consolidate the process of resistance to uniformity and standardisation.

2.3 The segmentation of countries and societies

The phenomena that have presented themselves are global, that is to say, the whole planet is and will be affected. However, this does not mean to say that every country will react in the same way. Globalisation is highlighted by the emergence of three types of players: those who globalise, those who are globalised and those who are left out by globalisation. Those who globalise concentrate on capital, resources, knowledge and the control of information. Those who are globalised are 'information poor' and 'knowledge poor' workers and consumers. Those who are left out have little or no access to information and knowledge, with no absorptive capacity as consumers and no relevance to production. This segmentation and division of both societies and the entire international community is becoming increasingly accentuated. These three types of individuals and groups exist in every country: those who globalise are, and will probably remain, a minority, but society will be affected by globalisation according to the strength of its social cohesion and the degree of integration of the institutions that belong to it.

Part II. Globalisation and Education: some precautions

When reflecting on the effects of globalisation on education reforms and changes, we should not overlook the fact that in the short term – with some exceptions – the perceived impact of globalisation on what is happening in the classroom, the school, or in the education process is likely to be minimal. The main reason is the remoteness – if not the absence – of any ties between educational institutions and other social institutions more directly linked with globalisation: the sectors of banking and finance, transport and communication, cultural industries, mass media, other producers and traders of goods and services. All this being said, like the deterioration of the terms of trade in the past, the collapse of the stock exchange in some countries today will have disastrous effects on their education systems.

Moreover, predicting the effects of globalisation on education reform is fraught with difficulties due to the many interdependent components of education and the fact that even the smallest disturbance of a system can have major long-term repercussions. Therefore, any statement on the effects of globalisation should be made with a great deal of moderation and should be interpreted with some scepticism. In this respect, I would like to add some caveats dealing with the effects that the globalisation process may have on education reforms.

There are at least two ways of looking at the effects of globalisation on education. The first is to what extent education systems are being 'shaped' by globalisation or, in prospective terms, what are the changes likely to affect education systems in the coming decades resulting from globalisation? The second is what kind of policy reforms should be adopted to address the consequences of globalisation? Should policy-makers accept globalisation as reality and an unavoidable trend that societies should adapt to; and is the purpose of educational reform to take into account and draw benefits from the positive social consequences of globalisation while maintaining within tolerable limits the negative consequences of globalisation?

To take the first point, in all societies, whether advanced or backward, at any point in time, a variety of patterns of education systems co-exist: poor or wealthy conditions of schooling; traditional or high-tech delivery systems; a diversity of teaching–learning strategies from rote memorisation to active child-centred education, etc. When referring to the links between globalisation and education, we are discussing changes only in the parts of the education system that might be exposed to globalisation. Inertia in the implementation of educational change is generally great – changes in education are slow – while, at the same time, the globalisation trend tends to be moving very rapidly. Therefore, it is safe to assume that (i) mismatches and discrepancies will prevail between the expected impact of globalisation on education and the actual changes occurring in education as a result of globalisation; and (ii) statements about expected changes and proposed reforms for education in an increasingly globalised world are not forecasts of reforms or changes, but should be interpreted as part of a framework for educational policies having some consistency with the trend of globalisation.

Taking the second point, a great deal depends on the assumptions made about the future of globalisation. Will the present trends continue peacefully and for how long? Will globalisation generate political and social resistance and turmoil, consequently leading to a 'swing in the pendulum' back to more controlled movement of people, financial resources, material resources and, as seen in some countries, of ideas? Are we assuming a Huntington or a Fukuyama [2], or a scenario that promotes the capacity of individuals to remain masters of their own destiny?

In what follows, I will refrain from stating the desirable or likely evolution of globalisation. Assuming the present trend of globalisation continues and its consequences become more tolerable, I will select five areas of concern for education policy-makers and propose some 'normative and prescriptive' views on how they could be addressed.

Part III. Education Reform: the tasks ahead

The five areas of concern are: the goals of education, the structure of the system, the educators, the assessment of outcomes, and the role of government and other protagonists.

1. Educational Goals: new emphasis

1.1 What globalisation highlights

(i) The loss of standards for individuals. The nation, the family and world of work are institutions that contribute to social cohesion. Their weakening by globalisation produces distressed individuals, unprepared to confront challenges, who lack faith in society and their future.

(ii) The breaking up of societies. Although certain elements of globalisation have enabled some societies to speed up their development process, the globalised world remains, for the most part, deeply unequal. Globalisation engenders exclusion, the development of economic and social differences, aggravation of conflicts between groups of different identities, the dislocation of societies and the dissipation of commitments to universal solidarity. At the same time, questioning of life's real aims, which could address these challenges, is blurred and biased by purely economic concerns.

(iii) The unequal participation in the development of societies. The unequal participation in the development of societies is particularly worrying at the economic level. Today, work is the main factor for social

integration, but the world of work is going through a fundamental and irreversible change. In order to understand it, we must specify that the concept of work has two actualities: 'work-action' and 'work-employment'. On the one hand, work is related to the 'doing' of an action and, on the other hand, work is made visible through employment, that is to say, a socially and legally defined task, which is considered as the principal factor for social integration. The current upheavals concern two actualities: employment-work becomes a rare commodity which contributes to the exclusion of a growing part of the population from the production of wealth as well as consumption; on the contrary, action-work tends to take on a more heterogeneous form that is necessary for civil society. Today we are happy to undergo change. But, we must accept the fact that employment-work will no longer be the only factor of social integration: the development of societies will take place through other forms of work-action with hybrid aims such as associative activities, political participation and personal investment in the definition of interest and common objectives.

1.2 What education goals highlight

Globalisation is not a radical revolution that is going to completely transform education: its impact will be more an emphasis of certain trends. Firstly, we should remind ourselves that education must not lose sight of its traditional basic goals: reading, writing, arithmetic, knowledge and skills development; in short, everything required to live and to communicate with the environment, everything that a person needs to participate in the life of his/her society. Secondly, faced with the consequences of globalisation on individuals and societies, other goals become relevant for educational reform.

More autonomy for individuals in a society of knowledge. Society must aim to allow every individual to develop freely. The individual will have to find his/her own points of reference in a society that is changing constantly and that generates short-lived values. It is therefore imperative that he/she succeed in delivering himself/herself from set types of stereotypical activity, both psychologically and economically, and discover a taste for improvisation, invention and discovery. School must give pupils the capacity to acquire the relevant knowledge and interpret new values that will, in turn, guarantee them the ability to remain up to date with the evolution of their environment. If a concerted effort is not made to strengthen the autonomy of the individual, then human integrity is under threat from influences that are replacing traditional standards.

Rebuilding the social link. It is through education – at school and in non-formal environments – that the desire to live together, and an understanding of the resulting benefits, are acquired by learning to work in teams, developing individual abilities, learning to listen to others and the events which surround us, and understanding our economic, social and political environment whether at a national or global level. Education should be the catalyst for the desire to live together at the heart of the same society and in the same 'global village', through the teaching of universal values such as tolerance and human rights, the diversity of culture, respect for others and for our environment, through searching for the right balance between society's concerns and the integrity of the individual.

More equal development of society. The workplace requires creative, talented and cooperative people. Education – like all social institutions – must contribute to a more equitable development of society, that is to say, where all members have a fair share in production as well as in consumption. Policies to fight economic exclusion and contribute to social inclusion include not only the acquisition of essential knowledge which can be used as a starting point for continuous learning, but also the building of autonomy and the readiness for a flexible lifestyle where employment will not dictate the provision of a status in society.

For example, individuals must learn how to cope with periods out of a stable job and choose to use these periods for education, voluntary work or participating in community and associative activities; in short, all other forms of work-action, synonymous with social use, and therefore with recognition and identity.

Altogether, in an increasingly global world, the concept of goals should gradually reflect the fact that educational institutions should strive together with other social institutions, to achieve those goals all too often proposed for and imputed to the education sector alone. It is only when education is regarded as an integral part of the social system that the goals proposed for education – identified as social goals – become meaningful.

2. Rethinking the Tasks of Each Component of the Structure

Strengthening individual freedom, re-establishing the social link, giving everyone the opportunity to take part in development – these are the proposed goals of education. Education must, in fact, contribute to revitalising a group of citizens who share the values, issues and challenges of their community, country and the world.

2.1 New requirements

A society of citizens. To build a society of autonomous, productive, participative and committed citizens will require a radical shift in emphasis of the division in tasks between different levels and types of education. Basic education for all – as promoted at Jomtien – will inevitably be the main concern of all policy-makers, in particular those in charge of education. Obviously, such a requirement will inevitably involve restructuring education as a whole.

An outdated traditional tasks assignment. Traditionally (leaving aside pre-school education), we find in practically every education system a three-tier structure: (i) primary/basic education to learn the '3 Rs' and a rudimentary introduction to different subjects; (ii) secondary education, expanding and deepening the learning of different subjects, linking the other two tiers or levels, preparing for higher education, in the case of academic success, and for the workplace for others, including via vocational education and training; and (iii) higher education, for the preparation of the cadres (engineers, managers, researchers, etc.) of the nation. This traditional trilogy loses its relevance in a more global world that requires better-educated citizens. We may well observe two contrasting scenarios: (i) a gradual demise of secondary education or its inclusion in basic education – a two-tier structure, which prevailed in Europe in the early Renaissance years; or (ii) some redeployment of tasks between basic, secondary and higher education. Although the four pillars of education highlighted by the Delors Commission ('learning to be, learning to know, learning to do, and learning to live together') apply to all the components of the education system, different goals would be attached to different levels of education.

The tasks of basic education. Globalisation entails an increase in the tasks of basic education. The globalised world needs a society that is made up of citizens capable of acting and thinking autonomously about rapid social evolution. These skills must be acquired by all citizens, along with the fundamental elements of learning – reading, writing and arithmetic. It is therefore the task of basic education to build the citizen at the heart of the 'global village'. However, it comes back to this sector of education achieving the majority of objectives defined earlier. If this level is to be the 'passport for life', then it must give children the opportunity to learn to be, to learn to learn and to learn to live together by relying on school and the multiple non-formal educational resources.

Higher education: traditional tasks and new social functions. The traditional task of higher education to produce the cadres of society should be revised in order to address the new demands generated by globalisation: demands from the state, which all too often lacks managers with the capacity to anticipate and adapt to changes; demands from firms that need technicians, engineers and managers able to fulfil new tasks and that are ready to adapt to the rapid evolution of innovation. For universities to serve societal need, they should not be – as they often are today – the depository of political conservatism. Universities must be avant-gardist: they must present arenas for debate, generate and assess innovative theories, and analyse political and social problems with political neutrality and scientific rigour. In addition to addressing the need for skills development at the highest level and contributing to the production of knowledge, higher education should be a chance for everyone to educate themselves within the framework of lifelong learning and a chance for society to address its challenges and problems.

Secondary education: reconciling the old dilemma between terminal and preparatory education. Between a strengthened basic education with far broader aims and a rich tapestry of tasks, on the one hand, and a higher education with revised responsibilities and new social functions, on the other, secondary education no longer remains a preparation for higher education for those who succeed and a terminal transition to the world of work for those who fail. In the context of lifelong learning, each level of education should be preparatory, and in the context of globalisation, each level should be in a sense terminal.

Given the diversity of social needs and the contrasts between, on the one hand, the common core to be offered by basic education and, on the other hand, the rich programme of specialisation in higher education, secondary education would attach particular importance to the preparation of individuals to take charge of their own lifelong learning while contributing to the development of skills needed by the economy and society, i.e. learning to do, and learning to learn. For instance, in addition to allowing pupils to understand the world they live in through science and technology and opening the way to specific skills development, secondary education would include learning about the main languages, civilisation and cultures, and how to use and adapt to the evolution of the new information and communication technologies, and the methods of research and selection of information, all with a self-critical mind.

3. Teaching

3.1 How to teach in a changing world

A profession with competing demands. There are nearly 60 million teachers around the world today. However, recruitment has been carried out in many countries with limited public resources following structural adjustment policies. This has not enabled countries to attract candidates with adequate qualifications; the teacher's function has been devalued and, due to low salaries and poor working conditions, a deterioration in the morale and motivation of teachers, as well as high levels of absenteeism, can be observed.

The teacher today also faces competition in his/her own field. Following the development of information services and new modes of communication, the teacher has lost his/her monopoly as a supplier of knowledge. Consequently, teaching and learning are no longer a protected area of competence of the teaching profession, but are gradually opening up to other public or private players. New teaching and learning theories are challenging the teaching capacity of a large number of educators who have been trained in and who practise traditional approaches to education. New ways of acquiring knowledge and new delivery systems, threaten the teaching profession, such as multimedia, including CD-ROMs with sophisticated devices for self-learning at one's own pace. This means that we are already in a world where the teaching profession will require radical adaptation to new skills and new demands. Some have already predicted that teachers will disappear due to the advent of these new learning possibilities. This is unlikely, but the role of the teacher will, on the other hand, evolve and become perfectly adapted to the new skills and new needs.

More responsibilities. At the same time, globalisation, through weakening the state and promoting the decentralisation of power to local entities, indirectly generates new responsibilities for teachers. In education, decentralisation – when it works – means a relocation of decision-making power to local authorities, schools, headteachers and, for classroom management, teachers. If the teacher is not trained to address these new managerial responsibilities, the future of reform that seeks more participatory school-based management may be jeopardised.

New tasks. Finally, globalisation, by relying heavily on new information technologies (NITs), generates additional demands for new teaching skills. Indeed, NITs require teacher training to address the acquisition of two kinds of skills. Firstly, the understanding of NITs requires knowledge centred on their technical functioning and the communication processes they use. Secondly, NITs make an enormous mass of information accessible, which must be dealt with to allow the transformation of information into relevant knowledge.

3.2 A teacher in the future

Back to basics: training 60 million teachers. How to upgrade and adapt the competencies of the 60 million practising teachers in the world today, knowing that they have not all had the required training in basic education and that they do not all have access to continuous lifelong learning opportunities? This is a massive task and a major challenge for the teaching profession.

A professional and a manager. The professionalisation of teachers means that methodological guidelines and rules are being replaced by autonomy, guided by clear objectives and by ethics banning practices that are against the interests of the community. To achieve the main goal – to educate and train an increasingly heterogeneous group of pupils and teach them sustainable and interchangeable skills – the teacher must enjoy autonomy in his/her different tasks: class management, teaching strategies, arrangement of furniture and work spaces, adoption of flexible hours, individualisation of training to meet different requirements of learners, etc. However, it is obvious that the professionalisation of teachers will never materialise if – as in other professions – salaries are not established according to performance criteria and accountability concerns.

A broker in the information society. Largely, the role of the teacher will remain traditional, as pupils will still require a teaching support in one form or another to understand the knowledge to be acquired, at least at the basic education level. With globalisation and the appearance of NITs, the teacher will cease to be a speaker and become more of a tutor. NITs will allow the teacher to use new educational methods and give pupils more independence. One of the teacher's fundamental roles is to guide and to survey the learning process. Through the role of a guide, the teacher can assure that the curriculum, defined according to the goals of education, will be well and truly followed. Finally, teachers will provide new kinds of support: s/he will teach how to deal with information; in short, give pupils the capacity to find information, interpret it and be a responsible information consumer.

4. How to Certify

4.1 Societies that need to recruit skills

The demand for certification. The increase in economic and financial flows, the organisation of regional unions of states, and the transnational scale of operations (production, commercialisation, delivery) of a growing number of companies have contributed to widening the areas of recruitment of workers and a rapid increase in geographic mobility of labour. The worldwide spread of the labour market has had two consequences.

Firstly, the need to compare competencies: how can a company compare a diploma, for example, from the University of New Delhi with one from the University of Canberra? How can it be sure that certain training has instilled a certain skill? There is high market demand for a system that compares skills and diplomas. Secondly, the race for excellence: the competition between educational institutions is very likely to intensify and promote the search for the best quality. Excellence becomes the norm of recruitment for multinational companies seeking to achieve the best in world market competition.

A shared need. If the market feels the need for certification, it is not entirely the responsibility of the private sector. The debate on the respective roles of the state and the market has continued throughout modern economic history. It is true that these last few decades have been marked with a determined will to take the state back to its symbolic functions and leave the market to regulate economic activity. But the state cannot act without taking into account the economic interests of its population; the primacy of the market in our society has imposed two constraints on action under state control: on the one hand, ensuring the industrial development and competitiveness of the economy – favouring multinational expansion of national companies – and on the other hand, promoting investment in the territory. Marketing has found a new field: the 'sale of territories'. The state markets the location of investment in national territories by using a variety of incentives. For this, fiscal policy and the liberalisation of investment codes is no longer enough; the existence of a qualified workforce on the territory is one of the biggest factors when deciding on the location of centres of production. The state must guarantee to potential investors that they will find on site a comparatively better qualified workforce adapted to their own needs and whose skills will be guaranteed by a certification system that is internationally recognised. Furthermore, economic theories and the practical experience of models of development show that the chances of economic development in a globalised world are strongly linked to the quality of training of the qualified workforce.

The culture of excellence and the standardisation of skills. The certification of skills by an international system represents a real chance for education if the race for excellence effectively means an improvement in the quality of education and transparency in the evaluation of skills. This improvement can only happen if skills acquired at school and through different forms of informal education fully meet the needs of the market. We have seen that the skills required will be increasingly of a non-cognitive nature (personal and autonomous development, capacity for participation and integration into society). These skills are difficult to quantify and standardise. Therefore, the means to standardise and evaluate not only cognitive skills (acquisition of skills and expertise) but also non-cognitive skills must be found. Failure to do this may entail two consequences: on the one hand, the existing types of certification system will become inefficient, as they will not meet market demands for a reliable and transparent source of information in order to establish recruitment criteria; on the other hand, the limited scope of the skill-evaluation system has every chance to influence the quality of education, which would tend to focus its action on the learning of cognitive skills.

4.2 A challenge for education

Education must succeed in providing society with an efficient and effective certification system. Increasing numbers of private companies today have created their own certification institutions in order to compensate for the shortcomings of traditional examination procedures managed by the public education authorities. However, leaving the private sector to monopolise assessment and certification – as is the case in some countries – may well prove to be against the cultural traditions of many societies. That is why it is time to think about the problems of responsibility for certification in each country and the need for comparison of the different types of certification between countries. It has been suggested by some who have studied assessment and certification problems that a qualification authority should be established. It should involve representatives of 'producers' and 'consumers' of education and training, as well as recognised specialists in different areas of assessment and certification.

Standardising and benchmarking. Skills and competencies can only be compared to a certain number of standards and benchmarks. By establishing standards required by local labour markets and benchmarks inspired by other competing markets, the qualification authority (with representatives from the public and the private sectors) would be able to publicise its certification system. Certification should not be limited to skills acquired when preparing for a diploma, but also to the skills and competencies that may have been acquired during professional experience or continuous training. In some countries, systematic approaches have been established to document the competencies of individuals by incorporating information on their learning achievement through life.

Searching for indicators of non-cognitive outcomes. With reference to non-cognitive educational achievements corresponding to new educational goals (autonomy of individuals, ability to integrate and participate in society), the qualification authority will have very little capacity today to address the needs for assessment and certification using scientific and transparent approaches. Study and research is required before a comprehensive system of certification can be developed with the potential of comparability of education/training systems across countries. Meanwhile, indicators of proxies of non-cognitive outcomes are being used either at country level (comparing countries) or within countries (comparing education/training institutions), but rarely at an individual level.

Can the qualification authority be legitimate? The qualification authority may prove to hold a key role of regulation and quality control. It might therefore gain some legitimacy in the eyes of education/training institutions, the teaching profession, the students, the state and the companies. However, even if its composition does reflect the interests of all protagonists, including a fair representation of companies and labour unions, no qualification authority can ever be fully legitimate, as it will always be influenced by either short-term concerns determined by the needs of the labour market, or long-term perceptions of what should be the goals of education according to the promoters of humanistic values of education. Put differently, a qualification authority will tend towards some legitimacy only if it can find a fair balance between social goals and the diversity of goals of the various protagonists of education.

5. Educational Policies

It is clear that education is a concern shared by all members of society. The adoption of goals, the mobilisation of resources, the approaches to administration and management, the rules and regulations of the sector, and the assessment and certification system would require some kind of participation from all social actors. At the same time, such a broad participation of diverse actors would significantly affect educational institutions.

5.1 The state's loss of monopoly

The erosion of its power of action. Until recently, with few exceptions, in most countries the state monopolised many of the responsibilities in education. Today, in most countries, the state has experienced erosion of its power, its credibility and even its legitimacy. The state is no longer in a position to decide unilaterally on public policy, notably educational policy. A redistribution of power is taking place between the state, companies (nationals and multinationals), news and media agencies, associations and NGOs (scientific, professional and cultural), and regional and local, public and private authorities. With decentralisation – when it works – and with devolution of power to educational institutions, further erosion of the role of the state is taking place. This trend is observed at a time when, for many, the public sector represents the epitome of a bureaucratic model. Proved to be inefficient, accused of being too slow, believed to waste public money and, in some cases, to support the corruption of the elected representatives, the public sector has lost the confidence of the citizens. This contributes to the delegitimisation of the state's action. With this lack of trust in the public's representatives, how can one ensure that the collective interests of society are not going to be undermined when entering into conflict with powerful individuals who are effective in preserving their private interest in policy-making and resource allocation? This is not a new dilemma; but it is raised in the context of globalisation when the definition of national entities is weakening and the state is proving its weakness in addressing economic and social issues faced by its citizens. The consequences – in some societies – are new opportunities to have access to power for demagogues and promoters of authoritarian regimes, with very little likelihood that such regimes will be inclined to adopt educational policies with universal goals. Therefore, establishing a counterbalance of state power to formulate and implement educational policies may be a much-needed task and a highly desirable evolution.

Education and the market. The weakening of the state and the erosion of its monopoly of educational policies is best highlighted by 'economism' or its reliance on the market. Nonetheless, almost all human activity is increasingly regulated by market tendencies. Even political and moral issues are expressed as economic issues. Terms such as cost, returns, profitability and efficiency now belong to the everyday vocabulary of the education profession as if schools and universities were firms selling learning. Due to economic considerations, structural adjustment policies are adopted, involving cuts in spending on education. The results are well known and depressing: increased segmentation between different types of educational institutions, a decrease in access to good quality education and limitations on those who could afford to pay, as well as a general drop in the quality of education.

This invasion of the education sector by economic concerns entails several other consequences: education must meet new requirements of efficiency and profitability, and listen to individuals and companies who consider themselves as consumers and who also act like demanding clients. This may have a positive effect on quality and accountability for those who can pay. The well-known distinction made by economists between public goods and private goods may well either disappear – in favour of the private goods – or become an excellent criterion for distinguishing between bad quality and good quality education. At any rate – and on a more positive note – in a global world led predominantly by market considerations, the assertion of requirements and demands by customers and users of education will naturally open doors to more collaboration and partnerships between all those involved.

5.2 What partnership?

Organising the partnership. Education should be dealt with through a partnership of all the social players. This partnership replaces hierarchical relations between the state and civil society institutions. Exchange and cooperation are developing based on the conviction that each party will gain from trust and sharing. For it to be a true partnership – and avoid the risk of 'some being more equal partners than others' – it must rely on new modes of exchange and, above all, on rules and safeguards which would offer some guarantee of a fair balance between partners whose resources and capacity for action are mainly very unequal.

New education protagonists. NGOs: The role of NGOs has become significant in the strengthening of education. They are regarded as guarantors of moral and voluntary commitment required for the development of education in sometimes difficult situations. However, recent evaluations of the actions of NGOs have posed a number of questions as to the cost-effectiveness of their actions in comparison to public administration, the sustainability and potential of the scale of their actions, and level of reliable data on their operational performances. These studies concluded with a great deal of scepticism and emphasised the need for both cautious and active policies to ensure transparency and efficiency in NGOs' operations.

Communities: The more global the world becomes, the more local the policy and action. 'Think globally, act locally' is a well-known slogan, which is self-explanatory in the growing role of communities – i.e. the families, the parents, the locally organised entities – in the social sector in general and in education in particular. Community participation may allow the mobilisation of additional resources and of new concepts and ideas:

(i) designing and producing more relevant and effective educational models with regard to the needs and reality of the population living in each community;
(ii) mobilising the contribution of local cultural resources, historical memories and social practices;
(iii) better addressing the needs of disadvantaged groups, the marginalised and the excluded; and
(iv) widening the access of education and improving school conditions.

The private sector: Whether we like it or not, market requirements – rationalisation, efficiency, profitability – are being increasingly applied to the definition of educational policies, management, and evaluation. Moreover, budgetary constraints, which lead to the diversification of sources of finance for education, are also demanding a growing financial contribution from the private sector. Finally, with globalisation, one observes an increasingly significant share in the provision of education and training totally controlled by multinational firms.

Partnership for better education. The different players that we have just described do not all have the same influence or power. Private companies are becoming increasingly important, even in education. To fulfil their own needs, companies have established successful educational and training institutions – oriented around their own objectives and very often covering more than just one country. The challenge, at national level, is how to reconcile the 'agenda' of the privately owned and managed education/training centres that enjoy a great deal of autonomy with educational goals adopted by society. The role of the state may prove to be crucial; for example, contributing to the development of efficient partnerships; promoting participation; ensuring the mobilisation of civil society; allowing initiatives to take shape; ensuring fair representation of protagonists; and ensuring transparency in the division of tasks and in the decision-making process. But will the state today be able to reinforce and re-establish its capacity to address the needs of civil society, to give priority to general interest while respecting individual interests, and to reconcile the preservation and development of national educational goals with the pressing demands of a global world?

A Final Consideration

In this chapter, I have raised more questions than provided answers; I have made speculations on the consequences of globalisation; and I have proposed normative (prescriptive) directions rather than well-documented recommendations.

Indeed, we have very few well-documented studies on the various topics discussed in this chapter. One of the main reasons is the tremendous change that has been experienced during the last decade in the organisation of the world economy, led by an accelerated path of globalisation. Another is the rather segmented and compartmentalised concerns of the educational research profession. A third reason is the absence of well-coordinated and well-codified multidisciplinary studies and approaches to address some of the issues raised in this chapter. Finally, the educational research agenda, in some parts of the world, reflects the professional background of the research community when, in other parts of the world, it is determined predominantly by the concerns of the donor community; and, in both cases, it is somewhat remote from the theme presented in this chapter.

Altogether, the programme of research and studies that this analysis has revealed is rich and daunting. We all need to mobilise our efforts to address it head-on in the coming years.

However, education will, without doubt, be the answer to the problems raised by globalisation. As a social reintegration factor, education will need to take a new and varied form but it will remain, especially in the future, the main element in allowing individuals to manage their own destinies. This, of course, all depends on the resources available for educational policies. Thus, it is necessary to convince the national and international decision-makers to mobilise resources for education in order for it to achieve its aims in optimal conditions and be able to meet the challenges raised by globalisation.

Notes

[1] At that time in, for example, the United Kingdom, France, Germany and some states in the United States.

[2] The reference here is to Huntington's claim of the 'wave of democratisation' in the latter part of the twentieth century and to Fukuyama's claim to the 'inevitability of modernity' in its Western guise. For details, see references.

Jacques Hallak

References

Delors, J. (1996) *Learning: the treasure within. Report to UNESCO of the International Commission on Education for the Twenty-first Century.* Paris: UNESCO.

Fukuyama, F. (1992) *The End of History and the Last Man.* Harmondsworth: Penguin.

Huntington, S. P. (1991) *The Third Wave: democratisation in the late twentieth century.* Oklahoma: University of Oklahoma Press.

World Conference on Education for All (WCEFA) (1990) *World Declaration on Education for All and Framework for Action to Meet Basic Learning Needs.* New York: WCEFA Inter-agency Commission.

Globalisation, Educational Reform and Language Policy in Transitional Societies

KEITH WATSON

Introduction

Speaking at a conference at the beginning of the twentieth century, Michael Sadler, one of Britain's greatest comparativists, made some insightful comments when he said: 'Great tidal movements of economic or spiritual change sweep over the world with irresistible force ... What the school (and teachers) can do is to bend all in their powers to the task of understanding the inner significance of each new and perturbing movement' (cited in Higginson, 1979).

This has certainly always been part of the role of comparative educationists. However, the changes that have taken place over the past 10 years or so – and that are still taking place – have transformed the political and economic structures of the world to such an extent that the comparativist's role has become both more important but also more difficult.

Given that 'all research that seeks to offer general explanations must be comparative' (Raivola, 1985) and that 'comparative education is a field of study that covers all the disciplines that serve to understand and explain education' (Le Than Khoi, 1986), including economics, politics, the social sciences and international relations, it may be that the traditional focus of comparative analysis is having to change. This was the nation state, and within that, the education system, or subsystem (e.g. primary or tertiary education) or even non-formal education. The setting was one or more particular social, economic and cultural context, depending upon whether the analysis was based on a single country or on a cross-country basis, though it was only truly comparative if it was the latter. The belief was that certain lessons could be learnt from identifying points of similarity or difference between countries (Hans, 1964; Mallinson, 1974; Watson, 1985). Indeed, this was the argument adopted by UNESCO in its 1993 World Education Report (UNESCO, 1993, p. 89):

> *At a time such as the present, when profound changes are*
> *occurring in the whole structure of global economic, social*
> *and cultural relations, and the role of education in these*
> *changes is coming to be recognised as fundamental, all*
> *countries can only benefit, from knowing more about the*
> *cultural premises of each other's education.*

However, in the new world order, the place of the state is being threatened and challenged from different sources. First among these are the economic forces of globalisation and free markets, which limit governments' ability to regulate, or control, their economies. Then there is the growth of regional supranational structures, such as the European Union, or the South African Development Community (Ilon, 1994; McGinn, 1994; Watson, 1997a), which have partly come about to withstand the pressures of globalisation through regional cooperation. In many other countries, the role of multilateral organisations, such as the World Bank and the International Monetary Fund, has become increasingly important. This is particularly true where nation states are imploding, or even disintegrating, as in the case of the former Soviet Union (FSU), the former Yugoslavia, Zaire and other parts of central Africa; or where they are being transformed from a centrally planned economy to a free market economy, as in central and eastern Europe (CEE). Since governments can only receive financial assistance if they pursue policies that are in accordance with the recommendations of these multilateral organisations, their control of their own affairs is, to say the least, limited – South Korea, Indonesia, Thailand and the Philippines have all recently experienced this external 'interference'. The comparativists' role then becomes more one of analysing the external influences bringing about change, as well as the resulting educational trends, in different contexts, though even this can be problematic.

Indeed, during recent years several American writers have developed theories of macro-analysis and world systems analysis as opposed to micro-studies 'in an attempt to resolve this problem' (Arnove, 1980; Ramirez & Boli, 1982), and for many years UNESCO and the Organisation for Economic Cooperation and Development (OECD) have been in the vanguard of identifying trends internationally, across diverse situations, to see what lessons or inferences could be drawn (e.g. OECD, 1987; UNESCO, 1993, 1995).

This chapter will be in this genre in so far as it seeks to take a broad sweep of developments in different parts of the world to see if it is possible to identify common developments that are currently taking place. It will therefore begin by looking at some definitions of transition and transformation. It will also use the nation state as the basis for comment since this is still widely used by international organisations and aid agencies for their points of comparison.

I. Theoretical Considerations

Terminology

During the past decade, the geopolitical structures of the world have been undergoing enormous and rapid changes, to such an extent that many regard these changes as little short of revolutionary. As with all revolutions, things are messy and confusing, changes are taking place with bewildering speed and it is difficult to know how to evaluate what is happening. It has been argued that the current transition has no historical precedent (Mercer, 1997) but in this century alone there have been at least three other major upheavals that have led to economic and educational changes of similar magnitude: the break-up of the old European order and empires following World War I, the creation of three major political and economic groupings following World War II, and the period of decolonisation of Asia, Africa and the Middle East during the 1950s and 1960s. One could go back further historically to see that the nation state is of relatively recent origin, and that great civilisations have risen and collapsed (Toynbee, 1954) and that in China alone every hundred years or so there have been cataclysmic social and political upheavals. We therefore need to treat with caution the current changes and what their outcomes may be. All that can be said with certainty is that the post-World War II understanding of the world no longer holds true. The world can no longer be divided into First, Second and Third Worlds, communist and non-communist, East and West, developed and developing. Countries can only be classified according to wealth, levels of democracy, sound governance, the rule of law and other social indicators (World Bank, 1996, 1997; United Nations Development Programme [UNDP], 1996, 1997), and even here there are different classifications, with some countries high on one indicator and low on another. The truth is that there is no longer certainty about global classifications; for how long will the World Bank, for example, be able to lump together the countries of CEE and FSU into 'Transitional Economies'? More importantly, what exactly is meant by 'transition'? As 'transition' is often associated with 'reconstruction' and 'transformation', let us unpack the subtle differences between the last two terms first.

'Reconstruction' implies restoration and rebuilding, for example, after a war. This would apply to Europe being reconstructed after World War II, to Cambodia, Eritrea, Mozambique, Namibia and Vietnam recovering from the ravages of civil war. 'Transformation' implies making 'a thorough and dramatic change' from one situation to another, or 'a change, modification, transfiguration or alteration' to what already exists. The implication is that there is a clear blueprint of where a country, and its education system, is going. At one level, this applies to countries like South Korea, Malaysia and Taiwan, whose economies have been transformed and whose education systems have been a key feature of this transformation. At another level, the term would apply to South Africa, which is seeking to transform itself from a nation based on racial superiority and inequality to one based on racial harmony and equality, though as Sayed (1997) has argued, the current policies will exacerbate inequality along social class terms rather than racial ones.

'Transition' implies a process or change from one place, state or condition to another, without necessarily being clear about where that 'other' is going to lead. This could, of course, be applied to nearly every country or society in the late twentieth century but it is more generally the term used to apply to the former socialist countries of CEE and FSU. Mongolia, China and Vietnam are also often lumped together as 'transitional', as are the former Baltic States.

The variations between these economies, however, are such that while there are similarities, the differences do not make it easy to lump them together as classified groups. Within the 'transitional' states, for example, there are:

(1) those states with strong natural affinities to western European culture from before World War II – the Czech Republic, Slovakia, Hungary, Poland – the Baltic States of Estonia, Latvia and Lithuania could also be classified with this group;

(2) those countries that formed the FSU, including Russia, Ukraine, Georgia, Tajikistan, Kazakhstan, Turkmenia etc., but even here a distinction needs to be drawn between Slav and Orthodox republics and Islamic or Caucasian ones;

(3) the Balkan states, with a history of social, and not state, ownership – Bulgaria, Rumania, the former Yugoslavia. Albania, both then and now, is very hard to classify;

(4) China, with its very different historical and cultural patterns, is also a 'transitional' economy. Vietnam and Laos would also fit this group as officially socialist countries but now embracing market economies;

(5) former socialist states, such as Cambodia, Mongolia and Myanmar (formerly Burma), which are 'reconstructing' as well as being 'transformed';

(6) those countries that have broken, or are breaking, free from colonial oppression and civil war, such as Eritrea, Mozambique and Namibia;

(7) South Africa, which, far from redesigning its whole economic structure from that of a command economy with central planning into a free market economy, so typical of 'transitional' societies, is seeking to

'transform' its economy, political system and educational system into a more just, and racially equal, system.

Given the variety outlined here, it can be seen that any comparative analysis, at this stage, is bound to be superficial, even if it may be illuminating.

However, moving away from specific definitions and classifications, there is a general assumption, at least on the part of aid agencies, and international educators and economists, that we are talking about societies that are moving away from rigid economic state planning and control to more market-oriented economies; from one-party states to plural democracies; from lack of competition to free market competition; from a situation where the state controls, directs and regulates to one where there is diversity, competition and choice; from a situation where ethnic divisions were not recognised and minority languages were largely suppressed to one where linguistic and ethnic diversity is recognised and/or encouraged.

Among key features of transitional economies identified by the Department for International Development (DfID, 1997) are 'the redistribution of rights and responsibilities between the State and its citizens; growing social and economic inequalities; the growth in corruption; environmental degradation; and the need to integrate these economies into global economic and political frameworks'.

The common features that link all these societies, however, whatever their geographical location, are: the rapidity of change, the weakening of state controls, the dismantling of one system and its replacement with another, and the 'messiness' of these reforms.

The remainder of this chapter will seek to explore: (a) why this phenomenon has come about at the end of the twentieth century, i.e. what forces have led to similar developments in different parts of the world, more or less simultaneously, which are very different from the 1950s and 1960s, the main period of decolonisation; (b) what are some of the constraints on the reforms; (c) what have been some of the key implications for education; and (d) what are some of the challenges for the early years of the next century.

Forces Leading to Change: globalisation

It would appear that the forces that have led to the political and economic upheavals in those parts of the world that sought isolation from, or immunity from, global economic developments, finally broke down the barriers of Iron Curtains, Bamboo Curtains, apartheid and every other system of repression designed to isolate countries and communities from developments that were taking place elsewhere in the so-called 'free' world of democracies and economic liberalism. These forces are what has increasingly come to be called 'globalisation' – but what is it?

The world is increasingly treated as one single, global, economic unit with transnational corporations (TNCs), operating in many countries, sometimes under different brand names, producing component A in one country, component B in another and assembling all the components into a finished product in a third country, as, for example, with washing machines, cars, or radios and televisions. Plants may open and close depending upon where labour costs are cheapest, with the result that local economies may be boosted or destabilised. 'The globe is now the primary operational unit and older units, such as national economies, defined by the politics of territorial states, are reduced to the complications of transnational activities' (Hobsbawm, 1994, p. 15). 'Globalisation is a buzzword, a term as ambiguous as it is popular' (Kofman & Youngs, 1996, p. 45), which seeks to show that in many areas of life we are dealing with relations that go beyond the confines of nation state or country boundaries. It 'entails the privatization and marketization of economic and political structures' (Reich, 1991) in which the ability of the state to control all the activities within its borders is becoming limited.

The main features of globalisation are these: the growth of TNCs and MLOs (multilateral organisations); the international division of labour; the encouragement of markets rather than government central planning (e.g. World Bank, 1996); the growth of offshore finance and telecommunications that can link banks, stock markets, companies and organisations together in a global network; increasing migration of peoples within and across national boundaries in the search for work; the growth of media by satellite that ensures programmes can be beamed across the globe regardless of national boundaries; and the growth of NGOs (non-governmental organisations), both international and national. However, we need to remind ourselves that globalisation is not new, is not global, only relates to certain aspects of life, is not benign, and it does have notable implications for educational provision as well as for how comparativists view the world.

Taking the first of these – newness – the globalisation of trade has been accelerating since the mercantilists of the sixteenth and seventeenth centuries, accelerated during the nineteenth century because of improvements in telecommunications and transport, and has further accelerated during the twentieth century because of Fordist means of production and developments in computer technology. It is part of a process, not an end in itself. The first telegraphic communication took place in 1840; time was synchronised on Greenwich Mean Time in 1854; global telecommunications links date from the 1880s; and airline and short-wave radio links from the 1920s. George V gave the first global broadcast in 1930 while global influenza killed millions in 1918/19

(Rowlands & Green, 1992). Global warfare was experienced for the first time in the 1940s.

Although all countries are directly or indirectly affected by globalisation, not all countries are linked into a global economy, especially in many parts of sub-Saharan Africa. Indeed, as Green (1997, p. 160) has argued, relatively few countries are affected by global TNCs; 24,000 out of the known 37,000 TNCs are based in only 14 OECD countries and 73% of accumulated stock is in the USA, Japan and western Europe. The volume of trade is less now than at different historical periods in the past two centuries (p. 158). Even global culture is exaggerated. Only in the areas of telecommunications, 24-hour financial markets linked through the Internet, environmental and atmospheric change, and the use of the whole world as a potential production line or for division of labour can it truly be called global.

Far from being benign, globalisation has had deleterious effects on millions. Although improved technology has brought benefits to millions – improved sanitation, healthcare, access to knowledge and literacy etc. – it has also led to ecological degradation, increased inequalities within and between regions and countries, to poverty for many and affluence for others, and to loneliness, isolation, selfishness and bewilderment at an individual level (Schluter & Lee, 1993). In many parts of the world, the pressures of global capitalism have led to a deterioration in working conditions, especially for women and ethnic groups, and a decline in social protection on the part of governments. This is particularly true in parts of the FSU and CEE. Moreover, Fukuyama's (1992) thesis needs to be challenged. This is that globalisation has led to the triumph of liberal democracy and Western capitalism and offers the best way forward to meet the economic and political needs of the world, the eradication of poverty in our times – so that we can now think of 'the end of history'.

Nonetheless, it needs to be recognised that these economic pressures, together with the growing influence of the media, which, because of satellite communications could no longer be blocked, and internal political and economic structural weaknesses in so many centrally planned socialist economies, finally led to their disintegration, dismemberment, reconstruction and/or transformation.

In the ensuing economic and administrative chaos many, if not all, the transitional, reconstructing societies have sought financial and technical assistance from MLOs such as the World Bank, the International Monetary Fund (IMF), the European Bank for Development and the Asian Bank for Development. Apart from demands for economic restructuring, currency revaluation, the encouragement of multiparty democracy and the rule of law, those MLOs have also advocated, amongst other things, the decentralisation of administration and decision-making, as ways of enhancing local democracy and public accountability; the encouragement of the private sector, as a means of introducing competition, choice and raising additional revenue; curriculum reform to allow for greater flexibility in the subjects taught and in ways of learning; and greater recognition of linguistic and ethnic diversity. How these proposed reforms have impacted in different situations will be the focus of the next section.

II. Areas of Reform

Administration and Finance

One of the main areas of reform in many countries during the past 15 years or so has been that of educational decentralisation. While this has become a key feature of many governments' stated educational policy, it is a central plank of major international efforts at restructuring education in transitional, transformational and reconstructing societies. Much of the thinking behind this approach comes from the World Bank and the IMF (Bloomer, 1991; Prawda, 1993; Watson, 1997a) and has been accepted in countries as diverse as Australia, Brazil, China, England and Wales, Holland, Mexico, Poland and South Africa, to name but a few. It is perhaps ironical, since at the time of post-colonial independence and the rapid expansion of developing country education systems, centralisation was seen as the way forward, for reconstruction, for the best use of limited resources and for giving a sense of direction, since the claims made for decentralisation have not always been realised (Hurst, 1985; McGinn, 1997) and since decentralisation inevitably leads to greater social inequality. In China, for example, some localities have now been recognised as so poor that they have no hope of making any progress without external assistance (World Bank, 1995a), while Bray's (1996a) study of household contributions towards educational finance in nine East Asian countries has revealed that the poorest members of society are contributing disproportionately from their meagre incomes towards education, largely because decentralised administration has created financial inequalities. In Russia there is considerable confusion because of a lack of clarification about levels of administrative responsibility (Heyneman, 1998), and in South Africa the lack of clarity over the role of Provincial Directors of Education *vis à vis* the Federal Minister of Education had to be resolved by the Supreme Court. Even so, there is sufficient ambiguity to cause potential conflict between different administrative levels.

Rondinelli et al (1987) have suggested that there are five types of decentralisation which have been applied in different countries. These have ranged from delegation, devolution and deconcentration, to deregulation and privatisation. This is not the place to explore the subtle nuances of these terms. Suffice it to say that the main arguments put forward for some form of decentralisation are usually administrative and financial, because of concern with the most efficient way to distribute, manage, utilise, or even raise educational resources. The delegation of powers to school governing bodies, the devolution of decision-making to regions, the deconcentration of bureaucracy to lower administrative levels, the deregulation of catchment areas or the privatisation of key parts of the system might, or might not, improve the efficiency of educational provision and might or might not weaken the power and control of the centre. Indeed, the more a system is regulated and privatised, the greater is the need for greater central control and monitoring of the system through the curriculum, the examination system, teacher regulation and inspection. Unfortunately, in many transitional and reconstructing societies, the infrastructure and personnel are simply not there, at least in the early stages of reform.

There are also political and ideological reasons proposed for decentralisation (Sayed, 1997). At one level, these may range from arguments in favour of community participation, local democracy and empowerment for local communities to those in favour of greater efficiency and accountability. Cynics would argue that governments use decentralisation as a means of getting local communities to finance education locally. At another level, a view put forward by the Radical Right is that decentralisation weakens central control, encourages individual choice and leads to improved standards (e.g. Chubb & Moe, 1990). The arguments put forward by the World Bank include a mixture of much of these, depending upon who is the audience/readership.

In the context of South Africa, according to Sayed (1997), there are two contradictory rationales behind the moves towards greater decentralisation, which have already led to conflict between regional and central government and which could lead to even greater conflict (Chisholm, 1997; Kruss, 1997; Sayed, 1997). The National Party advocated decentralisation on the grounds that it would enhance administrative and financial efficiency and that it would improve school effectiveness and quality, especially because localised financing would lead to greater accountability. On the other hand, the African National Congress and other anti-apartheid forces advocated decentralisation in the belief that local communities would develop politically and would mobilise grass roots resistance against the then oppressive Nationalist regime. The thinking behind this was that localised administration would give power to the people, as opposed to the state. Thus, Parent, Teacher and Student Associations were conceived as vehicles for community expression and participation.

In the post-apartheid South Africa, the official belief has been that decentralised administration would give power to local communities, thus enhancing the position of the poor and marginalised in society. This view was reflected in the first White Paper on Education in the new South Africa. However, as Sayed (1997) has observed, strong local democracy can work against central government if it is felt that the centre does not appreciate local/regional needs and aspirations. Indeed the Constitutional Court had to make a ruling in early 1997 over the National Education Policy Act as to where power really lies, with the Minister of National Education or with Provincial Ministers of Education. Perhaps inevitably, it ruled in favour of the centre. Even so, this is not the end of the matter. Although theoretically the state (i.e. the National Ministry of Education) regulates and controls the school system, particularly through the curriculum, textbooks and examinations, the provincial governments can decide on language policy and the detailed administrative responsibility rests with local communities. It is this latter issue which is tendentious since, while the South African Schools Act seeks to provide for a uniform pattern of school governance throughout the country, it devolves responsibility to individual schools, much as the local management of schools pattern in England and Wales, and allows individual school boards to raise additional funds by charging fees. The principle is that if parents, or local communities, desire quality schooling, they should be encouraged to pay for it. This was seen as a way of allowing elite white schools to remain so, but the effect is to encourage social and academic inequality through the development of a two-, or even three-tiered system. Sayed's conclusion is that educational decentralisation is 'likely to redefine inequities from a racially-based to a decentralised class-stratified, two-tier public school system in which neo-liberal market ideology will hold sway' (1997, p. 12).

In CEE and FSU, the problem of decentralisation was complicated in the early years of transition by economic decline, underinvestment in education, and by confusions over the different levels of responsibility. Whereas in South Africa the problems arose over clarifying decisions already broadly agreed across the political spectrum, in CEE and FSU the problems arose because of the perceived need to alter the balance of power between the centre and localities quickly, because administrative personnel and teachers were not used to showing initiative, having always implemented policies from above, because the economic and administrative structures varied considerably from region to region and because there still are unregenerate Communists who do not wish to see any reforms to the system. For example, Kitaev (1994) argues that, in Russia at least, in spite of moves towards greater democracy and a market economy, the education system still suffers from overcentralisation, overhasty reforms in the context of the curriculum and teacher training, a lack of process concerning orderly reform, and continuing resistance to any sensible change. In contrast, the World Bank (1996) has written that:

> most governments have substantially reviewed their roles to
> meet the needs of a market economy, but in such critical areas
> as tax administration, public administration, and fiscal
> decentralisation reforms are still in the early stages in many

countries. This has hurt the economy and in some cases has adversely affected regional equity.

It has also inevitably had a knock-on effect on to educational provision. To give some idea of the scale of the problem, Georgia's GDP has declined by over 60% since 1960. Romania's GDP fell by 67% between 1989 and 1992, Kazakhstan's and Uzbekistan's fell by 50% between 1989 and 1995, Russia's by 40% and Poland's by 16% though the latter has subsequently begun to rise. The expenditure on education has inevitably been affected. Thus, whereas Russia was spending 7% of GDP on education in the early 1970s, this had fallen to 3.8% by 1991, though it had risen to 4.4% by 1995 (see Table I). Poland spent 6.6% of GDP on education in 1989. By 1991, this had fallen to 5.4% and had risen to 6.2% by 1995. The most dramatic falls were in Mongolia and Kazakhstan and especially in capital investment in schools. This fell in Russia by 23% between 1991 and 1992 but in Mongolia there was no capital investment in education during 1992/93 and 1993/94 (Mercer, 1997). In Kazakhstan, Turkmenia and Uzbekhistan, many rural schools have fallen into disrepair as a result.

Country	State education expenditure as percentage of GDP				State education expenditure as a percentage of total state expenditure			
	1989–91		1992–95		1989–91		1992–95	
Poland	1991	5.4	1994	6.2	1991	14.5	1995	12.9
Romania	1989	2.4	1992	3.9	1991	15.0	1992	13.0
Mongolia	1990	11.3	1993	3.8	1990	17.6	1993	15.2
Russia	1991	3.8	1994	4.4	1991	5.1		
Kazakhstan	1990	7.0	1995	3.1	1989	20.0	1995	14.0
Ukraine			1992	7.8				

Table I. State education expenditure as a percentage of GDP and total state expenditure.

Although the CEE's percentage of total expenditure on education compares favourably with OECD countries (Table II), it compares unfavourably with newly industralised countries such as Mexico, Singapore and Thailand. When the GDP per capita is compared, the figures become even more problematic. However, these are bold figures. Add to this situation the confused transfer of administrative and financial responsibility from central to regional, local and even institutional levels, and the problems are compounded. This is particularly true in the FSU. Not only is there confusion over the ownership of educational property, buildings, land, and equipment, over the licensing, training and upgrading of teachers; but over such things as textbooks, clothing, repairs and maintenance. According to Orivel (1996), in certain parts of the FSU, especially Georgia, teachers' salaries no longer even cover the cost of transport to and from work. In Russia itself, teachers' salaries have fallen from 81% of the average industrial wage in 1970 to 55% in 1994, while assistant professors, who earned 123% of the industrial wage in 1960, now earn barely 62% (Heyneman, 1998).

	Percentage of total expenditure					Total Expenditure As a % of GDP	GDP per capita (1990 dollars)
	Social security Welfare, Housing	Health	Education	Defence	Other		
Economy							
OECD members							
Canada	36.4	5.2	2.9	7.4	48.1	23.9	20,440
France	46.4	15.3	6.9	6.3	25.1	43.7	20,380
Germany, Federal Republic of	48.9	18.1	0.6	8.3	24.1	32.5	23,650
Italy	-	-	-	-	-	49.6	18,250
Japan	-	-	-	-	-	45.6	26,930
United Kingdom	31.8	13.3	3.2	11.1	40.6	38.2	16,500
United States	28.7	13.8	1.7	21.6	34.2	25.3	22,240
Latin America							
Argentina	39.4	3.0	9.9	9.9	37.8	13.1	2,790
Brazil	25.5	6.7	3.1	3.5	61.2	35.1	2,940
Mexico	13.0	1.9	13.9	2.4	68.8	18.1	3,030
High-forming Asian economies							
Singapore	8.2	4.6	19.9	24.0	43.3	22.1	14,210
Thailand	5.9	7.4	20.2	17.1	49.4	15.5	1,570
Central and Eastern Europe							
Bulgaria	23.9	4.8	6.2	5.6	59.5	77.3	1,840
Czecho-slovakia	27.0	0.4	1.9	7.1	63.6	55.6	2,470
Hungary	35.3	7.9	3.3	3.6	49.9	54.7	2,720
Poland	20.5	16.1	14.3	7.5	41.6	29.3	1,790
Romania	26.6	9.2	10.0	10.3	43.9	37.0	1,390
Russian Federation	24.5	1.2	5.1	19.1	50.1	26.8	3,220
Yugoslavia	6.0	0.0	0.0	53.4	40.6	21.0	-

Table II. Components of central government spending in various sectors (1991).

The result of this scenario is what Heyneman (1998) calls 'spontaneous decentralisation', i.e. local authorities, private bodies or organisations and individual parents and communities have had to pick up the pieces. In Poland, communal authorities took over the running of 91.8% of pre-schools in 1991 and parents have been expected to meet the costs through fees. Local government bodies are responsible for primary and secondary education and by 1994, communes had assumed control of 15% of primary schools and 1% of secondary schools (Heyneman, 1998). In Russia and Ukraine, while local authorities might run pre-primary schools, parents are expected to contribute to teachers' salaries through fees. However, as the World Bank (1995b) points out, there is considerable confusion as to which level of government, and who within that government, is responsible for financing what. Inevitably, therefore, the success or failure of certain school systems depends on how wealthy a local community is and how resourceful are school principals. Regional, even local, discrepancies and inequalities are thus on the increase.

Along with financial contributions to the public school sector there has been widespread development in the private sector. There are many variations of this (Bray, 1996b), ranging from profit-making institutions run by individuals or groups through to joint public/private ventures. As Heyneman (1998) argues, 'In many instances the problem is not a lack of reform, but an incoherence of reform and a bizarre interpretation of a market economy'. The biggest growth areas have been at nursery and higher education levels, especially in Hungary, Kazakhstan, Mongolia, Poland, Romania, Russia and Ukraine. For example, enrolments in private higher education in Poland and Romania have risen from 10% to 27% in the 1990s. By 1995, over 100,000 students were enrolled in private education in Romania (Eisomon et al, 1995).

There has also been a widespread growth of private institutions in technical and vocational fields. To some extent, this was perhaps inevitable. Command economies, by their very nature, are inflexible, and adjusting to market economies and responding to the pressures arising from globalisation have proved very difficult. Table III reveals some of the employment changes that have taken place in selected economies during the 1990s. In those countries most rigidly controlled, and most cut off from Western market economies – Albania, Mongolia and Romania – there have so far been relatively few changes to cope with the new situation. In Hungary, Poland, Russia and Ukraine, however, specialist institutions in accountancy, business, commerce and law have begun to spring up apace. In Russia, there are now 200 non-public tertiary institutions, more than the total number in western Europe. Of the 141 that are officially recognised, 67 specialise in commerce and management, 13 in law and public administration and five in social work (Heyneman, 1998). In addition, private vocational schools, specialising in fields such as auto mechanisms, building and related fields in service industries have also begun to develop rapidly.

(% change)	Czech Republic	Hungary	Poland	Slovakia
Declining share of employment				
Agriculture	-5.5	-3.5	-7.9	-4.2
Manufacturing	-6.0	-2.5	-1.2	-8.1
Increasing share of employment				
Trade and catering	7.8	1.1	6.7	5.1
Financial services and real estate	1.2	2.4	2.3	0.3
Public administration	3.3	2.5	–	3.7

Table III. Employment changes (1991–97) (% change).

In east Asia, household contributions, fees and private education at all levels of education have also become common features of the 1990s (Bray, 1997; Bray & Lee, 1997). It is now acknowledged that education is no longer the exclusive provision of the state and that private schooling and/or fees need to be encouraged if shortfalls in state-funded education are to be overcome. The result, again and inevitably, is that there are new opportunities for some, hardship for others. In a recent World Bank study on Vietnam (World Bank, 1995c), it was shown that in 1992/93 52.2% of the costs of primary school, 67.7% of lower secondary and 72.2% of upper secondary school were met from private households in the shape of uniforms, books, transport, food and additional tuition fees. A more recent study undertaken by Bray (Bray, 1996a) reveals that the household contributions to primary education range from 30% in the Philippines, to over 50% in Vietnam and 75% in Cambodia. Moreover, these figures do not cover opportunity costs, that is the cost of young children not helping at home, or on the peasant land holding. Inevitably, therefore, the rural poor are the most adversely affected. In certain parts of China, parental contributions for books, writing materials and teachers' living expenses have risen so dramatically that many parents have opted for low cost private education (Tsang, 1994; West, 1995). By 1995, throughout China non-governmental/private resources accounted for nearly 30% of all educational expenditure, while central government financial contributions accounted for only 11% (Cheng, 1997).

The cost of fees in Mongolia, simply to cover the costs of food, especially meat, from which public subsidies have been withdrawn, and boarding, has led to a marked drop-out from schools (Subbarao & Ezenari, 1995, p. 13), while in China, Myanmar, Cambodia and also Mongolia, private tutoring has now become so extensive that the same teacher who taught in the public sector in the morning becomes a private tutor in the afternoon.

From Bray's research certain clear patterns are emerging: the poor in all countries are being hardest hit; the costs of secondary education are always higher than at primary school, so that even if poor families can afford primary education they are unlikely to afford secondary; rich families spend proportionately less of their income on education; school boards, which have the power to charge fees and which are invariably composed of local elites, often pay scant regard to the financial hardships of the poor. This merely confirms similar findings from East Asia (Bray, 1997; Bray & Lee, 1997); Bhutan, (Bray, 1996c); Uganda, (Opolot, 1994), Tanzania (Galabawa, 1994) and Kenya (Maku, 1985). Finally, whereas in socialist/communist societies before transition there was a belief that even if there was poverty it should be shared equally, now there is growing evidence, especially from China and Vietnam and Laos, that even if some communities may be poor, that is no reason why everyone should be poor, a precept long ago recognised by George Orwell in *Animal Farm*! On the other hand, in the context of Russia, Kitaev (1994) reckons that the inertia and resistance to change from many bureaucrats, older people and those living in rural areas is such that they would rather everybody was equally poor than that some are richer than others. The tragedy, however, is that in a world committed to Education for All (World Conference on Education for All [WCEFA], 1990), the World Bank (1991, p. 62) can acknowledge that 'Poor parents ... are finding it increasingly difficult to send their children to school and many parents have come to doubt the value of schooling'.

The Content of What is Taught

In all dictatorships, whether of the Left or the Right, especially in those states bent on creating a new society through 'the new Soviet Man' or Chinese citizens who were both 'Red and Expert' or based on racial supremacy, there is a certainty about what should be taught, the ideas that can be discussed and the questions that are not allowed to be discussed. Control is exercised through officially approved textbooks, an official curriculum, examinations and inspections. Those involved in education in all the countries under review would have been familiar with this scenario. Dismantling such a system can be easily done; replacing it with something of value is more problematic, especially given the confused process of administrative and financial decentralisation that has been taking place in most of the transitional and transformational states.

In China, for example, decentralisation has been both liberating and has created greater diversity. Whereas it used to be known for its uniformity of syllabus and rigidity of textbooks, it has now probably a greater diversity of textbooks than anywhere else in the world. Beginning in 1988, initiatives were taken to create diverse textbook editions of the national curriculum, with variations for specific regions. In what was initially called 'one syllabus, many editions', there were originally eight editions of textbooks for coastal provinces, students of advanced levels, advanced rural areas, new economic zones, etc. These came into being in 1991. As the 1990s have progressed, however, there has been a virtual open policy on textbooks and their contents (Cheng, 1997). As a result, there is now a considerable diversity in ideology, with varying degrees of enthusiasm for individualism, the market economy, new technologies, etc. The idea of a uniform pattern of 'national development' has long since been relegated to the past. Inevitably, the more urban and economically advanced the location (e.g. Shanghai, Beijing, Guangdong), the greater is the variation. In the underdeveloped rural areas, teachers still feel safe teaching from the standard national edition of the curriculum and the standard textbooks. The effect of this process is to further exacerbate the gulf between the sophisticated urban dwellers, with their many job opportunities, and the rural peasantry, where the pace of life and economic development are much slower.

Contrast this with South Africa's dilemma. The Government of new South Africa has been at great pains to eliminate the vestiges of the hated apartheid regime and to replace these with a new vision of 'the Rainbow Nation' and Curriculum 2005. Unfortunately, such have been the financial constraints on this aspect of the education system that many schools and teacher training colleges are still using textbooks that were issued by the Nationalist government and provincial authorities are expected to provide in-service training for teachers on the new curriculum without providing additional funds and with a lack of clarity about which language medium should be used.

In the CEE and FSU countries, at one level the picture is as much to do with how things are taught as with what is taught; at another it is to do with reasserting ethnic/national identity and with correcting historical inaccuracies in the previously highly politicised curricula. Transition has inevitably meant a revolution of the curricula and teaching methods so that they can reflect new values and objectives such as personal responsibility, intellectual freedom, creativity and problem-solving skills, as well as the need for new textbooks, often in different languages, which reflect these new ideas. Unfortunately, too many of the reforms have been too hasty and ill thought through, resulting in a degree of confusion. How can teachers, who have spent their careers in a system in which everything was carefully directed and controlled, be suddenly expected to change their whole approach, especially if teaching materials are still lacking and there is considerable uncertainty about the direction the system should take (Chapman et al, 1995)? Both at school and tertiary levels, 'The issues of preparing young people for a market economy have not yet been comprehensively addressed by the public and the local education authorities; they depend on the initiatives taken on behalf of educational institutions and by students themselves' (Kitaev, 1994, p. 127).

It is not difficult to see why this situation has come about. In all the Marxist/Communist/socialist planned economies the school system was used for political purposes: to stress the virtues of Marxist-Leninism, dialectical materialism and communist political economy. Although how far the ideology of the Marxist state was stressed varied from country to country and the success of the political indoctrination was called into question by numerous observers (Zadja, 1980; Grant, 1992), there were certain common features: an overt and covert attack on religious beliefs and an overwhelming emphasis on scientific belief. In January 1918, a decree from the Russian Ministry of Education stressed that 'the teaching of religious doctrine is not permitted in any state, public or private educational institution where general education subjects are taught'. Teachers had to create 'godless corners' and 'to teach atheism with enthusiasm, knowledge, care, devotion and dedication'. The decree was reiterated in 1930, although by 1954 Khrushchev recognised that the process had gone too far and had to be modified. By the 1980s, cracks began to appear in the anti-religious propaganda and Gorbachev made considerable concessions after negotiations with the papacy (Gorbachev, 1987). Since the collapse of the Soviet State and the independence of the CEE satellites, there has been a burgeoning of religious belief and practice, and a growth of religious schools, particularly fundamentalist Christian schools, especially in the Czech Republic, Hungary, Poland, Russia and Slovakia.

The emphasis on science and mathematics, to the extent that by Grade 8 (mid-teens) 60% of the school timetable was devoted to these subjects, was not only regarded as a counter-emphasis to religious belief but was also a result of political conviction that only through the mastery of science and mathematics could there be economic development and success and a triumph over the capitalist West. Thus, at university level, science, technology, mathematics, solid state physics, nuclear engineering and related fields were all 'protected' subjects, in so far as they received the cream of the funds, and the students. However, while the FSU and CEE education systems, with their stress on literacy, numeracy and factual information, were highly successful in providing knowledge, they failed on several counts. They were inflexible and they failed to develop problem-solving skills, higher order thinking, creativity, initiative and a spirit of inquiry. This can be seen from Figure 1, which contrasts certain centrally planned systems with others (World Bank, 1996; Heyneman, 1998).

In a centrally planned economy, where technological changes are predictable and the content of skill training is relatively certain, it is easy to plan the curriculum and training. The result was an excellent emphasis on vocational education in most of the CEE and FSU countries, where skill training and not initiative was the hallmark of the classes, as can be seen from Table IV. Unfortunately, this led to a distorted labour force. In 1991, for example, 71% of the adult population in Russia had qualifications in engineering compared with 27% in Germany and 9% in the USA (European Training Foundation, 1997).

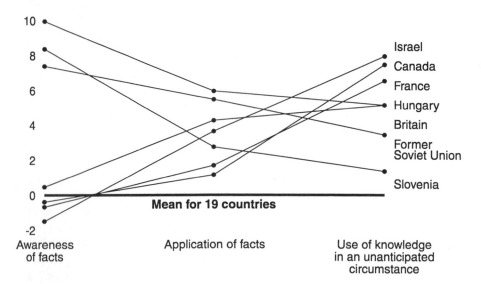

Figure 1. Socialist education emphasised accumulating knowledge rather than applying it. Source: World Bank, 1996, p. 125.

Remove the planned economy, however, and allow free markets and entrepreneurial skills to flourish and the need for higher order thinking, creativity and questioning becomes apparent. Unfortunately, progress and reforms in this direction, particularly in Bulgaria, Hungary, Romania and Russia, have been pitifully slow. There are several reasons for this. The costs of rewriting textbooks, or even of finding authors capable of rewriting them, have been considerable. Until these are readily available, it is not easy to retrain teachers. In any case, there is a growing concern over the quality of teaching and retraining of teachers in several countries. There has also been more interest in democracy, political freedom, progressive educational thinkers, new approaches to school management, at least in Russia, than there has in serious curriculum reform (Chapman et al, 1995).

In some transitional countries, most notably the Baltic States, Georgia, Hungary and the Ukraine, there has been greater interest in seizing the opportunity to re-establish a sense of historical accuracy about what is taught in an attempt to redress the teachings relating to the former oppression of Russian/Soviet imperialism (Dyezok, 1997; Heyneman, 1998).

Region, country and year	Basic or less	Vocational	Secondary	Higher
Central and Eastern Europe				
Bulgaria 1990	44.6	15.8	30.0	9.6
Czechoslovakia 1989	26.0	21.0	43.8	9.2
Hungary 1990	38.4	23.1	26.9	11.6
Poland 1988	34.2	29.5	27.9	8.4
Romania 1990	35.8	31.4	24.0	8.8
Western Europe				
Austria 1990	28.8	57.8	6.3	7.1
France 1969	35.3		46.0	14.6
Greece 1989	52.6		35.3	14.6
Ireland 1989	26.8		55.5	17.5
Italy 1990	26.6		66.2	7.2
Netherlands 1989	12.6		61.3	19.7
Spain 1990	48.4		46.1	3.3

Table IV. Level of education of the labour force in various countries and years (percentage of total labour force).

Curriculum reform in some countries, most notably Armenia, Georgia, Moldova, the Ukraine and the Baltic States, has provided an opportunity to reassert a sense of ethnic or national identity using local, national or indigenous languages as the medium of instruction or as the main language to be taught. Wherever possible, Russian is being replaced by English as the main foreign language to be learnt (Wright, 1994; Mitter, 1997).

In the area of curriculum reform, therefore, it can be seen that the transitional and transformational states are pursuing different routes, depending upon how far the authorities wish to redress past grievances and injustices. However, there is a recognition that, faced with the challenges of the global economy, there needs to be greater flexibility regarding what is taught and how students are encouraged to think if they are to acquire jobs in rapidly changing labour markets.

Languages of Instruction

The third area of reform is that of the language issue. There is not the scope here to develop this theme in depth. To explore the situation in each of the states of CEE and FSU would require at least a paper, if not a book, on the topic (Mitter, 1992; Wright, 1994). I have already explored the language issues facing many plurilingual and multiethnic countries in the light of pressures for globalisation, and the use of English, on the one hand, and the pressures for the use of local or indigenous languages, at least at the primary level, on the other (Watson, 1994, 1997b).

However, it can be seen that there are significant developments in both the transitional group of countries, as well as the transformational ones, and that there are two common trends across all of them: the rejection of the use of a language of repression (except in China) and the growing use of English.

The importance of language in terms of political power and the use of education to reinforce linguistic and/or political power have long been recognised (Watson, 1993, 1994). Two of the prime examples of this have been Russia and China, both of whose leaders used a national language as a means of ensuring political control over the territories that were conquered. The problem has been less acute in China where the 50 minority nationalities, with their own languages and customs, form a relatively small part of the total population – 6% – although they are spread over about 10% of the geographical land mass of the country. From ancient imperial times, Mandarin Chinese has been used as the language of unification and political control. In the old Soviet Union, however, there were over 130 nationalities, some of which were substantial numerically. The Soviet authorities perceived Russian as the language of unification and collective security: the minority nationalities saw Russian as a language of colonial dominance. From the late 1950s, there was an intense programme of Russification, intended not only to break down opposition to Russian Slav hegemony, but to develop Russian as the national language (Pipes, 1975). In the Baltic States, incorporated into the Soviet Union as a result of the Nazi–Soviet Pact of 1939, the process of Russification – and colonisation – was just as intense.

It was clear by the 1970s that the policy had failed in so far as there was no notable increase in non-Russian-speaking groups using Russian as their first language and because there was considerable resentment amongst non-Russian groups, who all had to learn Russian as a second language while only 3% of Russians ever bothered to learn a language other than Russian (Pipes, 1975). Similar resentments were felt in CEE, and in Poland, especially; despite having had to learn Russian in school, very few Poles would ever use it outside the classroom. It was inevitable, therefore, that if Russian control ever ended, there would be a resurgence in the use of local languages simply as a means of asserting national identity. This is precisely what has happened.

In 1997 in the FSU, 87 different languages were being taught either as part of the curriculum or as the medium of instruction, especially where Russians are in the minority (Heyneman, 1998). In the Baltic States, Hungary, Georgia and the Ukraine, the resurgence of the national language has made the minority Russians feel increasingly threatened.

In all the independent states outside the Russian Federation, the revival of national languages, along with national/ethnic identity and loyalty, have now become commonplace. According to Mitter (1997, p. 225):

> *Curricula and textbooks give ample evidence of how these new forms of identity, crystallizing into 'patriotism', are emphasised and reinforced. However, this is only one side of the coin. The other side is highlighted by the emergence of chauvinism and xenophobia whose potency is enlarged by fanatical teachers (who, unfortunately, are not rare).*

In other parts of the transformational, reconstructing world, the rejection of languages of oppression can also be seen. In Mozambique, the decision to reject Portuguese in favour of English as the national language, and the decision to join the Commonwealth, and Namibia's decision to choose English rather than Afrikaans or any other indigenous language as the national language reflect regional economic and political realities (Brock-Utne, 1997). Eritrea likewise rejected Amharic as a language of repression and has embraced English and eight other languages, both for educational and for communication purposes. In South Africa, where 11 out of 27 languages spoken have been recognised for educational purposes, and as an expression of both human and linguistic rights, the costs of providing materials in all these languages could prove prohibitive. In any case, English is rapidly replacing Afrikaans and all other languages as the dominant language. In Vietnam and Cambodia, English is also gradually replacing French as the major foreign language, largely because the Association of Southeast Asian Nations (ASEAN) conducts all its business in English and because English is the most widely used language in the Asia-Pacific region (Crystal, 1997). In the past two years, two other African countries, Algeria and Rwanda, have also replaced French with English as the most important foreign language to be learnt in school.

It is this latter development, the growth of English, which could prove to be the most significant, since it reflects a recognition that English is rapidly becoming the global language, because of the media, the Internet, the linking together of stock markets, banking and, above all, TNCs. The spread of English is part of the process of globalisation. In Russia alone, 50 million people are learning English. In China, it is the main foreign language. Throughout CEE, the picture is the same. In the transformational states of Africa, it is essential for the political leaders and businessmen to be conversant with English, as Mozambique and Namibia have shown. Such a situation is not without its problems, as Figure 2 shows, especially as it leads to growing inequalities between those who have access to the language – and all the opportunities this brings – and those who do not.

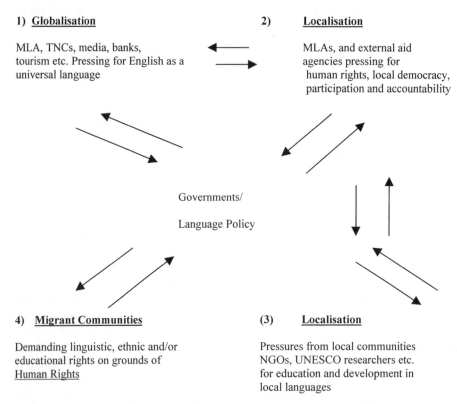

1) **Globalisation**

MLA, TNCs, media, banks,
tourism etc. Pressing for English as a
universal language

2)   **Localisation**

MLAs, and external aid
agencies pressing for
human rights, local democracy,
participation and accountability

Governments/

Language Policy

4) **Migrant Communities**

Demanding linguistic, ethnic and/or
educational rights on grounds of
Human Rights

(3)   **Localisation**

Pressures from local communities
NGOs, UNESCO researchers etc.
for education and development in
local languages

Figure 2. Irreconcilable pressures facing governments concerning language policies.

III. Challenges for the Future

It can be seen that many parts of the world are in the process of some very messy and confusing changes. What they are being transformed or changed into remains to be seen. Not all the trends and developments can easily be compared simply because of the speed of changes and because the initiators of change have been so varied. However, given that these changes will continue well into the twenty-first century, it could be salutary to identify some of the areas of concern that have become apparent during the past few years and that will need to be addressed if there is to be successful development in the future.

I perceive the following to be the main areas of concern. It is quite probable that other issues will also emerge.

Issues of quality and quality control. In systems that move from central (rigid) control to some form of decentralised and local control, especially when the private sector is also being allowed, or even encouraged, how can the quality of educational provision be maintained?

How to develop an inspection mechanism. One form of quality control is clearly a pattern of inspection, of buildings, of finance, of teaching, etc. to ensure that at least some minimum standards are adhered to, and that the regional and local disparities are not too considerable. How can this best be developed and regulated? This links in with:

The private/public sector balance. If the private sector is to be encouraged for some with the public sector for the majority, there is clearly a need to ensure that competition is fair, that certain groups are not unfairly advantaged while others are disadvantaged and that standards are maintained in all educational institutions.

How can this be done?

Ethnic nationalism. The excesses of ethnic nationalism have been most blatantly evidenced in Burundi, Rwanda and the former states of Yugoslavia but developments in the CEE and the FSU could also tip the balance. All those with political power and credibility need to be aware of these dangers and the international community needs to monitor potential trouble spots.

The impact of globalisation. Governments and teachers need to be aware of, and sensitive to, the impact of globalisation, not only on how this is shaping economies and the labour markets but also on how it impinges on the need to develop flexible teaching materials. Alvin Tofflers's *Future Shock* (1975) is no longer in the future: it is NOW.

Equality. One of the major effects of globalisation, privatisation, and decentralisation is the creation of social, political and economic inequalities. Should this be of concern? Should governments and those involved in education be more concerned with quality and standards, or should there be a greater concern for social justice? This issue does not simply affect transitional and transformational societies: it affects all of us. How should we respond?

References

Arnove, R. F. (1980) Comparative Education and World Systems Analysis, *Comparative Education Review*, 24, pp. 48–62.

Bloomer, K. (1991) *Decentralising the Education System in Quality in Basic Education*. London: Commonwealth Secretariat.

Bray, M. (1996a) *Counting the Full Cost: parental and community financing of education in East Asia*. Washington, DC: The World Bank and UNICEF.

Bray, M. (1996b) Privatization of Secondary Education: issues and policy implications. Paris: UNESCO, mimeo.

Bray, M. (1996c) Equity Issues in Local Resourcing of Education: community financing of primary schools in Bhutan, *International Review of Education*, 42, pp. 495–514.

Bray, M. (1997) Recognising the Burden on Household: family and community financing of primary education in East Asia, *Journal of Educational Planning and Administration*, XI, pp. 167–178.

Bray, M. & Lee, W. O. (1997) Education and Political Transitions in Asia: diversity and commonality, in W. O. Lee & M. Bray (Eds) *Education and Political Transition: perspectives and dimensions in East Asia*, pp. 3–16. Hong Kong: University of Hong Kong Comparative Education Research Centre.

Brock-Utne, B. (1997) The Language Question in Namibian Schools, *International Review of Education*, 42, pp. 241–260.

Chapman, J., Froumin, I. & Aspin, D. (Eds) (1995) *Creating and Managing the Democratic School*. London: Falmer Press.

Cheng, K. M. (1997) What have been Reformed? A Review of Two Decades' Reform in China's Education, paper presented at the Oxford International Conference in Education and Development, 'Education and Geopolitical Change', 11–15 September, New College, Oxford.

Chisholm, L. (1997) The Restructuring of South African Education and Training in Comparative Context, in P. Kallaway, G. Kruss, A. Fataar & G. Donn (Eds) *Education after Apartheid, South African Education in Transition*. Cape Town: University of Cape Town Press.

Chubb, J. E. & Moe, T. M. (1990) *Politics, Markets and America's Schools*. Washington, DC: Brookings Institute.

Crystal, D. (1997) *English as a Global Language*. Cambridge: Cambridge University Press.

Department for International Development (1997) *Eliminating World Poverty: a challenge for the 21st century*. London: The Stationery Office.

Dyezok, M. (1997) The Politics of History in Post-Soviet Ukraine, paper presented at the Oxford International Conference on Education and Development, 'Education and Geopolitical Change', 11–15 September, New College, Oxford.

Eisemon, T. O. (1995) Higher Education Reform in Romania, *Higher Education*, 30, pp. 135–152.

European Training Foundation (1997) *Report on the Vocational Education and Training System, Former Yugoslav Republic of Macedonia*. Turin: European Training Foundation.

Fukuyama, F. (1992) *The End of History and the Last Man*. Harmondsworth: Penguin.

Galabawa, J. C. J. (1994) Characteristics, Financing, Unit Costs and Selection Issues of Non-government Secondary School Provision in Tanzania, in M. Bray, Recognising the Burden on Household: family and community financing of primary education in East Asia, *Journal of Educational Planning and Administration*, XI, pp. 167–178.

Gorbachev, M. (1987) *Perestroika*. London: Fontana/Collins.

Grant, N. (1992) Education in the Soviet Union: the last phase, *Compare*, 22, pp. 69–80.

Green, A. (1997) *Education, Globalisation and the Nation State*. London: Macmillan.

Hans, N. (1964) *Comparative Education*, 3rd edn. London: Routledge & Kegan Paul.

Heyneman, S. (1998) The Transition from Party/State to Open Democracy: the role of education, *International Journal of Educational Development*, 18, pp. 21–40.

Higginson, J. H. (Ed.) (1979) *Selections from Michael Sadler*. Liverpool: Dejall & Meyorre.

Hobsbawm, E. (1994) *The Age of Extremes: the short twentieth century, 1914–1991*. London: Abacus.

Hurst, P. (1985) Decentralisation: panacea or red herring? in J. Lauglo & M. McLean (Eds) *The Control of Education: international perspectives on the centralisation–decentralisation debate*. London: Heinemann.

Ilon, L. (1994) Structural Adjustment and Education: adapting to a growing global market, *International Journal of Educational Development*, 14, pp. 95–109.

Kitaev, I. V. (1994) Russian Education in Transition: transformation of labour market, attitudes of youth and changes in management of higher and lifelong education, *Oxford Review of Education*, 20, pp. 111–130.

Kofman, E. & Youngs, G. (Eds) (1996) *Globalisation: theory and practice*. London: Pinter.

Kruss, G. (1997) Educational Restructuring in South Africa at Provincial Level: the case of the Western Cape, in P. Kallaway (Ed.) *Education after Apartheid: South African education in transition*. Cape Town: University of Cape Town Press.

Le Than Khoi (1986) Towards a General Theory of Education, *Comparative Education Review*, 30, pp. 12–39.

Maku, B. M. (1985) *Equity and Efficiency in Financing Secondary Education in Kenya: key issues in state community partnerships*, Working Paper No. 429. Nairobi: Institute of Development Studies, University of Nairobi.

Mallinson, V. (1974) *An Introduction to the Study of Comparative Education*, 4th edn. London: Heinemann.

McGinn, N. (1994) The Impact of Supranational Organisations on Public Education, *International Journal of Educational Development*, 14, pp. 289–298.

McGinn, N. (1997) Not Decentralisation but Integration, in K. Watson, C. Modgil & S. Modgil (Eds) *Educational Dilemmas: debate and diversity, vol. 3: Power and Responsibility in Education*, pp. 17–24. London: Cassell.

Mercer, M. (1997) Pre-university Education Finance in CEE and CIS Countries: re-drawing responsibilities, paper submitted to the Oxford International Conference on Education and Development, 'Education and Geopolitical Change', 11–15 September, New College, Oxford.

Mitter, W. (1992) Multicultural Education: basic considerations in an interdisciplinary approach, *Prospects*, 81, 22, pp. 31–40.

Mitter, W. (1997) Divergent and Convergent Trends in Multicultural Education in Russia and the Neighbouring Countries, in K. Watson, C. Modgil & S. Modgil (Eds) *Educational Dilemmas: debate and diversity, vol. 3: Power and Responsibility in Education*, pp. 221–228. London: Cassell.

Opolot, J. A. (1994) *Study on Costs and Cost-effective Approaches to Primary Education in Uganda*. Kampala: UNICEF.

Organisation for Economic Cooperation and Development (OECD) (1987) *Migrants' Children at School*. Paris: OECD.

Orivel, F. (1996) The Education Sector in Georgia: previous achievements, present problems and perspectives, mimeo, in S. Heyneman (1998) The Transition from Party/State to Open Democracy: the role of education, *International Journal of Educational Development*, 18, pp. 21–40.

Pipes, R. (1975) Reflections on the Nationality Problems in the Soviet Union, in N. Glazer & D. P. Moynihan (Eds) *Ethnicity: theory and experience*. Cambridge: Harvard University Press.

Prawda, J. (1993) Educational Decentralization in Latin America: lessons learned, *International Journal of Educational Development*, 13, pp. 253–264.

Raivola, R. (1985) What is Comparison? Methodological and Philosophical Considerations, *Comparative Educational Review*, 29, pp. 261–273.

Ramirez, F. O. & Boli, B. J. (1982) Global Patterns of Educational Institutionalization, in P. G. Altach, R. F. Arnove & G. P. Kelly (Eds) *Comparative Education*. New York: Macmillan.

Reich, R. B. (1991) *The Work of Nations: preparing ourselves for 21st century capitalism*. New York: Vintage Books.

Rondinelli, D., McCulloch, J. & Johnson, R. (1987) *Decentralising Public Services in Developing Countries: a framework for policy analysis and implementation research*. Charlotte: Research Training Institute.

Rowlands, I. H. & Green, M. (Eds) (1992) *Global Environmental Change and International Relations*. London: Macmillan.

Sayed, Y. (1997) Redefining the Public and Private Boundaries: discourses of educational decentralisation in post-apartheid South African education, paper presented to the Oxford International Conference on Education and Development, 'Education and Geopolitical Change', 11–15 September, New College, Oxford.

Schluter, M. & Lee, D. (1993) *The R Factor*. London: Hodder & Stoughton.

Subbarao, K. & Ezenari, K. (1995) *Transition, Poverty and Social Assistance in Mongolia*. Washington, DC: Education and Social Policy Department, The World Bank.

Toffler, A. (1975) *Future Shock*. London: Pan.

Toynbee, A. (1954) *Civilization on Trial*. Oxford: Oxford University Press.

Tsang, Mun. C. (1994) Costs of Education in China: issues of resource mobilisation, equality, equity and efficiency, *Education Economies*, 2, pp. 287–312.

UNESCO (1993) *World Education Report, 1993*. Paris: UNESCO.

UNESCO (1995) *World Education Report 1995*. Paris: UNESCO.

United Nations Development Programme (UNDP) (1996) *Human Development Report 1996*. Oxford: Oxford University Press.

United Nations Development Programme (UNDP) (1997) *Human Development Report 1997*. Oxford: Oxford University Press.

Watson, K. (1985) *Key Issues in Education: comparative perspectives.* Beckenham: Croom Helm.

Watson, K. (1993) Language, Education and Political Power: some reflections on North–South relationships, in M. C. Beveridge & G. Reddiford (Eds) *Language, Culture and Education*, pp. 19–41. Clevedon: Multilingual Matters.

Watson, K. (1994) Caught between Scylla and Charybdis: linguistic and educational dilemmas facing policy makers in pluralist states, *International Journal of Educational Development*, 14, pp. 321–337.

Watson, K. (1997a) Educational Provision for the 21st Century: who or what is shaping the agenda and influencing developments, in S. G. Weeks (Ed.) *Education in Southern Africa*. Gaborone: University of Botswana Press.

Watson, K. (1997b) Language, Power, Development and Geopolitical Changes, paper presented to the Oxford International Conference on Education and Development, 'Education and Geopolitical Change', 11–15 September, New College, Oxford.

West, L. (1995) *Regional Economic Variation and Basic Education in Rural China*. Washington, DC: The World Bank.

World Bank (1991) *China: Provincial Education Planning and Finance: sector study*. Washington, DC: The World Bank.

World Bank, (1995a) *China: regional disparities*. Washington, DC: The World Bank.

World Bank (1995b) *Russia: education in the transition*. Washington, DC: The World Bank.

World Bank (1995c) *Vietnam: poverty assessment and strategy*. Washington, DC: The World Bank.

World Bank (1996) *World Development Report 1996: from plan to market*. Washington, DC: The World Bank.

World Bank (1997) *World Development Report 1997: the state in a changing world*. Washington, DC: The World Bank.

World Conference on Education for All (WCEFA) (1990) *World Declaration on Education for All*. New York: Inter-Agency Commission, WCEFA.

Wright, S. (Ed.) (1994) *Ethnicity in Eastern Europe: questions of migration, language rights and education*. Clevedon: Multilingual Matters.

Zadja, J. (1980) *Education in the USSR*. Oxford: Pergamon Press.

Reflection on Megatrends in Education from a Polish Perspective

DANUTA ELSNER

Introduction

Since the peaceful revolution in 1989, Poland has been undergoing a period of great change, which has impacted on every sector of public life. This is particularly true for the education sector. The heart of the transition process lies in getting rid of principles, regulations and the way of thinking inherited from the communist period as soon as possible. This means returning to democracy, a market economy, and a pluralistic political system – phenomena that have existed without interruption for many decades in western Europe.

Poland, like other post-communist countries, aspires to be a member of the European Union. In practice, this means promoting many radical changes, which will harmonise Polish regulations and standards with those of the West. As a result, too much emphasis has been put on implementing Western solutions and ignoring characteristically Polish ones.

As far as education is concerned, one example of the Western perspective is given by Caldwell & Spinks (1992) in their 'megatrends in education'. The term 'megatrend' was popularised by John Naisbett (in Naisbett & Aburdene, 1990), a futurologist who tried to predict major trends in society. Caldwell & Spinks's 10 educational megatrends are not well known to all educators. This chapter aims, therefore, to identify briefly what these Western megatrends in education are, compare and contrast these trends with their Polish counterparts, and describe the extent to which they are relevant to the Polish context (or indeed to the eastern and central European post-communist societies which, like Poland, are undergoing a rapid period of transition). For the sake of clarity and brevity, the chapter will confine its discussions to two key questions.

To what extent are the Western megatrends in education relevant to Poland?

To what extent do trends specific to Polish education differ from those described by Caldwell & Spinks?

General Reflections on Megatrends in Education from a Polish Perspective

Megatrends in education and other problems connected with a vision of the future world and the role of education in it are not popular topics for discussion among Polish educators. Although education itself looks to the future and the transition period seems to be a good time to create long-term plans and policies, there is little discussion of longer-term trends. There are various reasons for this: first, teachers, headteachers, local education authority officers and ministry officials are so preoccupied with everyday, short-term problems that discussion of future trends and the vision of education seem to many to be fruitless; and secondly, for many of the older generation, the collapse of the communist regime has meant a good opportunity to restore the pre-communist past (regulations, institutions and standards from the period before the Second World War), which they perceive as a Golden Age (Kotasek, 1995). This situation is not only specific to Poland but also illustrates what is happening in other European post-communist countries too.

Here, then, is the first discrepancy between Eastern and Western perceptions. People from the well-developed Western democratic countries are more future-oriented, e.g. they outline megatrends, discuss future developments, create long-term plans and policies, while people from developing countries in central and eastern Europe are more preoccupied by the past and the present. Looking into the future seems for most of them to be a kind of luxury that they can not afford.

Specific Reflections on Megatrends in Education from a Polish Perspective – analysis

Specific reflections refer to the 10 megatrends cited as follows (in the order proposed by Caldwell & Spinks), and elaborated upon in the light of experiences of the Polish education system.

1. There will be a powerful but sharply focused role for central authorities, especially in respect to formulating goals, setting priorities, and building frameworks for accountability.

For the last few years, there has been a national debate on the role of central and local government in Poland. This has impacted strongly on education. After nearly five decades of excessive centralisation in the education system, during which decisions were made at the top and passed to schools for implementation, many politicians now wish to decentralise as many functions as possible to local councils.

This policy and practice of decentralisation, which appears to have been perceived by many as a cure for all 'educational diseases' (Radziwill, 1995), is not without its own problems. This is due to the fact that total delinking from the old system – and old practices – at least during the early stages of a period of transition, is unrealistic.

A second specific area worth reflecting on is the major curriculum reform that is under way. The main emphasis of this reform is to introduce a free selection of subject matter in the place of a monistic content and thus make the school curriculum more student-centred. This means that for the first time since the Second World War, Polish schools have the right to create their own curriculum as well as to set up their own student assessment system. It also signifies that local schools are responsible for their own curriculum development within a centrally defined framework. For many headteachers and teachers, this is a good opportunity to convert schools into more autonomous and self-managing organisations after years of regulation of nearly every aspect of school life by the Ministry of Education. Yet in spite of this opportunity and the prevalence of a commonly expressed desire that as many functions and tasks as possible should be decentralised, the division of role between central and local government in the field of education is not clear. Thus, the trend in Poland seems to be that even though the role of central authority is 'powerful' and is also sharply focused in terms of formulating goals, setting priorities and building a framework, it still has negative associations with the period of strong centralisation during the communist period.

2. National and global considerations will become increasingly important, especially with respect to the curriculum and an education system that is responsive to national needs within a global economy.

Nowadays in Poland, national and European considerations are recognised in respect of curriculum and educational policy. Both of these are new and seem to be equally important. Global perspectives, on the contrary, are excluded as far as the educational system and the curriculum are concerned. There are several reasons for this.

First, during the communist period there was a tendency to diminish national priorities in favour of so-called international communist considerations. This practice, which was common throughout the Eastern bloc countries, affected the aims of the school in many ways but particularly in promoting the ideology of communism, which was global in its orientation.

A second reason which boosted the importance of national and European considerations in educational policy and content was Poland's desire to join the European Union and NATO in the shortest time possible. This aspiration, it must be noted, was so strong that it led to the adoption of western European perspectives at the expense of central and eastern European ideas.

A third reason which explains Poland's indifference to the global perspective lies in the fact that most Poles seem to perceive the rest of the world (i.e. outside Europe) as 'peripheral' and of no interest to Poland. This led many of them to identify 'global' with 'European' and not to look further than the continent of Europe, with which they would like to strengthen their trade and political ties.

In the light of these facts, the Polish educational trend that emerges highlights national and European considerations at the expense of the global perspective. The weakening of the latter contradicts Caldwell & Spinks's observation.

3. Within a centrally determined framework, government schools will become largely self-managing, and distinctions between government and non-government schools will narrow.

During the communist period, virtually all schools were state schools. A small number of private schools were allowed in order to show the international community that private schools also existed under the totalitarian regime.

The first time non-government schools were established in large numbers was in 1990. Now, there are over 900 such schools in Poland as well as over 500 further education institutions and over 100 higher education institutions run by associations, churches and local chambers of commerce. Between 1990 and 1993, there was an explosion in the number of private schools and educational institutions but now the number has stabilised. Private schools are expensive and not many parents can afford to pay for them because of the lack of a well-developed middle class in Poland.

Private schools are much smaller than government schools. In order to attract parents they offer a more comprehensive curriculum and more attractive extra-curricular activities but this does not mean that pupils in such schools have higher achievement. Often, less gifted children and children with behavioural problems are enrolled in private schools. A trend that is worth noting here and which concurs with Caldwell & Spinks's observation is that the distinction between private and government schools is minimal in terms of organisation, content and educational goals.

4. There will be unparalleled concern for the provisions of a quality education for each individual.

This trend has an impact on education, although initially the focus of quality education was more on teaching and learning and less on management. This concern can be illustrated by the determination of schools to try to measure the quality of their performance and by the popularity of the concept of 'quality' as a topic for staff development meetings as well as for training events, organised for teachers and headteachers by Teacher In-service Training Centres. Quality assurance, quality measurement and indicators in education in general, and especially in schools, are also very popular topics of articles, books and training materials. This challenges local education authority officers to change the content and methods of teacher and school appraisal rather than to preoccupy themselves with collecting quantitative data as in the past.

Moreover, a spin-off of the concern for providing quality education is that 'education' itself has become more valued as a means of achieving a higher quality of life through a competitive labour market, which no longer heaps privileges on communist members alone. A good example of the value of education in Poland is the fact that the average rate of unemployment amongst individuals with university degrees is less than 1% as compared to 11% in the general population. Another example is the growing number of young people who, since 1990, have enrolled for under- and postgraduate courses at their own expense.

In the light of the preceding discussion, one can conclude, as did Caldwell & Spinks, that the provision of quality education is an emerging trend in Poland.

5. There will be a dispersal of the educative function, with telecommunications and computer technology ensuring that much learning which currently occurs in schools or institutions at post-compulsory levels will occur at home and the workplace.

During the communist period, access to higher education was limited by quotas at the post-compulsory level. Recently, higher education has become for many a desirable good and numerous higher education institutions – both government and non-government – have been established. Therefore, concentration rather than dispersion seems to characterise the situation in Poland.

Very few newly established institutions use telecommunications or computer technology to promote education due to lack of capital for software and hardware. This means that prospective students of such institutions are not properly equipped to make use of computer technology. Moreover, although business enterprises are equipped with computers and have access to the Internet, very few individuals have such resources at home and thus cannot use these tools for self-development. As far as computer technology as a medium of education is concerned, there is a noticeable shift from school-based to work-based (but not yet home-based) learning in Polish professional education.

6. The basic emphasis in education will be expanded to include problem-solving, creativity and capacity for lifelong learning and relearning.

Polish schools at all levels pay too much attention to academic knowledge and value most highly students with mathematical and linguistic intelligence and good memories. Problem-solving, creativity and learning and relearning are not yet popular with either teachers or students. This being the case, a new national curriculum framework was prepared in 1997 with the sole purpose of assisting Polish schools to shift their orientation from an overemphasis on academic knowledge towards building flexibility, creativity and the capacity for lifelong learning.

7. There will be an expanded role for the arts and spirituality; there will be a high level of 'connectedness' in the curriculum.

During the communist period, the ratio of vocational schools to grammar schools was 80:20. This is evidence of the educational priorities at that time. The main aim of schools then was to prepare workers for industry and agriculture rather than students who were aware of their human rights. As a result of that policy, emphasis was placed not on humanities and social science but on vocationally-oriented subjects.

During the last few years, however, there has been a major increase in the proportion of grammar schools. At present 56% are vocational schools and 44% are grammar schools, and the long-term target seems to be to reverse the ratio of the past. Irrespective of the ultimate target, this shift or trend is likely to continue into the next decade if the Polish education system is to converge with that of western Europe. If it takes place, the shift will signify an expansion of the role for the 'arts' and 'spirituality' as well as a higher level of 'connectedness' in the curriculum.

8. Women will claim their place among the ranks of leaders in education, including those at the most senior levels.

Position in school	Total no. of leaders	Total no. of women leaders	%
Headteacher	30,671	21,520	70.2
Deputy headteacher	13,623	10,541	77.4
Department head (general schools)	1,707	1,493	87.5
Department head (vocational schools)	3,222	1,074	33.3
Other middle managers	6,578	5,272	80.1

Table I. Proportions of women appointed to senior positions in Polish schools (1997).

As Table I illustrates (and in line with the experiences of other post-communist countries), more women than men are appointed as headteachers, deputy heads and other educational leaders in Poland (for details see Stepniowski, 1997).

However, these figures (as Table II indicates) are slightly toned down when we examine the position of women leaders within the local educational authorities.

Position in school	Total no. of leaders	Total no. of women leaders	%
Chief Education Officer and Deputy Chief Education Officer	103	29	28.2
Head of Department	149	79	53.0
Deputy Head of Department	32	20	62.5
Head of Section	134	69	51.5

Table II. Proportions of women appointed to senior positions in local education authorities in Poland (1997).

Overall, the dominant position of women as educational leaders is quite significant and encouraging. It is significant in that it surpasses Caldwell & Spinks's forecast. On the other hand, note must be made of the major contributing factor to the high proportion of women managers. In Poland, staff of educational institutions at all levels are poorly paid. Thus, to be a teacher or headteacher is less attractive to men, who tend to prefer better paid jobs in industry. This has led to the existence of schools with only one man (who usually is the caretaker) among the staff and to numerous problems connected with pupils' behaviour in school.

To date, there are no studies of women managers in education in Poland. Considering many factors, it is unlikely that such a theme will be topical in the near future.

9. The parent and community role in education will be claimed or reclaimed.

In the communist era, parents had few rights in relation to schooling. A more proactive involvement of parents in education has been noticeable since 1987. In that year, the first Civic Educational Association (CEA) was established and it now runs more than 400 independent schools. The CEA consists mostly of parents and has served as a role model for local communities throughout Poland. Seen from this perspective, one can safely conclude that parental awareness and involvement in education has been gradually increasing during the last few years.

10. There will be unparalleled concern for service by those who are required or have the opportunity to support the work of schools.

The idea of client orientation is very new within the Polish education system. In the last few decades, a preoccupation with the curriculum rather than with the needs of individual children has predominated. The reason for this was obvious, in that schools were perceived as institutions to mould obedient citizens.

At present, the trend towards good quality service for every child is recognised. This is being encouraged by local community councils, which are increasingly aware of the importance of education for the economic and spiritual growth of their regions. Open enrolment of children in schools according to the wishes of their parents, which was not permitted for years, is now being discussed. Such choice is obviously a feature of increasing concern to meet clients' needs.

Specific Reflection on Megatrends in Education from a Polish Perspective – synthesis

The reflections on megatrends from a Polish perspective that were discussed in the preceding section are summarised in Table III.

	The content of megatrends in education according to Caldwell & Spinks	The Polish perspective on megatrends
1	Powerful but sharply focused role for central authorities	Decentralisation of an overcentralised education system
2	National and global considerations	National and European considerations
3	A narrow distinction between government and non-government schools	No major distinction between government and non-government schools
4	Emphasis on provision of quality	A shift from a focus on quantity towards quality
5	Telecommunication and computer technology move post-compulsory education from schools to home and workplaces	Explosion in the number of institutions of higher and further education which have little money for modern technologies
6	Emphasis on lifelong learning	Emphasis on access to good formal education
7	Expansion of the roles of arts and spirituality in the curriculum	Expansion of the humanities in the curriculum
8	Growing number of women leaders in education	Existing high proportion of women leaders in education
9	Claimed or reclaimed role of parents	Growing activity of parents in education
10	Total client-orientation and support for schools	Expanding role of local communities in supporting schools

Table III. Summary of megatrends from a Polish perspective.

It is worth noting that a major criticism of the megatrends presented by Caldwell & Spinks is that no reference is made to the future of the teaching profession. This is a matter of great concern in Poland and indeed, in the other central and eastern European countries, too, especially when one reflects on the depth of the problem of training and retraining teachers. As we know, reforming teacher education is not simply a matter of changing teaching content and methods – important though these are – but also a matter of changing fundamental values and beliefs. Fullan sheds light on this when he opines that:

> *changes in beliefs are difficult to bring about: they challenge the core values held by a person ... and they are often not explicit or recognised ... Logically, one might think of beliefs changing first which, in turn, leads to new behaviours associated with the belief. Practically, however, there is considerable socio-psychological evidence to support the view that beliefs are learned through experience. (Fullan, 1988)*

Homo Sovieticus vs Homo Europaeus

An area of great concern in the current trends of the education system in Poland is the impact of the heritage of the communist regime and the beliefs and practices of the educators. The 45-year period of the communist regime, as argued by many writers, had a deep influence not only on society but also on the life of each individual. As a result of this influence, a certain type of mentality was shaped, the so-called Homo Sovieticus.

Dependence is the main feature of Homo Sovieticus, an archetype created by Polish philosopher Jozef Tischner (1992) in order to describe the mentality of a collective person moulded under the communist regime. Tischner employs the term 'sovieticus' in the generic sense of 'totalitarian man'. He applies it to all the communist societies of eastern and central Europe, emphasising not the particular dominance of the Soviet Russians over the ethnic groups, but the mentality that became widespread within totalitarian regimes. The roots of dependency, according to Tischner, are embedded in the lack of private property: individual property was always very limited under the communist regime; the ownership of the means of production was forbidden for individuals (Oldroyd & Elsner, 1994).

At the same time as Homo Sovieticus prevailed in the East, liberal philosophy and economics in the West encouraged a concept of the human being as an independent individual. That contrasting archetype can be called Homo Europaeus. Table IV gives a comparison of the main behaviours, beliefs and attitudes of people in western and eastern Europe. It must be stressed, however, that Homo Sovieticus is not a species limited to the former totalitarian nations, nor is Homo Europaeus absent there.

Homo Europaeus	Homo Sovieticus
Proctative	Reactive
Creative	Conservative
Responsible	Irresponsible
Independent	Dependent
Active	Passive
Optimistic	Pessimistic
Success-oriented	Failure-oriented
Open-minded	Narrow-minded
Outstanding	Mediocre

Table IV. Homo Sovieticus vs Homo Europaeus.

Concluding Remarks

In the preceding sections, we have seen how the difficulties experienced by those attempting to implement reforms in Poland (and other European countries) can be explained by the heritage of the communist regime. Indeed, the heritage of the communist regime can be considered as the most important factor explaining those difficulties. A whole range of aspects of this heritage can be identified, most of them of a sociological nature and relating to the inertia of acquired attitudes and behaviour patterns. More specifically, we can speak of work habits current in the old system, of the deeply rooted practice of acting only according to detailed instructions from above (e.g. following centrally prescribed curricula), of outdated teaching methods (e.g. authoritarian and encyclopaedic), and the like (Kalous, 1996).

We have also been introduced to the major curriculum reform currently going on in Poland. We argued that for the first time in decades teachers have to be responsible for their school curriculum based on the curriculum framework issued by the Ministry of Education.

Moreover, it was also suggested that the heart of this curricular reform lies in making teachers responsible for what happens in the school. This in turn led us to identify the characteristic features teachers will require in order to undertake their responsibilities. These, which are more in line with the qualities of Homo Europaeus, are: becoming independent, active, creative, open-minded and success-oriented. By contrast, this means getting rid of the features of Homo Sovieticus, which might take a considerable time. But *how much* time will it take to get rid of the features of Homo Sovieticus?

When the famous sociologist Ralf Dahrendorf was asked to predict the length of the transition period in central and eastern European countries (Dahrendorf, 1991), he said that the establishment of a new political system could be realised in 6 months; the transition in the economy could be achieved in 6 years; and the transition of people's attitudes and approaches would take 60 years.

If true, six decades is too long to wait for the peoples of Poland and other post-communist states. Given this predicament, what the educational systems of this region might be able to do is to treat the transformation of the teaching force as a megatrend. So doing will equip our schools not only with teachers who can teach and practise democracy but who can also provide suitable role models for the new citizens of the expanded European Union.

References

Caldwell, B. J. & Spinks, J. M. (1992) *Leading the Self-managing School*. London: Falmer Press.

Dahrendorf, R. (1991) *Reflexions sur la Revolution en Europe 1989–1990*. Paris: Seuil.

Fullan, M. (1988) Research into Educational Innovation, in R. Glatter, M. Preedy, C. Riches & M. Masterton (Eds) *Understanding School Management*. Milton Keynes: Open University Press.

Kalous, J. (1996) Transition and Transformation of Education, in J. Kalous & F. van Wieringen (Eds) *Improving Educational Management*. De Lier: ABC.

Kotasek, J. (1995) Vision of Education in Post-communist Era, *International Review of Education*, 36, pp. 473–487.

Naisbett, J. & Aburdene, P. (1990) *Megatrends 2000*. New York: Willian Morrow.

Oldroyd, D. & Elsner, D. (1994) Homo Sovieticus Meets Homo Europaeus. Coping with the Clash of Attitudes in East–West Collaboration, in K. Hamalainen & F. van Wieringen (Eds) *Reforming Educational Management in Europe*. De Lier: ABC.

Radziwill, A. (1995) Zakres Odpowiedzialnosci Panstwa za stan Edukacji. Dyrektor Szkoly No. 2.

Stepniowski, K. (1997) *Nauczyciele w roku Szkolnym 1996/9*. Warszawa: CODN.

Tischner J. (1992) *Etyka solidarnosci oraz Homo Sovieticus*. Krakow: Wyd. ZNAK.

Pedagogical Challenges in Post-Wende East Germany

BERNHARD THOMAS STREITWIESER

Introduction

This chapter emerged from research conducted in June 1997, in former East Berlin. During this time I was given the opportunity to visit the Max Planck Institute for Human Development and Education. My goal during this time was very simple: to learn as much as possible about the experiences of East German teachers before, during and after German reunification. Through discussion of a wide range of topics, covering a broad spectrum of time and experience, I hoped to learn about some of the important issues which these teachers today feel must still be resolved. More narrowly, the objective of my research was to learn about teachers' attitudes towards the West German educational system introduced after the Wende, and how they evaluate the system in light of their prior experiences as teachers in the German Democratic Republic (GDR).

Study Design

To conduct the study, I constructed guidelines to structure interviews with civics and history teachers. All the interviews were conducted in German, chronologically from the beginning of each teacher's career, through the days of the Peaceful Revolution, and up to the present. I explained that I was interested in learning their judgements about the two education systems, since as educators they are unique in having experienced both vastly different systems in their careers. For this reason I tried to structure the questions so that the interviewees would approach each question in terms of comparing life as a teacher in the GDR with life as a teacher in the Federal Republic of Germany (FRG): before and after reunification, then and now.

I conducted 25 in-person interviews with teachers from different neighbourhoods of former East Berlin. With the generous assistance of researchers at the Max Planck Institute [1], I had little trouble finding teachers from different school types and experience levels to meet with me. Except for one, all interviews were audio-recorded. Our meetings took place at the teachers' schools, in their homes, at the Institute or at local cafés. The duration of each interview on average was 2 hours. The demographics of the final pool of interviewees broke down along the following lines.

1. Gender:

> Women   18
> Men   7

2. Former German Democratic Republic school types represented:

> Polytechnische Oberschule (POS) (1–10 grade comprehensive 'polytechnical' vocational school)   13
>
> Erweiterte Oberschule (EOS) (11, 12th grade Abitur track extended secondary school)   2
>
> Berufschule (11, 12th grade trade school)   9
>
> Sonderschule (1–11th grade school for the gifted)   1

3. Federal Republic of Germany school types represented [2]:

> Hauptschule (5–9th grade lower track school of three main traditional German schooling tracks)   4
>
> Gymnasium (5–10th grade upper track college-preparatory school, leads to the Abitur for college entrance)   5
>
> Gesamtschule (5–10th grade comprehensive school; an alternative to the traditional 3-tier system)   6
>
> Berufschule (11–13th grade trade school)   8
>
> Sonderschule (1–11 grade special schools)   2

Except for one teacher, all of the interviewees had on average worked as teachers under the education system of the GDR for 8 years, and since reunification have worked continuously as teachers in the FRG. Again, except for one, all of the interviewees on average were in their mid-forties.

Background

Very few people will ever forget the amazing days in late November of 1989, when East and West Germans did the impossible and scaled the

Berlin Wall, bringing down an empire that only a few weeks before had vowed to live 'another 100 years'. Along with the death of the GDR's political and economic system, a way of life, a culture, and an education system also passed into history.

Objectivity, perhaps most possible because of the passage of time, has allowed some researchers today to recognise that much of what the West initially dismissed in its euphoric 'victory' over communism should perhaps be re-evaluated today. Research since 1990 has been conducted on various aspects of educational change in reunified Germany, such as the following:

- problems facing educational policy-makers (Anweiler, 1992; Mitter, 1992; Mintrop & Weiler, 1994; Phillips, 1995);
- structural adjustments (Anweiler, 1992; Costello, 1992; Mitter, 1992; Fishmann, 1993; Mintrop & Weiler, 1994; Rust & Rust, 1995);
- curriculum reform (Mitter, 1991);
- textbook reform (Fritzsche, 1990; Moldenhauer, 1991; Addick, 1992);
- changes in higher education (de Rudder, 1993; Weiler et al, 1996);
- educational adjustments to a free market economy (Latka-Johring, 1991);
- reflections on the purpose and place of secondary education within new German social policy (Behrendt et al, 1991); and
- teachers' adjustments to the West German education system (Doebert & Rudolf, 1995; Combe & Buchen, 1996; Hoyer, 1996; Mintrop, 1996).

To consider East Germany and its legacy, one finds it difficult in hindsight not to recognise that, along with a political and economic system that clearly had many repressive characteristics, there were aspects of the East German social system, including the education system, that were quite advanced and humanistic.

Over the past decade, studies on East German educational changes have moved from being largely descriptive of systemic changes, to being more oriented towards the individuals involved (administrators, teachers and students) and how they have met the challenges that the educational reunification process has presented. Many of these studies have considered the effects of systemic changes, or how new curricula and textbooks have affected outcomes. Fewer studies have considered cultural differences, such as how the social climate in schools and classrooms has changed. Only recently have a limited number of researchers begun to consider the question of teacher perceptions and behavioural reactions to their new roles.

I see research on educational changes in Germany in the post-reunification decade as essentially developing in three distinct stages. Stage I (1990–92) is characterised by the first studies which began appearing shortly after the fall of the Berlin Wall. In these early studies, many more questions were posed than answered. The main anxieties stemmed from questions about what challenges the GDR's education legacy would pose, and if policy-makers would handle the debates with sensitivity and patience when trying to work out how best to unite the two systems. This research was, out of necessity, in reaction to the unexpected historical events happening at the time. Many of these early studies extensively reviewed the creation and reform processes of each system as it had developed over the 40 years of separation, and they offered more of a chronological account than an analysis in their attempts to predict what might happen in the future.

From the early studies, which mainly reacted and predicted, those appearing 2–3 years later into the new system, representing Stage II of the research (1993–95), shifted from looking at what would happen to starting to consider what had happened so far. These studies often began their analysis with an overview of what reunification had done to German education from a system-wide point of view, and then moved on to a closer analysis of one aspect (e.g. the Gymnasium) or to a case study of a particular school, federal state, or some other type of comparative analysis. Studies moving toward the decade's close, representing Stage III of the research (1996–97), have been the first to truly move beyond descriptive, East–West comparative or highly critical studies, which so far have been quick to point out the limitations and failures of East German pedagogy without much to say for its strengths. Some of these recent works have begun to step back and re-evaluate the educational system of the GDR for aspects of its pedagogy and learning ethos which might have been positive. In this third research phase, an attempt has been made to consider the perspective 'from below' in an attempt to debunk the too-often reductionist perspective 'from above', which has portrayed the GDR teacher as nothing more than a propagandist (*der systemnahe Lehrer*). In this respect alone, these studies have been very important.

The region of eastern Germany officially became the German Democratic Republic on 7 October 1949, 4½ years after the end of the Second World War. From this date forward, for the next 40 years almost to the day, the eastern half of Germany became quickly shut off from the Western world, most dramatically by the building of the Berlin Wall in November 1961. The Iron Curtain ensured that East Germany would cease to be part of the culture of West Germany, and be left untouched to form its own culture as an independent nation. For the next 40 years, just as West Germany tried to convince the world of its alliance with the capitalist, democratic systems of the Western nations, so East Germany was committed to proving that not only did it have its own culture as a nation, but that it was also a showpiece for the success of communism. After the Soviet Union itself, East Germany's small economy became the strongest in the Eastern bloc, and its citizens enjoyed the highest standard of living (Siebert-Klein, 1980). Pivotal to the success of socialism in East Germany, as is the case for most successful political and economic systems, was of course its teaching force.

After reunification of East and West Germany was officially declared on 3 October 1990, the governments of the five new Eastern German Federal States, or Laender, adopted the traditional Western German model for secondary education, thus reimplementing the structure that had existed in Weimar Germany prior to the Second World War. A 'third way', as an alternative to socialist and capitalist education models, by which East German education on its own terms was to be gradually dissolved into the West German system, was discussed at length by East German educators but then quickly rejected by West German policy-makers in the sweeping school legislation of 1991. In its entirety, East German education was roundly discredited and its philosophy of education and teaching methodology dismissed as too tainted by communism to serve a useful purpose in the 'new' system. In a mere 6-week summer period, the educational structure of the former GDR was revamped along the lines of the Western German model. Although the majority of teachers (close to 80%) did not lose their jobs – unlike much of the rest of the population – their new roles were perhaps even more challenging than coping with unemployment: playing the same parts as before but in completely new characters. Mintrop & Weiler write that:

> *The transition process forced a large number of former East Germans to change ... [However] for the most part, teachers were able to keep their jobs ... It is this unusual coexistence of full-scale systemic change and the retention of the old teaching force that creates such an intriguing opportunity for studying the reaction of teachers – as micro-political actors, so to speak – to major changes in their professional and political environment. (Mintrop & Weiler, 1994, p. 257)*

In addition to operating within an altered school structure, teachers were given new textbooks to follow and, more importantly, were expected to pursue completely different methodological and ideological guidelines from those they had been charged with carrying out for the past 40 years. Concurrently, students and parents also began exercising freedoms that they had only dreamed of a few months earlier, thus adding another level of challenge to teachers' already daunting task. The result was that massive educational and societal changes were ordered from above, with the expectation that Eastern German teachers working from below would successfully bring about the transition in their schools. This was to be accomplished without their involvement in educational decision-making at the political level, and without their needing to have their new roles (what was expected of them and what they could expect in return) clarified. In short, a great many things were expected and yet, in a paradoxical reversal of what had been the norm before, it was suddenly left up to them as to how they would carry out their new tasks under the new system.

David Phillips (1995), in his excellent research on Eastern German educational changes, has written that a unique opportunity to study comparatively two systems in action was lost when West German policy-makers rejected the initial 'third way' proposal (which would have allowed for a differentiation in style but not necessarily of quality). Educators the world over might have had much to learn about pedagogy and its durability over social change by watching the education systems of the Eastern and Western Laender grow together over time, instead of one side coping with wholesale replacement by the other. The quick replacement of one system by the other forced Laender policy-makers, administrators and, most of all, teachers to scramble for new footing, opening up problems which today have yet to be resolved.

In having experienced the remaking of their entire educational system in the image of the FRG, there lies within every former East German teacher who taught during those years, and who continues to teach today, a remarkable portrait of how very differently people can choose to deal with life-wrenching change. The affective experiences of former East Berlin teachers, partly aware of the pedagogical liberation that the death of their nation has afforded them, and at the same time also still struggling to catch up to a faster, more impersonal system and way of life, are explored in the following sections.

Discussion of Main Findings

For the sake of brevity, I have chosen only a few quotations to make each point, although there were many very interesting ones from which I found it quite difficult to make a selection. I have tried, therefore, to choose only those data that highlight most clearly and succinctly the themes of my study.

1. The Transition and Perceived Criteria for a 'Successful' Umlehrnen *(unlearning and relearning)*

Much of the literature about educational change in Eastern Germany has painted a bleak picture of how it affected teachers and how in turn they coped, from unhappily conforming in order to save their jobs (Weiler et al, 1996) to conforming to an irreversible process which the population pushed onto them (Fishmann, 1994).

However, in my brief study, I found this not to be the case; teachers in East Berlin experienced a 'friendly' transition. Teacher K said that a feeling of arrogance on the part of West German teachers with whom she began working shortly after reunification was not evident. They worked well together and learned quite easily from one another. Teacher I added:

> *The West German teachers liked the kind of atmosphere which the East German teacher brought over. They just got pulled into the group with us. In the West, the mentality is usually 'Everyone for himself'.*

Teacher W argued similarly, saying that:

> *Our colleagues who came here from Spandau (West Berlin) showed a readiness from day one to be helpful to us here in East Berlin. Through working together, through being so helpful, they really gave us a lift and helped make this 'melting together' process a lot easier. Of course, there is still some tension between different employment statuses, but this has less to do with East–West differences than with professional differences, which would exist in any case. In my school at least there was no feeling of being colonised by the West; the teachers who came here helped build what really became a completely new school. They weren't colonisers, but just the opposite: colleagues. I really can't say it was any other way. I think many others had this experience too; not all, but many.*

2. Appreciation for the Pedagogical Freedoms the Wende has Introduced into Classrooms

While each teacher in the sample had much to say about how reunification in different ways has affected them, some very critically and negatively and others quite pleasantly, no one completely regretted that the political and economic constrictions of the former system were gone. In referring to the former system, in fact, nearly everyone at some point used the word '*Diktatur*' (dictatorship) to talk about their past conditions. The appreciation these teachers have for the freedoms that the Wende introduced was quite evident and eagerly expressed. Teacher P put it this way:

> *Teachers in the GDR are really, on average, the biggest winners of the Wende [but even so] in my school the majority of the faculty misses the GDR, they regret that it is gone. Shortly before elections you most often hear people saying, 'Before everything was better than it is today' and they complain about the school system. When I notice people like this, I think to myself that maybe they were in the Stasi (Staatssicherheitsdienst, state secret police) or something, and I keep my distance. Granted, there is a lot of joblessness today,*

> *and families are hardest hit in part, you hear people say, 'You never had that in the GDR' but that they are now driving a Mercedes and earlier had to wait ten years for a Trabant, well, that's all forgotten now. Before they earned 1000 East German marks, today they earn 3500 West German marks, and that too is forgotten: the percentage differences don't get calculated out.*

Teacher J, who only taught for one year before reunification, characterised his feelings about the transformation this way:

> *For me the Wende was like hitting the jackpot: I went from being a poorly paid GDR teacher to a relatively well-paid West teacher. Because I was young and only lived through the end of the GDR, and was not in the party and so did not have any political skeletons in my closet, it was very convenient that reunification happened. For me it was not too late, I could still go travelling. Some of the older generation weren't this lucky.*

3. Problems with a Decentralised Curriculum (Freier Lehrplan) and Nostalgia for the Old Centralised Education System

These problems were due to:

(a) difficulties imposed upon instruction in the light of vastly differing student abilities;
(b) appreciation for the pedagogical freedoms the Wende has introduced into their classrooms; and
(c) difficulties with taking on greater responsibility without sufficient guidelines for how to manage them.

Education in East Germany, as in all communist systems, was centralised. As Margaret Siebert-Klein (1980) explains in her work on East German education, it is clear that while ideally teachers at the local level were encouraged to make recommendations to successively higher levels of administration, in reality school structure and ideology was dictated completely from above and stringent controls on teacher methodology and use of teaching tools permeated every possible aspect of classroom instruction. Teachers in East Germany were among the key elements supporting the system and maintaining its legitimacy. However, the political system was also built in such a way as to make working as a teacher but not supporting the system virtually impossible. At least during the early and middle periods of the regime, up until the later years of the 1980s, thinking one way and acting another, as a teacher, was very difficult. The state security (*Stasi*) component stationed on each faculty made it very difficult to practise loyalty for show only, without believing in the system.

Every aspect of schooling was mandated in top–down fashion by the central government's Ministry for the Education of the People (*Ministerium für Volksbildung*). From school structure and curriculum formation to teaching methodology and lesson content, teachers had strict guidelines about what to teach when, and how to teach it, to whom and for what purposes. Teachers were extremely circumscribed in terms of being able to concentrate on stressing those areas which they might feel were important, or putting less emphasis on others, and also in the methodology they used in teaching lessons. *Lehr-* and *Lernfreiheit* (or learning and teaching freedom) concepts embedded in centuries-old traditional German educational philosophy were not words that existed in the East German teachers' lexicon. But today, among this particular sample of teachers, there has emerged quite a discrepancy on the merits of a circumscribed versus a freer curriculum.

On the one hand, Teacher L came down strongly in favour of the old, centralised system:

> *What I personally really liked were centralised lesson plans, I wish we still used them today, they are extremely sensible. I wish we still used the centralised textbooks and tests, where each school had the same materials. But of course these will never be used again. Each teacher knew the material they were supposed to teach and that made sense. Today each teacher can do what he wants, that is to say, when I don't feel like teaching something, I can just drop it. But before there were really hard and fast guidelines, this and this and this had to be in the lesson and someone checked that it was taught, and students were tested to see if they knew it.*

On the other hand, this clearly defined curriculum also had its restrictions. Teacher F represents the other viewpoint, saying:

> *It was not directly prohibited to bring other things into the prescribed lesson, but the problem was finding time to insert it into the plan. If, for instance, I had to teach on a specific topic, I had to figure the exact time needed, and if I left something out, someone would demand of me, 'What were you actually teaching if they don't know X or Y by now? Why can't they solve this?' There was always this risk. If you got the exam envelope and realised you had left something out [3], it would be bad. There was a problem if your students didn't do well.*

The Ministry of Education wrote the textbooks and examinations, which teachers were then sworn by oath and required by law to carry out exactly as stipulated. Not only was each subject in the curriculum very carefully selected for fulfilment of the underlying Marxist-Leninist economic and political goals of the socialist state, but each day of every teacher's lesson plan was also planned down to the very hour. Unannounced inspections to ensure compliance with the lesson plan were not uncommon. But, more importantly, teachers knew that if they deviated from the socialist dogma and insisted on bringing in elements from personal opinion not shared by the Ministry of Education, the danger was that any student in the class might relate to his parents what he or she had learned in class and set off, innocently or deliberately, suspicion about the teacher and then swift action by the authorities. The parents might not like what the student was learning, or the student might not like it, and a teacher under suspicion quickly became a danger to the state's goal of producing a productive and dedicated workforce.

Teacher W explained how this took effect:

> *As a teacher, one was often afraid. One never knew what kind of parents were hiding behind their child, so that if you had a conversation with a student in which you were critical of some aspect of the system and voiced your personal opinion, then you were always a little afraid that somewhere a father or mother would get upset and bring pressure to bear on you.*

This said, however, it must also be realised that this strictness was an ideal, whose manifestation was more apparent in the early and middle years of the GDR's lifespan, and less so near its collapse. Teacher W, who began her teaching career in 1980 and still teaches today in a Berlin vocational school, explained:

> *The reality with which students were confronted looked of course much different from what was on the lesson plan, so that as a teacher one often said, 'You have to know this for the exam, you want to pass, don't you? And what you think, well, that may be the truth but if you write it on the exam you'll get a zero'. It was a kind of double meaning for us teachers. We tried to say, 'You have to learn this regardless of how you feel about it, you have to learn the content, and your private opinion may be right and good, but we aren't interested in that'. One knew that reality looked different so that in effect we ended up teaching a dual lesson.*

4. A Perception of Less Competent Students, Greater Social Problems

Since almost all parents in the GDR worked during the day, the mother equally as the father, had it not been for afternoon school-organised activity clubs, students would have had little to do during this time. The lack of these organised, state-funded activity groups as a part of today's education system is a problem which nearly every teacher in this sample pointed out as especially problematic. Teacher M explained his concern:

> *Today's society is so stressful, so dangerous ... there are no more after school hobby clubs as there were before where they could be busy in their free time. These would have to be financed by the state and the state just doesn't put money toward that any more. Everything that costs money is being reduced. In terms of societal needs, whatever costs money is being reduced, and in terms of culture and education most of all.*

During the years of the GDR, teachers often ran the youth party organisations, such as the Young Pioneers (*Junge Pioneere*) for students in 1–7 grade, or the Free German Youth organisation (*Freie Deutsche Jugend*) for students in the 8–12 grade before they were strongly encouraged to join the Socialist Unity Party (*Sozialistische Einheitspartei Deutschland*). Although the political purpose of each of these organisations was obvious and should not be discounted, they also gave students a better chance to foster closer relationships with teachers and form bonds of friendship that even those teachers who were very critical of the former system find greatly lacking today. In addition to teaching in the classroom and conducting regular parent–teacher conferences, teachers were also required, and had the right, to make regular home visits to the parents of each student (*Eltern Abende*), and also, in the case of vocational schools to visit the students at their places of apprenticeship. This ethos of responsibility was both a requirement but also something which many teachers expressed willingness towards. Teacher W2 spoke about this, saying:

> *Sure, we had things like afternoon learning clubs which we were required to lead, but it was duty in a different sense. Our way of regarding this duty was different. Today society is quite oriented toward the individual, everyone is most concerned about him/herself ... The whole society [in the GDR] was just so different. There's no other way I can say this.*

Teacher F explained how he felt about state-mandated responsibility:

> *Teachers felt very responsible for their students. A bad grade for a student was always seen as a failure on the part of the teacher. The teacher would ask him/herself, 'What did I do wrong? What do I have to do to bring this student up to speed?' Few students were left behind. The weaker students were helped so much, and the teacher organised students to help one another. We always found someone to help. Today in my school, students are much less motivated. Before, students were very motivated, I think, because they knew what they*

> *wanted in the future, and what kind of grades would be
> required. Today, many know that when they get out of school,
> there won't be a job waiting for them. Today they think, 'I
> don't mind if I have to stay in school another year'. Before, if
> someone stayed behind it was a catastrophe. Today if students
> are disappointed by having to repeat a year, they aren't
> showing it. They have no motivation.*

This ethos of responsibility fostered in many ways a very constructive learning environment, in which those less capable students were pulled along, while they might have fallen through the cracks in a more impersonal system. For all of its control, if one takes performance as the criterion alone, the East German school system functioned remarkably well. The achievement of its students was high when judged by Western standards. East German students tested shortly after the collapse of the Wall for competency levels in non-political subjects like biology and physics scored higher than their Western counterparts. In fact, the transformation from the GDR's school system to that of the GFR did not drastically impair the performance of East German students in comparison with their West German counterparts. Instead, Schnabel et al (1996) at the Max Planck Institute in Berlin found that differences in achievement were far more pronounced between students of different school types, than between students from East or West.

Mintrop (1997), in a study on tracking, found that the POS teacher's job was not so much to help as many students as possible qualify for the EOS, but rather to pass on to the next level as many students as possible through the 10-year system and thus avoid the stigma of failure, for which he or she would be held personally and primarily responsible by the authorities. Thus, unlike teachers in a tracking system, a POS teacher's job was not so much to assess a student's academic potential and to channel him or her into special courses to foster that ability, but rather to pass students forward to the next level – which sometimes required going to great lengths for them through extra work, setting up tutoring arrangements, putting pressure on parents and employers and, as a last resort and if absolutely necessary, just brushing those deficiencies under the carpet. Teacher F said:

> *This led to what appeared as a homogeneously achieving and
> equally intelligent student population, when in fact that was
> not so. It must really be said that teachers, because of pressure
> 'from above', were often just not in a position to do otherwise.
> This was a real problem. If two or three or so students failed,
> the principal would demand you answer exactly what in fact
> you had been teaching, it was seen as unacceptable that
> people failed.*

The apparent drive in East German education to homogenise student body achievement was one of the variables empirically investigated in the BIJU study (*Bildungsverlaeufe im Jugendalter*, or 'Learning Processes, Educational Careers and Psychosocial Development in Adolescence') conducted by researchers at the Max Planck Institute (Schnabel et al, 1996). The BIJU study found that for the first year of the 'new' school system (1991–92), there were fewer East German students in the lower achieving level, while in the upper achieving level there were equal numbers of East and West students, thus contradicting the idea that the uniform school structure may have homogenised the overall achievement level by hindering more capable students from achieving highly. In other words, improving the performance of lower achieving students was accomplished without it also impairing the high-level achievement of more capable students. The authors attribute part of this success to the extra-school learning activities (*Außerschulische Unterrichtsangebote*) which existed in the GDR, such as learning clubs (*Schuelergesellschaften* or *Schuelerkabinetten*) of the Free German Youth Organisation, teacher-organised tutoring relationships among students (*Lernpatenschaften*), closer school–employment–family relationships, and a more focused, teaching methodology.

While this ethos of responsibility helped students who might otherwise have been much lower academic achievers, it also had its problems. Sometimes the kind of control and monitoring of students could go too far. Teacher PV explained:

> *This brings us to a very important point. If a student was doing poorly at school, it was the teacher's job to investigate outside of school, even, for possible causes. During the GDR, teachers were permitted to pick up the telephone and call the parents' employer if the student acted up in class. And that was abuse of power.*

And, while fostering lower achievers apparently did not keep more capable students from high-level achievement, as the BIJU study shows, teachers took liberties in terms of presenting the most realistic judgement about a student's academic accomplishments to save themselves from embarrassment, or worse, trouble with higher authorities. It could be argued that this reaction may not actually be all too uncommon in any school system, but I think the point is worth noting nevertheless. Teacher F elaborated the negative elements he felt about this ethos of responsibility:

> *This responsibility of the teacher for his students was a problem. If you had the misfortune of having a class of 25 poor students, you did all you could to prevent poor performance; if they did poorly anyway, it was generally believed that the*

> *teacher was not competent. Therefore, teachers often let*
> *students pass who really should have stayed behind.*

5. A Perception that Teacher–Teacher, Teacher–Student and
Teacher–Parent Relationships Are Less Friendly Today

A concern shared by most of the teachers with whom I spoke was over
the fate of today's youth. Teacher W explained the disillusionment she
feels:

> *In terms of their future employment possibilities, the youth in*
> *the GDR grew up in a worry-free environment; the fear of*
> *finding a job was a foreign concept to them and their parents.*
> *The saying 'He who wants work will find work' meant*
> *something, and those who did not work were just regarded as*
> *too lazy to work. Many of those who work today and even*
> *those who pass their certification tests don't know what their*
> *next step will be. This is really one of the biggest differences*
> *between then and now.*

Teacher P added:

> *Teachers today have different things to contend with: drugs,*
> *criminality, Mafia, other types of social relations, these are*
> *things which naturally make the work of a teacher more*
> *difficult. It was easier in this sense in the GDR. Teachers get*
> *mad that before they were able to punish kids through the*
> *mechanisms of the FDJ [Free German Youth] or the JPs [Young*
> *Pioneers] and that these no longer exist today and the youth*
> *are now so free and so different. The power teachers had to*
> *control their students has been taken away.*

Teacher H also attributed some of his concerns about today's youth to
problems caused by a more consumer-oriented society:

> *Between the students relations seem much different now.*
> *Violence seems more prevalent; before this was much less. Of*
> *course there were fights before too, but they weren't started*
> *because 'You have Adidas shoes and I have Nike's', or over*
> *drugs. The problem of joblessness is also a huge factor.*

Teacher H, a former leader of a Young Pioneer group, noted that:

> *There is a very noticeable decrease in social relations among*
> *teachers today in comparison with before; it was much*
> *stronger before. As I perceive it, today teachers do less together*
> *socially, outside of school. Everybody does what he wants*
> *today. For many teachers, when the school bell rings and the*

day ends for them, they think, 'I don't have to do anything
more' [Germans call this a Beamtenmentalität, *or what in*
English we might call a 'nine-to-five attitude']. The solidarity
which existed before is no longer evident. Even in schools
where the entire faculty are all former East Germans, the
atmosphere is different now. Reasons I can think of for this are
threefold: (1) there are less requirements from the state today
than before, so they do what is in their job description but not
more; (2) many work in schools where they feel they don't
belong; (3) teachers haven't identified with the new
atmosphere yet. The work climate before the Wende was better
... or different.

6. Die Mauer im Kopf ist noch da *(There's still a 'Wall in the Mind')*

East and West Germany must be viewed as having been two quite
distinct cultures. After 1949, each country developed on such vastly
different social, cultural, political and economic levels that the citizens
of each country were conditioned to regard the other, even if historically
and linguistically the same, as different in almost every way. Remember
that, in a very real sense, Germans collectively as a people had been used
as political and cultural pawns throughout the cold war by each
superpower trying to ideologically outdo the other. Germany, East and
West, became the showpiece for the two larger bipolar political systems,
and each side was made to be the extreme example of its bloc's
ideological and structural identity. It is no wonder that when the two
nations were thrust together again – much faster than anyone could ever
have anticipated and, in retrospect, much faster than many people today
wished had happened – Germans were primed to see each other in the
starkest of terms. Teacher M expressed some of this anger quite
forcefully:

One has a tendency to judge the others in an instant. Many
West German students are very full of themselves, they think
they are special as Westerners. They think, 'Our Deutschmark
saved those lazy East Germans who sat around for 40 years
doing nothing but allowing themselves to become dumbed by
socialism'. But let me tell you, we are ahead of them on one
certain point: namely, we've now gotten to know both social
systems and they only know theirs. I know both and can see
things through two glasses, I can judge from two points of
view, and that's an area of experience that only we have and
they don't. No 'Wessie can see things this way'. ['Wessie' is a
term for a West German, as opposed to an 'Ossie' for an East
German.]

Conclusion

Today – 7 years after the Berlin Wall was ripped down – many Germans admit that there is a psychological wall still dividing them. This difficulty in seeing the 'other' in more objective terms has also manifested itself in channels of communication between both formerly separated societies. Understandably, this has made research by Germans on Germans, and particularly by West Germans on East Germans, more difficult. Many of the conversations I had with teachers, as an American and an outsider to Germany's most recent events, was by their own admission less guarded than it would have been with a West German interviewer. While this state of affairs is unfortunate and, it is hoped, soon to change, it also points to a unique and slight window in time when research by outsiders is of the essence. I hope through this study that I have been able to demonstrate this to some degree.

German reunification presents one case study of how two societies and their different educational sectors manage to come together based on a mutual desire to do so, but also to do so because it happens in an unstoppable and irreversible manner. The coming together of different cultures is serendipitous, surely, as often as it is planned, and the German case is a good example of a most surprising coming together. In observing this encounter, I think that comparative educators, as well as other social scientists, politicians and lay people of any culture have much to learn, and may therefore approach the next social and educational upheaval with greater sensitivity and insight.

A Note on Interpreting this Study

This research project has documented the experiences of 25 teachers, and then only a very small slice of their overall school transformation process. My reasons for concentrating only on teachers from former East Berlin were simple: one month was not enough time to justify a broader investigation; and having little prior experience in interviewing and field researching, I felt it best to start modestly rather than be overambitious. The study does not claim to represent East Berlin teachers as a group, and certainly not the entire body of East German teachers. The work environment described in schools and the characteristics of the student population for Berlin teachers should not be taken to represent conditions as they existed for the rest of former East Germany, nor for Eastern Germany today. The situation for teachers in the capital of East Germany and its biggest city was quite distinct from that of teachers in smaller cities and in the countryside. Finally, it should be noted that soon after the Wende, the situation between East Berlin teachers and teachers in the rest of Eastern Germany again was different as regards income and employment status. This was because of the difference between civil servant status (*Beamterstatus*), granted to Berlin teachers, and state employee status (*Angestellterstatus*), offered to the rest of the population of Eastern German teachers.

Notes

[1] My gratitude goes especially to Dr Juergen Baumert, Dr Christa Haendle and Dr Detlef Oesterreich.

[2] Strangely, but not by design, I did not have any Realschule teachers in my sample.

[3] Tests were written by the education ministry and sent to each school, so that the teachers had just as little idea of what the test questions would be from year to year as the students did.

References

Addick, C. (1992) The Development of Textbooks, Curricula, and Educational Reform: the case of pedagogics as school subjects, *Zeitschrift fuer Pedagogik*, 38, pp. 703–724.

Anweiler, O. (1992) Some Historical Aspects of Educational Change in the Former Soviet Union and Eastern Europe, *Oxford Studies in Comparative Education*, 2, pp. 29–39.

Behrendt, W., Knoop, J., Mannschatz, E., Protz, S. & Sladek, H. (1991) Discussion of School and Educational Reform: secondary education in renascent GDR society, *European Education*, 23, pp. 37–50.

Combe, H. & Buchen, S. (1996) *Belastung von Lehrerinnen und Lehrern: Fallstudien zur Bedeutung alltaeglicher Handlungsablaeufe an unterschiedlichen Schulformen*. Muenchen: Juventa.

Costello, K. (1992) After the Wall: the remaking of Eastern German education, *Executive Educator*, 14, pp. 38–39.

de Rudder, H. (1993) Transforming Higher Education in East Germany, *Review of Higher Education*, 16, pp. 391–417.

Doebert, H. & Rudolf, R. (1995) *Lehrerberuf – Schule – Unterricht: Einstellungen, Meinungen und Urteile ostdeutscher Lehrerinnen und Lehrer – Ergbebnisse einer empirischen Untersuchung in Berlin-Ost, Brandenburg und Sachsen.* Frankfurt am Main: Deutsches Institut fuer Internationale Paedagogische Forschung.

Fishman, S. (1993) After the Wall: a case study of educational change in Eastern Germany, *Teachers College Record*, 94, pp. 744–760.

Fritzsche, K. P. (1990) In Search of a New Language: textbooks in the GDR, paper presented at the Annual Scientific Meeting of the International Society of Political Psychology, Washington, DC.

Hinke, B. (1991) A Challenge: confrontation or encounter between the educational systems of East and West? *European Education*, 23, pp. 74–96.

Hoyer, H. (1996) *Lehrer im Transformationsprozess*. Muenchen: Juventa.

Latka-Johring, S. (1991) East Germany's System of State Planning Faces a Thorough Free-market Shake-up, *European Education*, 23, pp. 31–36.

Mintrop, H. (1996) Teachers and Changing Authority Patterns in Eastern German Schools, *Comparative Education Review*, 40, pp. 359–376.

Mintrop, H. (1997) Retracking on a Grand Scale: policy and pedagogy in the reform of Eastern German secondary schools after the fall of socialism, paper presented at the Comparative and International Education Society Conference, Mexico City, Mexico.

Mintrop, H. & Weiler, H. (1994) The Relationship between Educational Policy and Practice: the reconstruction of the college-preparatory gymnasium in East Germany, *Harvard Educational Review*, 64, pp. 247–277.

Mitter, W. (1991) Comprehensive Schools in Germany: concepts, developments, and issues, *European Journal of Education*, 26, pp. 155–165.

Mitter, W. (1992) Educational Adjustments and Perspectives in a United Germany, *Comparative Education*, 28, pp. 45–52.

Moldenhauer, G. (1991) 2x Germany; 2x Political Education, *European Education*, 23, pp. 51–58.

Phillips, D. (1995) Educational Developments in the New Germany, *Compare*, 25, pp. 35–47

Rust, V. & Rust, D. (1995) *The Unification of German Education*. New York: Garland.

Schnabel, K., Baumert, J. & Roeder, P-M. (1996) Zum Wandel des Schulsystems in den neuen Bundeslaendern, *Neue Sammlung*, 4, pp. 531–544.

Siebert-Klein, M. (1980) *The Challenge of Communist Education: a look at the German Democratic Republic*. New York: Columbia University Press.

Weiler, H. N., Mintrop, H. & Fuhrmann, E. (1996) *Educational Change and Social Transformation: teachers, schools and universities in Eastern Germany*. London: Falmer Press.

Estonia in the Grip of Change: the role of education for adults in the transition period

TALVI MÄRJA & LARISSA JÕGI

Introduction

This chapter highlights the nature of the transformation that took place in Estonia following the demise of the Soviet Union in the early 1990s. It maintains that Estonia's transformation from socialism to capitalism had numerous advantages, although not without a high social price. It argues that the role and the importance of adult education in a society in transition is or should be different from that of a society that is relatively stable. This is substantiated by the growing number of adult education training centres, coordinated and led by the Association of Estonian Adult Educators (Andras), and by the nature of the content they cover in order to meet the demands of the labour market and the new awareness required by the general public. The chapter concludes with an expression of hope that Estonia is on its way to become a learning society and that the traditional open universities and other institutions will become the modern centres for a new kind of adult education.

Transformation in Estonian Society

The beginning of the 1990s might be remembered as a period of radical political, social and economic changes in the world, especially in Europe. It marked the end of the cold war, the collapse of the Berlin Wall, the fall of the Soviet Union and the end of an occupation which had lasted in the Baltic States for nearly 50 years. The changes led to a process (never before experienced in history) of transformation from socialism to capitalism, from a totalitarian to a democratic society, and from a planned to a market economy in Estonia and the other post-socialist countries in eastern and central Europe.

According to the Swedish–Estonian Balticom research programme (Lauristin & Vihalemm, 1997), changes in all east European countries, including the Baltic States, were accompanied by the opening of trade relations as well cultural contacts and communications with the West. Although there is a lot of truth in this view many political analysts believe it is erroneous to assume that these transformations are the sum of 'positive changes' inspired and assessed from the Western perspective. It is erroneous, they feel, because changes cannot be planned from above or from outside; rather they result from the interplay between social and political actors in various fields.

However, such an assumption is also suspect because societal, social and individual levels of change in Estonia are integrated into the systemic whole by common cultural characteristics, partly rooted in national culture, but at the same time strongly influenced by the all-European cultural environment and by global processes (Lauristin, 1997, p. 25).

The political, ideological, cultural, technological and social changes, and labour market development in Estonia over the past 30 years can be divided into five subperiods. These are:

- from the mid-1960s to the mid-1970s – a time characterised by economic growth;
- from the mid-1970s to the mid-1980s – a subperiod characterised by economic and political stagnation;
- from the mid-1980s to 1991 – the era of *glasnost* and *perestroika* in the Soviet Union and the beginning of national awakening and struggle for independence in Estonia;
- from 1991 to 1994 – a time of rebuilding the independent democratic state and developing a market economy and a system based on private property rights; and
- from 1994 to the present – a time of economic and cultural development.

Estonia's recent progress in the different areas of economic liberalisation has been relatively successful. This can be substantiated by the European Commission's evaluation, announced on 16 July 1997, of Estonia's readiness to join the European Union among the first group of post-communist countries. Compared to the countries of central Europe, politically, the main risk was the presence of a large Russian minority in the country. They accounted for about 40% of the population, and had to be integrated culturally and politically with the native population.

On the other hand, transition has not been easy and Estonia has paid a high social price for the changes in the 1990s: the birth rate has declined by about a third (this is a problem in Estonia which has a declining economically active population demographic trend); the success of the economic reforms has been overshadowed by increases in crime, drug addiction and social inequality (Estonian Human Development Report, 1996); and the new social situation creates countless psychological problems for individuals and communities in their dealing with everyday life.

The transformations have placed heavy pressures on the Estonian people. The most dramatic aspect of Estonian transition is the so-called transitional stress and growing disillusionment ('transitional shock') created by rapidly expanding differences in people's living conditions and by growing uncertainties about personal life-perspectives (Kutsar, 1996). New situations have created new demands on everyone, requiring them to add to their knowledge and skills, to learn. This has given rise to an increasing demand for adult education as a mediating force.

The role of adult education is often misunderstood. In many industrialised countries, adult education is a process by which interested people opt to learn about things they are interested in or to catch up on skills which they require. Roger (1994) attributes a larger responsibility to adult education in societies in transition. Here it is seen to be an active agent in the middle of the changing processes. Thus, the importance and role of adult education in a period of change differs from that in a relatively stable society where the aim of education is to acquire already existing knowledge, skills and values.

Education for Adults in Estonia

The role of adult education and the structure of the adult education system, as well as the training programmes and target groups, have changed as society has changed. In Estonia, a number of new developments can be noted.

First, private schools, universities and training companies exist in a mixed mode of provision beside public schools, training centres and universities, and new curricula have been developed at all educational levels. Second, a new round of educational legislation was begun in April 1996. Third, a growing awareness of the role and an increased demand for education has emerged. Distance education, continuing education, mixed-mode learning models, new learning and teaching environments, access to the Internet, are all examples of this. Finally, structural changes in the universities have been started – open universities, centres for educational technology, cooperation between universities, training centres and private institutions have all begun to take shape.

However, it should be stressed that, at the same time, Estonia is facing many problems during this period of transition. Some of these problems include the following.

1. There is no clear strategy for adult education; particularly, there are no long-term partnerships with enterprises or municipalities.
2. Cooperation of public educational institutions with those from the private sector is still weak and fragmented.
3. Universities are still not ready to cope with the increasing demands for educating and training adults and as such are being left behind in developments.
4. Developments in the system of vocational education in the transition period have not been in correspondence with rapid changes in society.
5. There are insufficiently qualified teachers, trainers, and adult educators to meet the current demands in education (Märja & Jõgi, 1996); and where teachers are trained, the level and capacity of training does not respond to the requirements of the labour market and the state economy (Pärnapuu, 1997).

Education, especially adult education, has two important responsibilities in the process of building a new society: it must support rapid and radical changes in society by providing people with the knowledge and skills needed for development. It needs to facilitate adaptation to new social, economic and technological conditions; and the education system has to become democratic in its orientation and practice (Märja, 1997). Moreover, as coping with change demands a higher level of knowledge, particularly 'new knowledge', traditional adult and higher education or employment education and training are not and cannot be sufficient (Jõgi, 1996).

Radical changes are needed in the education system, which has to incorporate wide goals, standards and approaches. According to many researchers and adult educators (Krajnc, 1995; Bron, 1995; Jarvis, 1992), the main function of adult education is not only to help adaptation to the market economy and labour market, but also to develop readiness to learn, readiness for continuous self-improvement, and to develop the abilities necessary for leading the process of development.

Thus, the main objectives for adult education in our society are:

- to disseminate knowledge, wider understanding and awareness of the new political and social system;
- to prepare people to take an active part in the life of society;
- to make people aware of political, economic, social and ecological problems and to develop their abilities to solve them;
- to teach people to identify their own needs, goals and aims; and
- to develop readiness to learn and to analyse their own behaviour and competency.

To further the transitional process in Estonia, the main objective of adult education is to achieve the competence and conscious efficiency of the whole population, their participation in all spheres of life, and their self-development (Märja, 1992). In this sense, adult education in Estonia becomes increasingly important and develops into 'a platform' of learning and consulting, and a 'platform' for socialisation and development.

The importance of the role of social movements and community-based organisations in promoting political transitions and acting as catalysts for educational transformation has been raised in this volume and elsewhere (see Groves & Johnson, N'zimande & Mathieson, and Allsop, all in this volume). In Estonia too, the role of non-governmental organisations (NGOs) in transforming education is of particular interest. Indeed, the leading role in adult education in Estonia has been in the hands of NGOs, especially since the establishment of Andras, in 1991. Andras has more than 100 member organisations, which are involved in general, labour market oriented and/or popular adult education. Andras is a member of the European Association for the Education of Adults, European Society for Research on the Education of Adults (ESREA) and International Council of Adult Education (ICAE).

The main goals of Andras are:

- to integrate activity in the field of adult education in Estonia;
- to upgrade and preserve the professional level of adult education;
- to gather and disseminate information;
- to train trainers (adult educators);
- to carry out research in the field of adult education;
- to publish and distribute materials about research and training methods; and
- to cooperate with adult education institutions around the world.

The role of Andras in the process of formulating adult education policy in Estonia is significant. Andras has participated in preparing:

- the Estonian Adult Education Act (adopted in 1993);
- the National Programme of Adult Education;
- the Euro–Delphi comparative research with 16 European countries;
- an adult education terminology dictionary; and
- research on the 'Estonian population in the labour market'.

The law (act) on adult education was put forward for discussion and was accepted by the Estonian Parliament in November 1993. Three areas of adult education are regulated by this Act: general adult education, labour market oriented education and popular adult education. Following this Act, subsidisation for adult education came directly from the state budget from 1995 onwards. The Society for Voluntary (popular) Adult Education Teachers was also founded in 1993. Moreover, the role of adult education institutions is expected to grow considerably. At present, the total number of the various kinds of establishments involved in adult education in Estonia is 900. Furthermore, it can be argued that, as a result of the Act, an increasing number of decision-makers in Estonia today understand the importance of education for adults in a period of transition, an understanding which, in turn, helps adult education to grow in importance and to shape the profile of the education system. Thus, we are in a position to choose the most adequate form and content of adult education and to take the best solution from different systems.

From the evidence, it would seem that Estonia is on the way to becoming a learning society. A number of adult education centres, evening schools for adults, open universities and other institutions are all gearing up to provide courses for adults and they are rapidly developing into modern centres for adult education.

The Training of Adult Educators

In recent years, growing attention has been paid to the training of adult educators for at least three reasons. First, teachers and adult educators are, clearly, the key group in the rapidly changing educational situation. Secondly, teaching adults demands a very high degree of involvement, not only professional but also personal and emotional. Thirdly, in spite of a rapid growth in the number of different kinds of adult education training centres, there is an acute shortage of competent adult educators. Given this situation, the Chair of Andragogy at the Tallinn Pedagogical University has been working on preparing the academic staff for training adult educators. Together with Andras, various programmes, courses and other activities are offered.

The successful development of a small democratic country can be guaranteed by a carefully planned and coordinated adult education system. However, it is not possible to speak in these terms about the adult education system in Estonia yet, since it is fragmented and there is a lack of cooperation between many public, private and voluntary associations. The structure of adult education is in a formative phase and educational opportunities vary between different regions of Estonia. Big cities like Tallinn and Tartu are growing economically and offer better opportunities, while economically less developed areas have fewer opportunities.

Conclusion

The role of adult education in Estonia's future will depend on what decisions the country makes in other areas of national life. If we choose the model of an open society – integration with the European Union, which is the strategy favoured by the present government – European educational values and principles will stand as a road mark for us. However, although it is likely that we will adopt European systems of education, we are open to all kinds of information and are ready not only to learn from our international partners but also ready to teach them, to share experiences, and to take part in different projects, seminars and conferences with them.

Estonia is in the grip of change. The expected changes in adult education resulting from Estonia's transition are fundamental. New parameters in theory and practice are essential and the extent to which Estonia is willing to learn from the experiences of others and to reflect and share its own experiences will determine the extent of our success in transforming education.

References

Jarvis, P. (1995) *Adult and Continuing Education: theory and practice*. London: Routledge.

Jõgi, L. (1997) Adult Educator Training at Tallinn Pedagogical University, *Baltic Dialogue*, 2, pp. 6–8.

Krajnc, A. (1995) Role of Adult Education in the Transition Period from Totalitarianism to Democracy, *Adult Education and Democracy*. Tallinn: United Nations Development Programme.

Kutsar, D. (1996) The Imprint of the Transformation on Living Conditions in Estonia, in J. B. Grogard (Ed.) *Estonia in the Grip of Change*, FATO Report, 190. Oslo: FATO.

Lauristin, M. (1997) Context of Transition, in M. Lauristin & P. Vihalemm (Eds) *Return to the Western World*. Tartu: Tartu University Press.

Lauristin, M. & Vihalemm, P. (Eds) (1997) *Return to the Western World*. Tartu: Tartu University Press.

Märja, T. (1992) Adult Education in Estonia, *Adult Education and Development*, 39, pp. 8–20.

Märja, T. (1997) The Role of Education for Adults in the Transition period in Estonia, in T. Märja, *Global Transformation and Education of Adults*, pp. 187–199. Estonia: International Institute for Policy, Practice and Research in the Education of Adults.

Märja ,T. & Jõgi, L. (1996) The Role of Universities in Education and Training for Adults in Estonia, *International Journal of University Adult Education*, xxv, pp. 31–43.

Pärnapuu, E. (1997) Job-related Adult Education in Estonia, *Baltic Dialogue*, 2, p. 4.

Rogers, C. (1994) *Adult Learning for Development*. London: Cassell.

United Nations Development Programme (UNDP) (1996) *Estonian Human Development Report 1996*. Tallinn: UNDP.

Educational Transformation in South Africa's Transition to Democracy

BLADE N'ZIMANDE & SUSAN MATHIESON

Introduction

The holding of the first ever democratic election in South Africa on 27 April 1994 and the inauguration of Nelson Mandela as President and Head of State of a democratic South Africa marked a milestone in the struggle of the South African people, and indeed the whole world, against apartheid. It was a truly historic moment in the struggles against colonialism both on the African continent and internationally. While the election marked the formal end of white minority rule and apartheid as a statutory system, it also marked the beginning of a struggle for the transformation and reconstruction of South Africa. The emergent democracy in South Africa was characterised by a government of national unity, which incorporated elements of the previous apartheid ruling bloc.

Given this reality, it is therefore important to contextualise and locate educational transformation in South Africa within the broader character of South Africa's negotiated transition. This chapter will firstly attempt a brief characterisation of the current conjuncture in South Africa, as a basis for understanding the current processes and contestations over the nature and pace of educational transformation. The second part of the chapter will be a continuation of the first part, whereby an attempt will be made to identify the key contending social and political forces in South Africa's transition, so that it is properly understood which forces stand for which policies and programmes in the unfolding educational changes and struggles.

The aim of undertaking such an analysis is primarily based on our belief that the only way to analyse and understand education transformation is by understanding it as a struggle reflecting the broader contradictions in South African society. However, in so doing, we will try to avoid a reductionist approach, whereby every education struggle can simply be read off from the broader political struggles. This is because education struggles, much as they are connected to the broader struggles around the transition, at the same time have their own specificities, which need to be understood on their own. But to analyse the specificities of educational transformation outside of the broader struggles would be to lose sight of the nature of educational transformation in South Africa.

The third section of the chapter will focus on the tensions, dilemmas, prospects and possibilities for education transformation in South Africa. Within this section there will be a brief discussion of some of the key advances made in educational transformation. Finally, in the last section, some of the key challenges facing educational transformation in South Africa within the context of the transition to democracy will be identified.

Characterising the Current Conjuncture in South Africa

The complexity of the present period in South Africa defies any simple characterisation. Nonetheless, it can be stated that the present period, and its unfolding struggles, substantively reflect the balance of forces in South Africa by the end of the 1980s. By this time, a situation had developed whereby the old apartheid regime could no longer continue to rule in old ways, nor to guarantee its hold over state power for any foreseeable period. Nevertheless, the old apartheid ruling bloc still had firm control over key state apparatuses, particularly the repressive state machinery of the police, army, the justice system and key sectors of the economy. The national liberation movement, on the other hand, led by the African National Congress (ANC), was holding the moral high ground both with the mass of the people inside the country and internationally, but it was not strong enough to move the revolution forward and impose its own advanced political alternatives. This interregnum gave birth to the unbanning of the ANC and other political organisations and the beginning of the era of negotiations.

The decision to unban and negotiate on the side of the white minority regime was precipitated by the profound social, political, economic and moral crisis that the regime faced. On the side of the national liberation movement, failure to forcibly dislodge the regime after the wave of semi-insurrectionary struggles of the mid- to late 1980s left the national liberation movement with little choice other than to seize the opportunity to participate in a negotiated settlement. This reality was also brought about by the change in the international balance of forces where the apartheid regime and its Western backers realised that the collapse of the Soviet Union and the socialist Eastern bloc lessened the threats of a communist onslaught.

The decision by the white minority regime to negotiate could also be located within the theoretical framework of democratic transitions in developing countries. These are attempts to defeat revolutionary movements – in the era of the decline of the socialist bloc and the growing confidence of imperialism to experiment with shifts from authoritarian to democratic regimes – by opening the political process to open electoral contests between these regimes and revolutionary movements. The transition in South Africa can also be theoretically located within the decolonisation model as advanced to explain the capture of state power by national liberation movements. In fact both these capture the dual character of the South African revolution: democratisation and decolonisation.

Despite the massive victory of the ANC nationally and in seven of the nine provinces, it only attained some elements of state power. This is for two main reasons. First, winning elections is not equal to winning state power. The latter, particularly in negotiated transitions, is a process that takes place over time. The speed with which it is done depends on the nature of the negotiated transition and the balance of forces at the time of assuming political office. Secondly, the Government of National Unity (GNU) was not an ANC government, but a government where the ANC – and indeed the dominant party – still ruled together with elements of the old apartheid ruling bloc. This made the GNU itself a site of contestation and struggle, with the national liberation movement attempting to speed up the process of transfer of power, whilst elements of the old regime within that Government were struggling to keep control over as much of the state structures as possible.

Thus, the GNU was characterised by contradictions. The main contradiction within the GNU was that it comprised of forces whose interests were fundamentally conflictual: the national liberation movement on the one side, and on the other, forces of apartheid colonialism, albeit the latter operating under completely new and different conditions.

The period of the GNU is a transient phase towards national democracy – arguably the stage that lays the firm basis for the resolution of some of the key problems facing South Africa, of which educational transformation is one of the major ones. Similarly, the transition to national democracy based on majority rule will be a contested one, with the elements of the old regime trying as much as possible to block a genuine transition to national democracy and installing what is sometimes referred to as low-intensity democracy.

However, much as it was expected that the constraints of the GNU would impact more on the ANC as the majority party in taking the process of democracy forward, it seems to be putting more pressure on the minority parties in this Government. The National Party was faced with the contradiction of being the largest opposition party and yet simultaneously operating within a government and an executive led by its principal adversaries. This created severe tensions within the party such that in June 1996, it decided to pull out of the GNU and remain purely a party of opposition in parliament.

It is in the interstices of this contradictory character of the GNU, and the continuing struggles to deepen democracy, that educational transformation will have to be deepened and consolidated.

Globalisation and Education in South Africa

It would be inadequate to understand the current conjuncture in South Africa without relating it to the place of South Africa in the current global conjuncture. Our approach is that the international terrain – particularly the current globalisation processes – is not merely an external factor to the political economy of South Africa, but is an integral component. This is because South Africa is a medium-earning country, but with a majority of its population living in some of the worst poverty that one can find in the developing world. Furthermore, the South African economy itself is highly dependent on the export of its mineral resources to the industrialised world, thus being integrated in the same way as some of the developing countries into the global economy. As a country, South Africa has not escaped the pervasive impact of neo-liberalism and the structural relationship between industrialised and developing countries in the current globalisation processes.

The implications of globalisation for education are principally that education increasingly becomes a commodity and subjected to market forces, thus making it increasingly inaccessible to the poor. In the developing countries, this is largely an outcome of the scaling down of the role of the state in the provision of social services, as well as the concentration of state resources in creating conditions for the capitalist market – liberalisation, privatisation, deregulation and devaluation of the currency. In the last 20 years or so, the achievements made by many developing countries, and African states in particular, in the sphere of education have been eroded as the World Bank and the International Monetary Fund (IMF) prescribed their structural adjustment programmes.

One of the effects of this in the new global order on education in developing countries is that these countries are directed, mainly through aid loans, to concentrate on basic education, whilst scientific, technical and higher education suffers cutbacks. This then creates a perpetual cycle of dependency on industrialised countries for high-level research and scientific work. This dynamic is reproduced within South Africa's own higher education institutions, whereby white academics are the leading researchers and scientists and black academics are mere cycles of this knowledge.

Advances and Challenges in the Transformation of Education in South Africa

Because of the long history of democratic struggle around education, a fairly comprehensive policy framework for the transformation of the education system had been developed by 1994 and the election of an ANC Government. This policy was based on the premise that the inherited education system would need to be fundamentally transformed if it was to overcome the legacy of the past, while at the same time becoming responsive to a new set of challenges. The transformed education and training system was to be a unified system based on the principles of equity, quality, non-racialism and non-sexism, and that was more appropriate to the socio-economic needs of the emerging democratic society. These goals would be met by moving towards the provision of lifelong learning, so that workers, adult learners and others who had been denied access in the past would gain access to education and training opportunities. It was asserted that the state would have to play a leading role in overcoming the inherited fragmentation and achieving these policy goals.

In terms of legislation and policy, significant strides have been taken towards achieving these goals. The legislative frameworks for a single coordinated school system and higher education system are in place. In addition, the South African Qualifications Act lays the basis for a single qualifications framework for education and training that facilitates multiple entry and exit points and promotes accessibility for all learners. Another key policy initiative has been the introduction of a new national curriculum, which is learner-centred and based on the achievement of specified outcomes and core competencies, in place of the rote learning so common in the majority of South African schools. Policy frameworks have been developed for adult education, early childhood education, learners with special educational needs and gender equity. This policy framework has not shifted significantly from the pre-election agenda that was mapped out by the national liberation movement for the most thorough transformation of the education system.

However, the record in terms of the implementation of this policy has been less successful. One of the key obstacles to transformation has arisen as a consequence of the compromises agreed to during the negotiated settlement, in particular the acceptance of a semi-federalised structure for the new South African state, with the creation of nine provinces which would have responsibility for the implementation of general education policy, as well as control over the budget. However, policy-making would remain primarily a responsibility of the national

Ministry of Education. This separation between policy and implementation has created a schism in the education system that is causing a number of problems in the delivery of a transformed education system. It has severely weakened the capacity of the national Ministry of Education to ensure the implementation of policy, while also allowing the national Ministry to shed responsibility for the practical consequences of implementing policy. As stated earlier, the pressure for provincial autonomy was a key demand of the National Party and its allies as a mechanism for weakening the capacity of the ANC to effectively transform society, and thus enable old elites to hang onto pockets of privilege within the system.

This new provincial structure for the South African state was a reality that was not adequately planned for by the ANC in the pre-election period. The National Education Policy Act (NEPA), passed in 1995, sought to address this problem by establishing the structures through which the National Ministry and Department of Education would relate to the provinces: the Council of Education Ministers (CEM) and the Heads of Education Departments Committee (HEDCOM). Essentially, this relationship was premised on the notion of cooperative governance. The legislation does provide teeth through which the Minister can hold provincial Ministers to account, but in practice, these have not been implemented. At the same time, the NEPA gave the national Ministry powers to determine national norms and standards for education, which have increasingly been implemented to bring about the redress of education resources. This was re-enforced in the South African Schools Act, which legislated that the national Ministry must develop national norms and standards for school funding. These guidelines came into force from April 1999. They lay down national criteria for education expenditure premised on the drive for redress and equity in state resources, with greater state allocation of non-personnel costs to the poorer communities.

However, it has been a much longer process to develop the managerial capacity to make national norms and standards a reality. This is largely a consequence of the weak structural relationship between national and provincial ministries and departments. The ANC-led Government took over a racially fragmented system in 1994. The 19 apartheid departments of education were amalgamated, but with new divisions generated between the national department and the nine provincial structures. In addition, there was only a limited management capacity, most of it concentrated in the former departments for white, Indian and coloured education, with extremely poor management capacity in the black and Bantustan education departments. The provinces that have performed most badly are the ones that had to incorporate Bantustan administrations into the new provincial structures. Education management was generally characterised by an authoritarian and bureaucratic style that was not geared towards social delivery. There has been an attempt to transform this culture, while at the same time developing capacity in the new provincial structures. However, much more needs to be done to improve management capacity and to transform the management culture. The absence of effective consultative mechanisms between the national and provincial departments is mirrored at a provincial level with a poor understanding of the new policy framework at a district level. The primary casualty of all this is the quality of education in schools, which are operating with minimal support from their provincial education departments.

The problem has been exacerbated by the new budgeting framework, which puts provinces in control of their own budgets, while in many cases they inherited a limited budgeting capacity. At the same time, policy-making, which is largely a national competence, has been separated from the budgeting process. This has led to what has become known as the problem of unfunded mandates. The most severe case of this was the absence of costing for the scrapping of the apartheid salary scales and the employment of additional teachers in overcrowded classrooms. These agreements were reached through the national bargaining chamber, but were not checked against the provinces' ability to fund the agreements. This created a budgeting crisis so extreme that provinces were unable to fund basic needs such as the provision of textbooks or even to pay for basic services such as water and electricity bills.

This overexpenditure was taking place in a context where the ANC Government had adopted the Growth, Employment and Redistribution policy (GEAR) as its macro-economic framework. Essentially, this bound the Government to bring down the budget deficit and to maintain tight constraints on budgetary expenditure. The approach of Government towards the overexpenditure of provincial budgets has been to enforce budgetary discipline, even if this results in the non-delivery of essential services.

The crisis in the education budget has made it clear that the ANC Government is not in a position to spend its way out of the inherited inequalities in the education system. The transformation of the education system will have to be achieved within the existing education budget. This can only be achieved if effective management and information systems are established that make it possible to plan for new priorities.

The national Department of Education has invested considerable resources in developing databases and information systems as the basis for monitoring and transforming policy priorities. The recently completed School Register of Needs Survey mapped for the first time ever the 32,000 schools that exist countrywide, revealing the grossly inadequate conditions pertaining in many schools. An Education Management Information System (EMIS) has also been established.

These databases will provide the data on which the new funding priorities being developed as national norms and standards will be implemented. This marks a growing concern to professionalise the education system and to bring it up to the standards required by a modern developing society.

However, implementing transformation is more than simply a matter of developing management capacity within the system. A Culture of Learning, Teaching and Service Campaign (COLTS) has also been launched as an ongoing initiative, which seeks to mobilise teachers, learners, parents and the education bureaucracy in the challenge of overcoming the demoralisation that had set into the education system during the apartheid years. There is an attempt to galvanise communities into rebuilding the education system. The COLTS campaign is to an extent an attempt to revive the tradition of popular democratic organisation that was so successful in the apartheid years.

However, with the ANC in government, it is the state and not communities that will have to lead the process of reconstruction and development. This means building on the traditions of democracy and consultation by making these principles the basis for relations between the Government and stakeholders in education. This involves the transformation of relations with educators, with school governing bodies and institutional councils, and with learners.

What this period has seen, then, is an attempt to adapt to the new environment of managing a modern democratic state within a globalised capitalist environment, while continuing to assert a transformative national education agenda. It has involved building on the policies and democratic practices developed during the struggle years, while developing the capacity to implement these policies.

Within this broad picture, certain issues have come to the forefront as key debates around which the struggle for educational transformation has taken place in South Africa. We deliberately pose these issues as dilemmas, precisely because they magnify most clearly the issues on which educational transformation is taking place in South Africa.

Autonomy versus the State

As stated earlier, one of the key sites of political contestation in the post-1994 era has been around the authority of the democratically elected Government over the public education system. The National Party, the Democratic Party and others representing the white minority have sought to limit the powers of the national Ministry of Education in order to limit the capacity of the ANC to effect its policy of educational transformation. The primary struggles of the minority parties in the education sphere have been to protect the pockets of privilege established by the apartheid Government, which they see as threatened by a too powerful state controlled by the ANC. They have sought to position themselves as the champions of institutional autonomy and minority rights against the dangers of state interference. It is quite ironical that the party that built such a centralised and authoritarian structure as the apartheid state should, now that it is out of power, be the greatest enemy of a centralised state. Most of the political struggles involving education in the post-election period have been about this issue, with the ANC asserting the powers of the Minister of Education over education policy and implementation, while opposition parties have sought to limit the powers of the national Minister.

However, the ANC has also built its politics out of the struggle for participatory democracy against the highly centralised and undemocratic apartheid state. It therefore has an interest in democratising the state and ensuring greater participation in decision-making from below, while at the same time strengthening the capacity of the state to implement policy, in particular its powers to redress the inherited inequities in education provision. At the same time, there are lessons from the rest of Africa in the dangers of a fragile state falling back on the despotic abuse of state power. The ANC has therefore had to steer a course that gives sufficient powers to the centre to implement national policy, while at the same time seeking to democratise the exercise of that power by making the state more answerable to a range of constituencies for its actions.

The struggles involving higher education highlighted these contradictions. There was an urgent need for the state to play a leading role in the overhaul of the higher education system in order to deal with the legacy of the past and to prepare for the higher education needs of the emerging democratic state. But at the same time, there was a strong concern to protect academic freedom and to defend institutional autonomy from an overinterventionist state. However, while a degree of academic freedom and institutional autonomy is a necessary condition for a healthy higher education system, some of the resistance to the state playing a greater role came from institutions that benefited from the existing *status quo*. The Afrikaans language institutions, which are most clearly the products of an apartheid state, have been the most staunchly opposed to state intervention under an ANC government. It is not just about state intervention as such, so much as the nature of the state that intervenes and the vested interests it threatens that is at issue.

In response to this situation, a model of cooperative governance was developed in the context of the leadership of the democratically elected state. The exact balance between the powers of the state and the role of institutions and other stakeholders in transforming the higher education system was fiercely contested. The greatest resistance to state intervention came from the historically advantaged institutions, in part because they had enjoyed a greater degree of autonomy and so had more to lose. The historically disadvantaged constituencies, on the other hand, were in favour of a greater role for the state, in part because they believed that the state would shift the balance of power in their favour, and would allocate more resources to their institutions. The Higher Education White Paper and Higher Education Act represented a complex balance between national planning and institutional autonomy in the implementation of those plans.

A Council for Higher Education (CHE) was established as a statutory advisory body, which could act as a zone of negotiation for the state and higher education stakeholders. The exact relationship between the branch for higher education in the Department of Education and the CHE is still being negotiated. The success of this will be an indicator of the practicability of cooperative governance as it has been conceptualised in the education sphere.

In practice, most state intervention has been in the historically disadvantaged institutions in response to the crises of debt and mismanagement that have beset many of these institutions. Some doubts have been expressed as to whether the state is sufficiently empowered to deal with these crises, and whether it is appropriate for the state to sit on the sidelines while public money is being squandered. However, there are no plans to change the legislation to give the state more powers of intervention at this stage.

The policy that is being developed for transforming higher education is premised on the need to improve the technical and management capacity of the state and institutions in order to make them more responsive to societal demands. Of course, it also involves an emphasis on participation in decision-making structures by a wider range of constituencies, but it is a significantly different route to democracy than that pursued by the popular democratic movement in the apartheid era, with its focus on mass organisation and resistance politics. However, its success is already being felt as institutions find themselves having to justify their missions and plans within a framework of institutional transformation. This attempt to implement a transformation agenda through more effective management of the system runs the danger of making educational transformation a function of technocrats. However, it also has the potential for furthering democracy as the system becomes more accountable, and as it becomes possible to link policy to budgeting priorities.

Re-establishing Democracy in the New Environment

This shift away from popular forms of organisation towards a more professional, state-driven transformation process has raised questions about how this process can also be used to strengthen democracy, and what forms democratic participation can take in the new environment. The problem is that, at least in the early years of democratic governance, the organisations of the middle classes and not of the majority of the South African people have been most able to make use of the democratic process. Many of these organisations, in particular those that mobilised around the South African Schools Act, represented groups that were beneficiaries of the apartheid order, and their aim has been to use the democratic aspects of the new legislation in order to further their own agenda of putting elements of the state education system beyond the reach of the democratic forces. The democratic movement, on the other hand, with some notable exceptions, such as the South African Democratic Teachers Union (SADTU), has found it difficult to shift from the opposition politics of the past to the more sophisticated terrain of engaging with the state and making use of the avenues for democratic participation that are opening up.

This raises fundamental questions about the possibilities of establishing a meaningful democracy in this transitional period. Democracy depends on creating a balance between the state and civil society. However, given the present balance of forces, a strong state is the necessary condition for redressing the inherited social inequities and establishing a non-racial democracy. The state to an extent has had to act on behalf of a still marginalised and silent majority by pursuing policies aimed at equity and redress, while at the same time seeking to open up new channels through which this majority can begin to voice their own demands. However, it is dangerous to assume that the state, even under an ANC-led government, will be able to continue to speak on behalf of the majority if they remain silenced and marginalised. Unless the majority are able to develop effective vehicles for asserting their demands, it is likely that the state will be pulled by the more powerful forces, in particular of globalised capital, and move away from the agenda set by the ANC of social reconstruction and development.

These issues have emerged in the process of implementing the South African Schools Act, the focus of which is to establish democratic school governance structures with considerable powers over the day-to-day running of schools. The situation in the majority of schools before the 1994 elections was that parents and school communities had been extremely disempowered. However, with an ANC government on the horizon, the outgoing Government gave the previously white schools special status as quasi-independent schools, and handed over responsibility and control for much of the day-to-day running of schools to school governing bodies. The intention of the National Party was to use school governance structures to put these privileged schools of the white minority beyond the power of the new government, and so protect them from the new policies aimed at redressing the inequities in education provision and opening up access to all. However, within the progressive movement there was also a strong tradition of community participation to improve the quality of black education through the

Parent, Teacher, Student Associations (PTSAs [1]). The new school governance structures thus had two very different origins – one within the democratic movement as a means of furthering the struggle for democracy, and the other as a strategy of the outgoing elite in order to defend their privileges.

However, a new dynamic also emerged after the 1994 elections of a weak and poorly resourced state that was keen to shed some of its financial and managerial responsibilities onto communities and parents. In this context, the demands of the quasi-independent schools to continue to take responsibility for their schools was seen in a reasonably favourable light, albeit within a new framework of democratically elected governance structures and within clear parameters regarding access and a national framework determining the rights and freedoms of language, culture and religion. However, while wealthier communities have been able to use the new policy and legislative framework to mobilise the resources of parents, it has had the effect of entrenching the existing divisions within the state education system. The limits to which parents in poorer communities can be mobilised to play an active part in developing schools are becoming painfully clear. At the other extreme, many of the quasi-independent schools are now more similar to private schools in terms of their fee structures and access to resources.

In this sense, the legislation has proved more effective in responding to the demands of the vocal minority in these schools, and at least initially, it is this constituency that has set the political and media agenda with debates about the autonomy of public schools, and concerns about protecting the quality of these elite schools. At the same time, with the shift of the ANC into government, the old structures of the mass democratic movement in education, such as the National Education Coordinating Committee (NECC [2]) and the PTSAs, with their capacity to mobilise around education issues, have waned. Where before communities in certain areas were very involved in struggles concerning education, there is now a tendency to rely on the state to transform schools.

The ANC has attempted to revive the old traditions of political mobilisation by spearheading the launch of an association of democratic school governing bodies. This association could play an important role in lobbying government and in refocusing attention on the pressing concerns of the majority of schools. It also aims to reinvigorate the latent energy, particularly in the black community, to actively participate in transformation, and to reverse the tendency to depend entirely on a state-driven transformation process. However, ultimately, the state must assume primary responsibility for building a quality education in the majority of schools. The state will have to accept the reality that community participation in school governance in poorer communities will require more, not less, state resources. In a context where education expenditure on non-personnel and development costs is severely curtailed, this will be a long and slow process.

Education and Nation Building

One of the key issues of contention in the development of education policy has been concerning the nature of the South African state we are building, and the terms on which the different language and cultural groups participate within a single national education system. However, in the South African context, the debate about language and culture is inextricably linked to the struggle of the Afrikaner elite to hang onto the privileged position they enjoyed in the apartheid state. The response of the ANC to this has been remarkably restrained, given the history of injustice that has been suffered in the name of Afrikaner nationalism. Rather than deny the Afrikaans language and culture, the ANC has sought to redefine it as one among many in an equality of languages and cultures that comprise the South African nation. The ANC, and the government it leads, has argued for multiculturalism and multilingualism, which implies a recognition of diversity and difference. However, it has argued that these should not be barriers to integration, but rather should be the terms on which integration takes place.

For the National Party and Afrikaner groupings, cultural and language differences have been the basis on which they have sought to justify their continued access to a segregated and privileged state education. They have argued for their right to control what they see as their own educational institutions within the state system as a means of perpetuating an exclusive Afrikaner culture within the broader state.

This issue was fought out fiercely in the writing of the new Constitution, with the National Party and Freedom Front arguing that the right to single-medium institutions should be embedded in the Constitution. The ANC, on the other hand, argued that the Bill of Rights should uphold the right of individuals to be taught in the language of their choice where reasonably practicable. This principle of upholding individual rights was fundamentally different to the notion of entrenching group rights and privileges within the public education sector.

Language, and the appeal to the ethnic nationalism of Afrikaners, has continued to be a key rallying call of the National Party in the unfolding debates about education policy. What the ANC has sought to do in response to this is to deconstruct the language debate, and to focus on the key issues of concern for the ANC, which are the question of meaningful access to all educational institutions, equity in education provision, the transformation of curricula and the democratisation of governance structures. If single-medium and dual-medium Afrikaans institutions do not contradict these fundamental principles, then the Government will accommodate them.

However, because of the nature of apartheid, debates about the Afrikaans language inevitably become debates about the entrenching of racial privilege. Some schools and higher education institutions that have in the past been dual medium, with an English-medium white class and an Afrikaans-medium white class, are now trying to stop the English-medium class, as they fear the demands of black students for access to these schools. Language thus becomes an effective way of excluding blacks. This is not just a struggle to entrench racial privilege, but is also about defending class interests, as it is a means of protecting white middle-class schools and universities from the challenges of providing an appropriate learning environment for educationally disadvantaged students, which in the context of apartheid education policies affects the majority of learners.

While the broad ANC policy on multiculturalism and multilingualism is clear, it is in the implementation process that this has often broken down. Provincial education departments are not clear about their role in supporting the process of racial integration in schools. As a result, many schools have been left to cope with the challenges of integration on their own. Flashpoints have arisen in some schools where the integration of black children has been resisted.

Here again is a case where the issues affecting the minority have become the issues that are recognised, while the major problems concerning language and the medium of instruction continue to be marginalised in the public discourse. At present, the majority of children whose home language is an African language are caught between learning in a home language that is marginalised in society, and having English as an often very poor second language as the medium of instruction. The Ministry of Education has adopted a *laissez-faire* attitude by leaving it to parents and schools to decide on the medium of instruction. However, given the high status of English, many parents and schools choose it as the medium of instruction. Research is beginning to show the damaging effect of this on the learning of many children who do not have sufficient mastery of English, and who are being taught by teachers who also do not have command of the English language.

A framework for managing multiculturalism and multilingualism at a micro-level, based on the principles established in the Constitution and by education legislation and policy frameworks, is urgently required. This will require a major investment by the state in management training and development throughout the education system. Here again it is not the policy itself, but the capacity of the Ministry and Departments of Education to manage the implementation of policy that is in question.

The State and the Market

In the present context of globalised economic markets, the South African state is under enormous pressure to limit the role of the state in providing the social and economic infrastructure of society. However, while there seem to be few viable alternatives to this in the current context, there are considerable dangers in such a policy, particularly given the enormous social inequalities that we have inherited. If the state retreats from assuming responsibility for financing the social and economic reconstruction of our society and depends on the market to fill the vacuum, it is likely that the existing inequalities will remain largely intact.

These difficulties have been encountered in the implementation of a policy for financing state education. It was clear that the existing education budget was not sufficient to provide a quality education for all. At the same time, a minority have come to expect a level of state investment in education higher than that enjoyed in many countries of the West, and far beyond the means of a middle-income country like South Africa to provide.

Given these constraints, the state was unable immediately to provide a free quality education to all, and instead opted to allow school governing bodies to collect fees from parents to supplement the provision the state was able to provide. It was intended that this would free the limited state resources to focus on the education of the most needy. This policy has been accepted by the majority of former model C schools, as they see it as a means of maintaining the quality of state education that had been established for the minority by the apartheid state in a context where state resources will be shifted to the disadvantaged.

However, there is a real danger that this will entrench the two-tier public education system that was inherited from the apartheid state, since those schools with a wealthy parent body will be able to raise more revenue than those schools with a poor parent body. Increasingly, the question of school fees is becoming a means of restricting access to the more advantaged public schools. Education policy has sought to avert this problem by legislating that only those parents who are able to pay school fees can be made to pay, and by entrenching the right of access to all public schools.

However, the common perception of schools and parents is that only parents who can afford the level of school fees can send their child to a particular school. The gap between the quality of the best-resourced and the least well-resourced public schools will remain for the foreseeable future. There is also a danger that the state will become dependent on parental contributions, and will retreat from taking responsibility for providing a free public education to all. If this happens, it is the least well-resourced schools that will suffer, and a quality education will remain a privilege for the rich, rather than a right for all South African citizens. This has profound implications for our ability to transform society, since education is a key factor in the allocation of life chances.

The question of implementing the election promise of providing 10 years of free and compulsory education has re-emerged within the ANC in response to concerns at how rapidly school fees have risen and as the state is retreating from financing even basic expenditure items such as electricity and water accounts. The ANC initially accepted the compromise of school fees based on a pragmatic acceptance that to introduce free education immediately would lead to chaos and non-delivery in education. However, it was accepted as a short-term solution, since initially the Government would only be in a position to provide free education to the poorest, but that this should be made progressively available.

At present, the debate is focusing around the draft policy for national norms and standards for school financing, which seeks to ensure that state funding is channelled to the poorest schools, while also placing restrictions on the amount of school fees that can be charged and ensuring that poor parents are not liable to pay school fees.

While an ANC-led government has not substantially increased the overall responsibility of the state to provide a quality education, progress has at least been made in redistributing state resources more equitably. However, it is questionable whether this is the first stage towards an integrated public education system that is accessible to all, or whether the existing class divisions will remain intact within the education system. This reflects the broader context in which the ANC has negotiated its policy for social reconstruction and development while accommodating market demands for a macro-economic policy that can keep the overall commitments of the state to social expenditure relatively low.

Equity versus Quality

The debate about equity versus quality has taken on a new bite given the present constraints on education spending, since equity can only be achieved by redistributing the existing education budget. Since educator costs account for approximately 90% of the education budget, demands for equity have focused on the question of equity in teacher–pupil ratios. The move towards equity both between provinces and within provinces has put pressure on the better-resourced schools to shed teachers and increase class sizes. This policy has been fiercely resisted by school governing bodies in the better-resourced schools, while on the other side the democratic teacher unions that support redistribution in principle have expressed grave reservations about the redeployment process.

The enormity of the challenge of shifting teachers from the rich to the poor has been hard to scale, given the resistance of teachers to moving schools, the poorly developed management infrastructure to manage the redeployment process, and difficulties in reaching an agreement that is acceptable to all the key stakeholders. Media attention has focused on the disruptions to better-resourced schools caused by the shift towards equity, while the impact of employing 40,000 additional teachers since 1994, both in creating a financial crisis in education and possibly in improving the situation in overcrowded schools, has hardly been acknowledged in the media. Many of these extra teachers have been employed in rural schools where the problems of overcrowding in the past have not been in the public eye. Hence, any improvements there have also not been recorded. Given the poor systems of information, it is not possible to determine exactly where teachers are deployed, or how the situation has changed since 1994. Certainly, personnel continue to be managed in a very haphazard manner, with a number of teachers who are considered to be surplus but who have not been redeployed drawing a salary, while new teachers are employed to fill existing vacancies, sometimes even before classrooms are built.

The national Department of Education is beginning to depend on the macro-planning instruments they are developing, in particular the School Register of Needs and the Education Management Information System, so that just, rational and educationally sound macro-planning decisions can be made in the allocation of resources. At the macro-level, decisions can more easily be made that balance the losses in education quality at the top end of the scale with potential gains at the bottom end from increasing access to resources. However, the question of equity in expenditure is less important than equity in outcomes if one is seeking to improve the overall quality of education. Performance indicators and rewards for improved performance are becoming an area that the national Department of Education is increasingly focusing on, particularly in a context where the shift towards equity in expenditure is not yet leading to an improvement of measurable standards.

There is a growing sense that the emphasis on shifting towards equity in teacher–pupil ratios has been at the expense of other more urgent resources that could have had a more immediate impact on improving the quality of education for the majority. Basics such as textbooks, school infrastructure and investing in management development are beginning to take over as priorities from equalising pupil–teacher ratios. However, this may be coming too late as the inflated personnel budget has crowded out other expenditure for the foreseeable future.

Elitism versus Massification

This tension between demands to maintain the educational standards that have been enjoyed by a racial elite, while at the same time spreading state resources more broadly, has been a source of considerable political debate. The ANC has addressed this issue by shifting the starting point for the debate away from the question of simply maintaining existing standards. Instead, the ANC has argued that we have to have a radical rethink of our educational priorities based on the socio-economic needs of the emerging South African nation.

This debate has been particularly heated in the context of higher education, where the ANC has argued that we need to move away from thinking only in terms of an expensive and elite higher education system for the few towards the provision of mass higher education. However, mass higher education will be difficult to achieve within the present financial constraints, and will require a radical rethink of the kind of higher education that can and should be provided. There needs to be a conceptual shift away from seeing the traditional university-based 3-year residential degree as the only valid form of higher learning. Other forms of learning need to be introduced, including distance education and shorter courses.

In addition, there will need to be fundamental pedagogical shifts if education is to cater effectively for the needs of a very different student body. The inherited concepts of quality will need to be interrogated to ascertain their appropriateness in a changed learning environment. For example, the lecturer transmission mode is becoming increasingly inappropriate as a means of communicating knowledge and understanding, in particular to second language students who may not know how to interpret the academic discourse. In addition, the kinds of knowledge that are required have also changed fundamentally.

While the ideal of extending higher education opportunities much more broadly is supported by the ANC, there is considerable caution from the Ministry and Department of Education about the implementation of such a policy, given that the higher education budget has remained fairly static. The present model of institutional autonomy within a national planning process means that changes in programme offerings will be driven largely from within institutions in response to incentives and directives coming nationally. There has not been a significant increase in student numbers in higher education since 1994, although the financial footing of poor but needy students has been stabilised through increases to the national student financial aid scheme. In addition, the distribution of students has shifted, with increasing numbers of students at technikons, and considerable increases in the proportion of black students that are registered.

South Africa faces enormous challenges in turning the education system around into one that provides for the whole population, rather than just a small elite. It has to deal with inertia and resistance to fundamental change within the education system, and the difficulties of creating new capacity where it has not existed before. It has to deal with political opposition from those that benefited from the old state education system that served a small minority. It has to build capacity within the bureaucracy to manage the process of change, and a framework for consultation and negotiation with stakeholders in the achievement of change. And it has to do all this in the context of a limited budget and a global environment that is not supportive of the role of the state in social investment. It is hardly surprising that it has been much slower to achieve the development of a mass-based education system that is of an appropriate quality than was anticipated by the ANC when it came to power. However, while the present plans for extending educational opportunities may be more moderate, they are also more concrete and realisable than the policies with which the ANC came to power in 1994.

Conclusion: challenges of educational transformation in South Africa

One of the key strategic challenges facing South Africa's transition to democracy is the rapid transformation of the very state instruments that are needed to take the broader transformation process forward. In education, for instance, the apartheid state structures require radical transformation, whilst these are being simultaneously used to advance transformation. This requires ongoing mobilisation of the democratic forces behind the transformation process. This is not easy, given the fact that the democratic movement itself is in the process of redefining its role and repositioning itself to play a critical role in the transformation process. It requires a shift from anti-apartheid mobilisation to mobilisation for transformation. What this means in practice is an issue that still needs to be addressed by the democratic forces as they seek to reposition themselves in relation to the transformation of the education system. Certainly, the ANC inside the state will have to assume greater responsibility for creating avenues for popular participation in education transformation. At the same time, the democratic movement has to position itself to take advantage of the steps taken towards democracy; and the degree of cooperation and consultation between the ANC inside the state and the ANC outside of the state needs to be considerably increased.

The second challenge is that of translating broad policy frameworks into workable programmes to impact immediately on the delivery of quality education, particularly to the majority of the people in the country. There is a whole range of mediating factors between macro-policy frameworks and effective implementation. The one critical mediating factor is to strike the correct balance between the respective roles and responsibilities of the various levels of government in the area of education. Of course, this requires more than the imposition of national policy and legislative initiatives on the provinces. An interactive and responsive relationship has to be built between the various levels of the state so that policy and implementation become more of a continuum.

The challenge of educational transformation, as with the transformation process more broadly, is the challenge to transform the state into an effective and responsive vehicle for delivery to the majority of the people. The election of an ANC government created the space for this to happen, and the legislative and policy framework is largely in place. However, the next phase will be a much longer and slower process that will be fiercely contested. It is by its success in achieving these longer-term changes that the present Government will ultimately be judged. In terms of education transformation, it is towards achieving the effective delivery of a quality education system for all that the present ANC-led Government is now oriented.

Notes

[1] The Parent–Teacher–Student Associations (PTSAs) were school-based organisations that were formed as part of the organs of people's power in the semi-insurrectionary struggles against apartheid. These bodies were made up of parents, teachers and students, and were developed as a counter to the official, apartheid school governing bodies, which were powerless, known generally as school committees.

[2] The National Education Coordinating Committee (NECC) was an umbrella body formed in 1986 to coordinate what were before highly localised and fragmented struggles against apartheid education. It was principally made up of PTSAs and sectoral national organisations representing parents, students and teacher unions. The organisation collapsed in the early 1990s largely due to financial constraints and failure to meaningfully adapt to the post-1990 negotiations phase.

The Challenges of Educational Reconstruction and Transformation in Eritrea

PETROS HAILEMARIAM

Introduction to Eritrea and its Educational System

Those who are not familiar with the new state of Eritrea may presume that there is no direct correlation between the country and the processes of 'globalisation' (or its precursor, colonisation), 'transition', 'transformation' and 'reconstruction'. Without getting entangled in a semantic squabble, this chapter hopes to dispel the aforementioned presumption by providing a brief overview of the history, geography, demography, economy and the education system of Eritrea.

Location and History

Eritrea, which covers an area of 125,000 sq kms, is situated in the north-eastern part of Africa, with a coastline of 1200 kms lying along the Red Sea. This new nation state, which obtained its name from the red colour of the algae in the Red Sea, shares its borders with Ethiopia to the south, the Sudan to the north and west, and Djibouti to the south and east.

The history of present-day Eritrea dates back to the third century when parts of it, known as 'Medri-Bahri' – land of the sea – were separated from what was then Abyssinia by the river Mareb and ruled by local chieftains known as 'Bahri Negassi'. By the sixteenth century, parts of this 'land of the sea', including Massawa, the port, were conquered by the Uthman ('Ottoman') Empire and/or its vassals in the neighbouring area. With the opening of the Suez Canal in 1869, the control of these lands was taken over by the Egyptians. During the scramble for Africa by the European powers, Italy gained a foothold in the Horn of Africa in 1885 by taking Massawa from the Egyptians and by controlling parts of the highlands ('Medri Bahri'), some of which were under the control of Emperor Yohannes IV of Ethiopia. By the early 1890s, the Italians had consolidated their power in the lowlands and highlands of present-day Eritrea and ruled this new colony until 1941. The defeat of Italy by the Allied Forces in the Second World War meant that Eritrea became a British mandate and remained so for 10 years until 1951. From 1952 to 1962, Eritrea, which had a democratically elected government and freedom of the press, was federated to autocratic Ethiopia in order to provide the latter access to the sea and to safeguard the geopolitical interests of the West. The situation was aggravated when the then Emperor Haile Selassie of Ethiopia annexed Eritrea to Ethiopia in 1962 by abrogating the United Nations (UN) resolution. This blatant violation of the democratic rights of the Eritrean people led to a costly and protracted war of liberation, which spanned 30 years and culminated in the liberation of the country on 24 May 1991. Following a UN-sponsored and internationally supervised referendum in 1993, Eritrea was officially declared an independent nation on 24 May 1993.

Demography and Ethnic Composition

Eritrea has a population of about 3 million, growing at an average of 2.7% per annum. A sizeable portion live in the diaspora as they were forced to flee their birthplace and seek asylum elsewhere due to the excessive oppression of the Ethiopian occupation force from 1962 to 1991.

Because of the successive waves of occupation by foreign powers, which included the Uthmans, the Egyptians, the Italians, the British and the Ethiopians, Eritrea remained a country of nine nationalities. These are Tigrigna, Tigre, Bilen, Saho, Nara, Kunama, Hedarib, Rashaida and Afar. Each of these ethnic groups has its own distinct culture and language. Two distinct values that permeate the cultures of all the nine ethnic groups are their strong sense of Eritreanness and the respected social standing accorded to elders. The fact that men and women and members of all the ethnic groups fought side by side for liberation also implies that some of the traditional conservative perceptions about the role of women in society have been transformed.

Economic Overview

About 80% of the population live in the rural areas where subsistence farming is widely practised. Nationally, the contribution of agriculture to GDP is small (Economic Policy, 1995) and its productivity rather low. This is partly due to reliance on rain-fed subsistence farming, little use of modern agricultural inputs (like fertilisers and machinery), progressive environmental degradation and long-lasting, inappropriate economic policies. The latter have had an equally negative impact on the industrial sector in Eritrea. In the 1950s and early 1960s, Eritrea had a thriving industrial sector accounting for about 40% of the industrial output of Ethiopia. However, the rate of industrialisation started to stagnate after Eritrea's forced annexation to Ethiopia and declined rapidly from the mid-1970s onwards. This was partly due to Ethiopia's decision to transplant major factories and industries from Eritrea to Ethiopia and partly due to the Dergue's (the Marxist-Leninist Ethiopian military junta) policy of putting all industrial establishments under state ownership.

Since liberation, the Government has put in place a macro-policy in which agriculture and industry occupy a prominent place. Moreover, both the Government and people have been actively engaged in rebuilding infrastructures that were destroyed and in constructing new ones to keep the economy moving. As a result of this combined effort, Eritrea's economy has grown at an average of 6% per annum for the last 5 years consecutively.

Education System

Prior to liberation, the education system in Eritrea followed a 6–2–4–4 pattern (i.e. 6 years' elementary schooling, 2 years' middle schooling, 4 years' secondary schooling and 4 years of university) and adopted Amharic as the medium of instruction at both the primary and junior secondary levels. The imposition of this medium of instruction, which is alien to all the nine ethnic groups in Eritrea, coupled with deliberate neglect by the occupation force resulted in a poor quality of education and a system characterised by crises. The impact of some of these crises is still being felt, as explained later.

Since independence, the education system has been restructured into elementary (5 years), middle (2 years), secondary (4 years) and university (4 years). The elementary and middle school cycles combine to form the basic education level.

In recognition of its contribution to human resource development in particular and to national development in general, education is given high priority within the government agenda. Thus, the Ministry of Education in conjunction with the support of local communities is determined to promote equal opportunity in terms of access, equity, relevance and continuity of education for all school-aged children.

The Challenges of Educational Reconstruction and Transformation in Eritrea

The Legacies of War and Neglect

At the end of the war in 1991, Eritrea inherited a depressed economy, dilapidated infrastructure and an educational system on the verge of collapse. The occupation of Eritrea and the war that followed had destroyed schools and wasted enormous resources that could otherwise have been allocated to education and other development programmes.

The educational system in Eritrea shows all the symptoms of prolonged neglect under conditions of colonialism and war. At the time of independence in 1991, 84% of the existing 190 schools were rated to be in serious disrepair. The remaining 16% were far from providing a satisfactory learning environment. Disparity in the geographical distribution of schools was sharply marked. For example, the number of schools, and particularly the number of secondary school students in the highlands, was far higher than those in the lowland areas of the country. Today, over 730 government and non-government schools are functioning, but many of these still need much improvement, expansion and/or replacement.

Eritrea is undergoing a process of rehabilitating educational institutions and services that were devastated during the long war. Decades of war and conflict have led to the accumulation of a huge backlog of primary-age children who missed schooling. At the time of liberation, the gross enrolment rate at the primary school level stood at 30%. The curriculum was so inappropriate that it generated thousands of unemployed and unemployable youth every year. Teachers were poorly trained. Moreover, since over 50% of the teaching force was composed of Ethiopians, a serious gap was created in the educational system when these teachers returned to Ethiopia immediately after liberation. To fill this gap, untrained high school graduates, retired teachers and ex-fighters were dispatched to schools after only short emergency courses in pedagogy.

EPLF's Experience in Education

The Eritrean People's Liberation Front (EPLF) operated its own educational system during the protracted liberation war. The central tenet of EPLF's educational policy was extending access and equal opportunity to all citizens, both among children and adults. This was expressed through the opening of primary schools and adult education centres in liberated and semi-liberated areas.

To facilitate accessibility, instruction in primary schools was offered in the mother tongue. Using the mother tongue as a medium of instruction assisted children to develop their cognitive skills more fully and promoted the consolidation of their cultural identities. To this end, the EPLF mounted a programme of further developing the various vernaculars by conducting ethnographic and orthographic research.

A major feature of the EPLF's educational policy was the integration of theory and practice. Students in EPLF-administered schools did not only study conventional subjects such as mathematics, language, science, geography and history, but, by participating in productive activities (e.g. gardening, farming, repairing roads, digging wells and constructing houses) they also made conscious efforts to apply what they had learnt. A big challenge in this context is the issue of how to adopt EPLF's fairly rich educational experience to the realities of the present day.

Current Educational Policies and Issues

Ever since liberation, the Eritrean Government has been making strenuous efforts to address the needs of national reconstruction as well as the wider needs of a developing economy. Within this framework, educational planning has assumed a two-pronged approach. On the one hand, it is aimed at rehabilitating the school structures and facilities destroyed during the war. On the other hand, efforts are being made to expand the school system and to lay a firm foundation for the provision of relevant education.

The principles underpinning these strategies, which have been enunciated in the Declaration of Policy on Education (Provisional Government of Eritrea [PGE], 1991) and other government documents (e.g. Ministry of Education [MOE], 1996), include:

- promoting basic education for all;
- extending equality of educational opportunities;
- ensuring that education makes a substantial contribution to reconstruction, national unity and the promotion of the social values of the people;
- developing scientific, technological and artistic skills;
- using the mother tongue as the medium of instruction in primary schools;
- adopting English as the language of instruction in post-primary institutions; and
- encouraging communities to play an ever-increasing role in the management of education by strengthening linkages between the school and the community.

Access and Equity

Within the parameters of these policies and principles, a top priority for the MOE has been expanding access to education. This is being carried out by increasing the number of schools, classroom units, students and teachers. In addition, the MOE is in the process of preparing a strategic plan, with a view towards attaining universal primary education by the end of 2010.

Compared to the 190 schools that existed on the eve of liberation, the present number of schools (730) represents an increase of 284%. The total number of students in primary, middle and secondary schools has increased from 168,803 in 1991 to 349,514 in 1997. A further breakdown of these figures indicates an increase of 128, 112 and 33% at the primary, middle and secondary school levels respectively. The number of teachers has increased from 3672 in 1991 to 7764 in 1997. This represents an increase of 177, 48 and 14% at the primary, middle and secondary school levels respectively.

Nevertheless, in spite of the rapid expansion of the school system, a very large number of children and youth are still deprived of access to education. For example, the gross enrolment rate (GER) indicates that in primary education, access to schooling was 52.2% in 1995/96, but the estimated net enrolment rate (NER) was only 28.8%. This suggests that nearly three-quarters of the children in the primary age group (7–11) were out of school. Since independence, there has been an enormous demand for more schooling. The high level of demand for schooling arises not only from the cohorts currently eligible to attend school, but also from the large backlog of those who have either never attended school or dropped out early. This explains the wide gap between the net and gross enrolment rates.

Another challenge facing the MOE is the big disparity in educational opportunity among the various regions – a legacy of social deprivation and inappropriate educational policies. Gross enrolment rates for primary schools located in the lowlands of Eritrea are significantly lower than those for the rest of the country. The gross rates for the former provinces [1] of Gash-Setit, Dankalia, Barka and Sahel were 31, 19, 16 and 11% respectively in 1994/95, whereas the national average was 52%. Consequently, the Ministry of Education is working hard to redress the imbalance by focusing on and giving priority to the needs of the more deprived areas.

Another imbalance that needs to be addressed seriously is that which pertains to girls' education. The national figures, which suggest a rapid expansion in student enrolment, conceal a large gender gap. For the country as a whole, 45% of primary school children were girls in 1995/96. However, in the lowland province of Sahel, girls constituted only 28% of the primary school population during the same period. It is also estimated that class repetition rates are higher for girls than for boys: primary, m = 13%, f = 23%; middle, m = 9%, f = 19%; and secondary, m = 13%, f = 27%. The demand for girls' labour at home, long walking distances to school, and traditional norms and beliefs (e.g. early marriage) are crucial factors militating against greater participation and retention of girls in the school system.

Relevance and Quality

Having expended considerable time, energy and resources on the quantitative expansion of the educational system, the MOE is now turning its attention to the provision of relevant and quality education. The centrepiece for this provision lies in reforming the national curriculum. Baseline studies have been conducted to obtain some indicators of the learning needs and circumstances of students at various levels in the school system.

In addition, at the macro-level, a needs assessment survey was carried out with a view to gathering relevant data from governmental and non-governmental organisations, employers, unions, professional associations, teachers, students, parents, local assembly members, community leaders and other groups with various interests in education. The results of the needs assessment survey will be matched with the priorities of the Government as outlined in the macro-policy and in the recommendations of the forthcoming report on Human Resources Development in Eritrea. This analysis, along with the situational analysis of the curriculum, will be used to inform the development of a revised national curriculum for Eritrea.

A curriculum that is relevant and of good quality would still be inadequate without the development of professionalism among teachers. As Stenhouse (1975, p. 83) rightly said in a memorable statement: 'there can be no curriculum development without teacher development'. Innovations in education cannot be effective unless teachers acquire the competence and skills required to initiate and implement new ideas and practices in actual classroom situations. Consequently, we are in the process of mounting large-scale pre-service and in-service training and retraining programmes that would buttress and facilitate the implementation of the new curriculum.

School managers and supervisors can also assist in the diffusion of educational and curriculum innovation by serving as vital points of personal contact between the initiators of change (e.g. policy-makers) and the implementers of change (i.e. teachers). Coombs (1970, p. 121) once suggested that 'if we want a meaningful revolution in education, it is with educational management that we need to begin'. To this end, Eritrea has already embarked on a long-term scheme for developing the professional competence of school managers and supervisors, an important component of which is a training programme initiated in partnership with the University of Bristol.

Community Empowerment and Sustainable Development

Since independence, the government of Eritrea has embarked on a wide-ranging programme designed to revitalise and develop the shattered economy and to promote its long-term growth. The overall vision of the country's future progress is based on the concept of human capital formation, with education and health as key inputs (Government of the State of Eritrea [GSE], 1994).

It is argued that investing in education, training and human capital is a prerequisite for sustainable development. The education–development interface may not always be axiomatic. However, where an expansion of educational opportunities takes place within the framework of economic growth and where this expansion is characterised by the incorporation of new knowledge and skills, it is highly probable that human capital will be enhanced.

In this context, education promotes higher productivity and provides people with the knowledge, skills and attitudes they need in order to be more effective in their everyday life. In a world that is increasingly being dominated by economic concerns, the nurturing of our future workforce is gaining a position of paramount importance. It is becoming even more apparent that human resources development, rather than the possession of natural resources, is the key factor in shaping a country's well-being and prosperity. This calls for more synchronisation between education and the world of work. In this context, education in Eritrea must support the creation of a competent, adaptable and highly productive workforce. Education must also enable our citizens to acquire new and valuable knowledge and skills throughout the course of their working lives.

In order to facilitate the consolidation of behavioural changes that are conducive to sustainable development, the Government is now making great efforts to encourage community participation in the planning, management and implementation of educational programmes. At the level of basic education, for example, participation in cost-sharing (in the form of cash and/or labour) is being complemented with community participation in making decisions about school location and educational programmes. This kind of participation can assist in improving the relevance and quality of education, in creating a sense of ownership and in establishing consensus among community groups. It is also an important step in promoting self-help activities for social development.

The Eritrean Government envisages greater mobilisation of resources by parents and communities through cost-sharing schemes both in terms of capital expenditure (community contribution for school facilities) and recurrent costs (paying small fees in all schools and covering the costs of teachers in community-based schools). It intends to sustain and deepen this cost-sharing scheme as part of a complementary programme of mobilising resources and extending ownership to local communities. However, as a matter of principle, a parent's inability to pay must not become a barrier to his/her participation in educational affairs.

Partnership, Collaboration and Development

The process of empowerment is an integral part of a wider policy of partnership, collaboration and sustainable development. This policy takes equal partnership as its starting point and is based on a model of horizontal communication and interaction leading to local decisions on development action.

To facilitate this process, the Eritrean Government has enacted a local government reform, which, among other things, provides an institutional and legal framework for allocating and sharing responsibilities in educational development among the central government, regional and subregional administrations and village/community clusters. The Ministry of Education is thus responsible for formulating policy guidelines and strategic macro-level plans, standardising and regulating educational activities, managing the overall development of human resources and undertaking research on key issues. The regional authorities are responsible for micro-planning and for the operation and management of the educational system, in partnership with the subregional and village/community-level administrations.

The same policy of collaboration and mutual benefit guides relationships with external partners. Eritrea welcomes international cooperation and experience sharing based on equitable relationships. At the same time, however, it is also argued that the educational system in Eritrea must be self-supporting in the long term and that it is unrealistic to expect any viable educational programme to be sustained indefinitely through external assistance.

Concluding Remarks

We live in a world that is becoming increasingly interdependent. Modern technology has integrated the world, and the world economy is gradually becoming frontierless. Technology is fast opening the possibilities of sharing information and experience with other nations and societies. Consequently, our citizens must be trained to access information through modern communication media and to use relevant and up-to-date information in decision-making processes.

One of the Eritrean Government's national development objectives is to promote 'an internally peaceful and stable nation, at peace and in harmony with its neighbours' (GSE, 1994, p. 11). The desire to stay at peace and in harmony with one's neighbours can and must be extended to cover the rest of the world. Whatever the case, this calls for the promotion of Eritrean as well as world citizens who perceive themselves as integral parts of a global community of people with common aspirations and a common commitment to peace and harmony. In this context, the challenge before us all is to create a learning environment in our schools that is conducive to the development of well-informed, outward-looking, conscious and responsible citizens.

Note

[1] The provinces have recently been reorganised into regions or 'zobas'.

References

Coombs, P. (1970) *The World Educational Crisis: a systems analysis*. London: Oxford University Press.

Government of the State of Eritrea (GSE) (1994) *Macro-policy*. Asmara: Government Printing Press.

Ministry of Education (MEO) (1995) *Eritrea: basic education statistics and essential indicators 1994/1995*. Asmara: Eritrea.

Ministry of Education (MOE) (1996) *Eritrea: basic education statistics and essential indicators 1995/1996*. Asmara: Government Printing Press.

Ministry of Education (MOE) (1996) *Eritrea: quest for education*. Asmara: Government Printing Press.

Provisional Government of Eritrea (PGE) (1991) *Declaration of Policy on Education*. Asmara: Government Printing Press.

Stenhouse, L. (1975) *An Introduction to Curriculum Research and Development*. London: Heinemann.

Transforming Teacher Education in a Small State: potential for distance education in Belize, Central America

CYNTHIA THOMPSON & MICHAEL CROSSLEY

Introduction

It is widely held that the strengths of a country's educational system are reflected in the quality of its teaching force. As reforms are introduced and as standards of education rise, the need intensifies for improved systems for the training of teachers to meet new demands. Over the past decade, Belize, along with many other developing countries, has been preoccupied with improving the initial and in-service training of teachers. Many schemes aimed at increasing the number of professionally trained teachers or with improving the quality of teaching and learning have, nevertheless, met with limited success. This chapter examines the nature of the latest teacher education initiative in Belize and considers the main lessons that can be learned from the experience, especially for other small states that may attempt similar types of educational reform.

On a broader level it can be seen how many recent initiatives designed to transform Belizean education have, to a significant extent, been inspired by global trends and developments. While there may be some advantages in this, the present study suggests that the chances of successful policy implementation are increased when local ownership is enhanced in all phases and at all levels of development initiatives. Belize has increasingly recognised the importance of critically evaluating the appropriateness and relevance of international trends and developments – while working collaboratively with external agencies to formulate development initiatives that are more closely related to perceived local

137

needs and the Belizean context. In the case reported here, this often necessitated significant modifications to externally inspired project proposals, the prioritising of human resource development, and increased involvement of local personnel. In the light of this experience, Belize's successes and challenges can serve as an example to other small states and transitional societies that are undertaking widespread educational transformation.

Background to Educational Reform in Belize

Belize: the context

Belize (formerly British Honduras) is a young nation on the Central American mainland that gained independence from Britain in 1981. It is bounded in the north and north-west by Mexico, on the east by the Caribbean Sea, and on the west and south-west by Guatemala. The country is sparsely populated, with a landmass of 22,000 sq km, and a population that has grown from approximately 184,000 in 1989 to 222,000 in 1996 (Belize Information Service, 1997). This is attributed mainly to the influx of Central American refugees and to the increase in Asian immigrants in the 1990s. The average population growth rate is now estimated at 2.6%. Belize is the only English-speaking country on the Central American mainland, and it is home to a mix of many ethnic groups, with five main languages or dialects being spoken. The country's economy is based on agricultural exports along with tourism and light manufacturing. In 1993 the GNP per capita was US $2440 per head, and the country is divided into six administrative districts.

A key feature of the educational system is the partnership that exists between the churches and the state. Under this partnership, government pays teachers' salaries, contributes to the cost of capital expenditure, assists with maintenance, develops curricula and standards, and trains teachers. The churches are responsible for the management and maintenance of their respective schools and for all related personnel matters. Despite the role of the various denominations, some fully state schools exist, government is the major contributor in the financing of education and, in 1995, spending on education comprised 20% of the Government's total expenditure.

Primary schooling runs from Grades 1 to 8 (Infant 1–Standard 6), with just over 53,000 pupils enrolled in the 280 primary schools during 1996, representing 84.7 % of the 5–14 year-olds in the population. Some 195 of these schools were in rural areas and 1994 teachers were employed in primary schools during that year, yielding an average pupil–teacher ratio of 26.6:1. The transition rate from primary to secondary schools stood at 80% (Belize, Ministry of Education, 1997).

Central to the goals of the Ministry of Education is a demand for greater access and participation in education and for the improved quality and efficiency of the system. Emphasis is placed on the development of the individual to ensure that every Belizean is afforded an opportunity to participate fully in the development of the country. The Government's policy of free tuition puts emphasis on 'quality enhancing inputs in education such as the development of sound administration and accountability, the supply of curricular materials, in-service training of teachers and the introduction of appropriate educational technology' (Belize, Ministry of Education, 1997, p. 7).

The Belize Primary Education Development Project: origins, goals, and components

The Belize Primary Education Development Project (BPEDP) sought to address many of the problems identified in the primary sector, which are related to the training of teachers, pupils' access to texts, curriculum development and implementation, assessment policies, the teaching of languages, school facilities improvement, and Ministry of Education planning and management capacity. The ongoing changes have far-reaching implications, some of which will need to be addressed beyond the phase of project funding.

The BPEDP was a 7-year initiative aimed at transforming and upgrading the primary sector of the education system. The project, which was the first in this sector in Belize, grew out of a Sector Review held in 1989. The Government of Belize subsequently initiated preparatory work in 1990, and in 1992, the project began implementation. In addition to a loan from the World Bank, the project received a grant from the British Overseas Development Administration (now known as the Department for International Development, DFID). The ODA part of the project had three interrelated components: Teacher Education, Education Development, and Planning and Management.

The main objectives of the BPEDP were:

> *to introduce a new system for the training of primary school teachers in order to improve the quality and relevance of teacher training and increase the number of teachers with professional qualifications; improve the quality, availability, and efficient use of educational facilities and resources for teaching, learning and assessment in primary schools; and strengthen the planning and management of education to enable the government to develop policies and implement programmes to improve the cost effectiveness of its expenditures on primary education. (World Bank, 1991, p. 10)*

The expected outputs of the project were to include an increase in the percentage of trained teachers in the primary sector from 45% to 80%; renovated primary classrooms to reduce overcrowding; all primary school children equipped with a basic set of texts; a revised and standardised primary school curriculum; and a ministry with the capacity for more effective planning and management, skills for data collection, analysis and research and increased numbers of professional staff.

The Teacher Education Component of the BPEDP

A brief overview of the history of teacher education in Belize helps to set the stage for the discussion of more recent initiatives.

The history of teacher training in Belize dates back to 1894 when the Board of Education Rules introduced the Pupil Teacher System of recruiting and training primary school teachers. The West Indies Royal Commission (Moyne, 1938), appointed to investigate the social and economic conditions of the territory, recommended that the Pupil Teacher System be replaced by a more systematic method. In 1941, a scheme was introduced and the first set of teachers went abroad for training. Shortly after, the Evans Commission (Evans, 1947) recommended the establishment of local training colleges and in 1954, two training colleges were established. The number of teachers to be trained was too small to accommodate two colleges and by 1965, they merged to form what is now Belize Teachers' Training College (BTTC), the only one in the country. From its inception, the college offered a 3-year programme of studies known as the 'Two Plus One Certificate', which included 2 years of intramural studies followed by 1 year of supervised 'internship'. In the same year as the merger, the ministries of education of Belize, Bahamas and Jamaica joined forces to form the Joint Board of Teacher Education (JBTE), which now serves as the accrediting and monitoring body for teacher training in the three countries. From 1966 to 1969 the two plus one programme was shortened to 1 year of intramural studies and 1 year of internship. During the same period, the college also mounted a 1-year intensive programme for junior secondary school teachers. In 1970, the two plus one programme was reintroduced and all other programmes were discontinued.

At its inception, BTTC was concerned with training only serving primary school teachers. It was not until 1988 that any attempt was made to introduce pre-service training. Attempts to attract secondary school graduates to the college met with limited success. Paradoxically, the requirement for admission to the college remains higher than the requirement for employment so it is easier, and financially more profitable, for secondary school graduates (and drop-outs), and for some primary school leavers, to seek employment first and to gain entry qualifications while they are teaching.

Notwithstanding the various development initiatives carried out over the past three decades, and the college's annual output of trained teachers, the country has until recently been unsuccessful in raising the percentage of trained teachers to an acceptable level (see Tables I and II). The college has often been held responsible for this slow rate of increase (Thompson, 1991). However, existing policies of recruitment into the profession, employment practices, and teacher attrition, are among other factors that explain the nation's failure to increase the percentage of trained teachers in the system. In 1992, only 45% of Belize's primary teaching force and less than 30% of its secondary teaching force had any professional training. The situation in rural Belize was even more disappointing. Ministry of Education figures for the same year show that only 35% of rural teachers were trained, compared with 64% in urban schools.

Year	1963	1968	1971	1975	1987	1990	1992
% trained	13	20	27	31	44	44	45

Table I. Trained primary school teachers 1963–92. Source: BTTC records.

Year	1978	1979	1980	1981	1982	1983	1984	1985	1986	1987	1988
No. graduated	45	52	52	48	27	43	41	36	43	17	35
% of cohort admitted to BTTC	83	69	71	66	37	47	50	40	57	27	49

Table II. Graduates from BTTC 1978–88. Source: BTTC records.

In an attempt to address this problem once again, the teacher education component of the BPEDP considered strategies that required more fundamental policy changes for the training and employment of teachers. The Government of Belize pays the full salaries of all teachers, even those in training. This means that for every teacher enrolled in the full-time programme, the Government pays for a replacement, who for the most part is less experienced and less competent. Besides being financially burdensome, this system has contributed to the slow rate of increase of trained teachers throughout the system.

Strategies adopted for the reform of teacher education through the project related directly to the following:

- a focus mainly on serving teachers;
- the largely academic orientation of the programme and the school curriculum;

- the piecemeal approach to the delivery of in-service teacher education;
- limited access to training for teachers in rural schools;
- the disproportionate distribution of trained teachers in rural and urban schools;
- the lack of physical outreach capacity to support in-service activities;
- lack of clear management and planning policies with respect to teacher posting, and to teacher demand and supply; and
- the absence of an attractive career path for faculty at the training college.

The overall goal of the new system of teacher training as implemented under the project is:

> to establish a structure of support, qualifications and incentives which will permit Belize to improve the competence of its teachers, to reinforce their professional identities, and to attain and maintain a more efficient and fully trained teaching force. (World Bank, 1991, Annex 5, p. 19)

This goal was to be achieved through:

- strengthening the teacher training system to provide professional certification and academic upgrading for some 700 untrained teachers;
- enhancing the quality and relevance of teacher training by providing assistance in staff development, course design and instructional materials development;
- providing incentives by offering salary upgrading for the successful completion of each level of the new programme;
- improving efficiency by placing less reliance on training in a full-time mode; and
- training principals as managers and instructional leaders in the primary schools.

Implementation Strategies

Introducing a New Training Model for Teachers

One major area of reform in the teacher education component was the phasing out of the Two Plus One Certificate, which had been offered since the establishment of the college in 1965. This programme was often criticised for its low completion rate and for being too theoretical and too heavily oriented to the academic school curriculum. In its place a new system called the Three Year Certificate with School Experience was introduced. This new programme offers training at two levels, Level 1 and Level 2. Level 1 offers 14 courses that provide essential skills and knowledge for practising teachers and places greater emphasis on developing the trainees' classroom teaching methodologies. The Level 2 programme supplements the training received in Level 1 and draws on the classroom experience of 1–2 years, which all applicants are required to gain between levels.

There are two modes of delivery for the new system: (a) full-time and (b) part-time. In the full-time mode, teachers complete 1 year (two 15-week semesters and one 6-week summer session) of intramural coursework. This is followed by one semester of supervised student teaching in a primary school where teachers are required to manage a class independently. Regulations require that teachers remain for an additional 6 months to 1 year in the schools to gain experience before returning to Level 2, which also consists of 1 year of intramural coursework. Teachers receive a certificate and salary upgrading after completing each level of training. The Ministry of Education certifies training at the completion of the Level 1 programme and the JBTE certifies training at the completion of Level 2. In the former system, certification and salary upgrading was only given at the end of 3 years of successful study.

In the part-time mode, teachers complete Level 1 through 2½ years of study, following the same course structure as in the full-time programme (Verbakel, 1997). The main difference is that teachers study while they continue to teach. There are four components to the part-time programme.

Self-study: teachers study using distance learning materials prepared by the college. They pursue two courses per semester.

Face-to-face summer sessions: teachers attend sessions for 4–6 weeks at the BTTC Belize City campus during the summer. During this time they pursue those courses which are difficult to deliver by distance or which require more hands-on activities, i.e. music, art, physical education, instructional aids.

Monthly workshops: teachers are required to attend monthly 1-day workshops held at District Education Centres. The workshops are designed to reinforce main concepts and teaching strategies as well as to provide a forum for dealing with issues and concerns held by both supervisors and students.

Classroom visits: field supervisors are assigned with between 8 and 12 students. They visit each student a minimum of once per month for a day. These visits are meant to provide professional assistance in general, and assistance with specific issues related to the module being studied in particular.

After successful completion of Level 1, teachers can apply for admission to Level 2.

Upgrading for Primary School Principals

In responding to its mandate to train principals 'to provide instructional leadership at the school level' (World Bank, 1991, p. 10), the college introduced a 1-year in-service programme for all primary school principals. A committee of managers, principals, college tutors and representatives from the Ministry of Education was formed to examine the new roles and functions of principals and formulate the resulting training programme. The group concluded that this should target only those principals who had completed the former BTTC programme or the newly introduced one. Of the 250 principals at that time, 204 were eligible. This programme is the first in the country that formally addresses the need for continuing professional development for teachers.

The structure, content and length of the programme resulted from the following concerns: the needs identified were too many to be taught in a short summer course; schools are scattered across the country and some principals in remote locations find it difficult to come to a central place; the provision should be practical and should address school improvement needs; and the human resources available in the college were insufficient to run another intramural programme.

In view of these concerns, the committee decided to offer a programme which followed the same basic structure as the Level 1 part-time design, except for the face-to-face summer component. The main characteristics are therefore as follows.

Self-study: using materials derived from seven modules developed by the Commonwealth Secretariat (1993) for a group of African countries entitled *Better Schools Resource Materials for School Heads*. Belizean principals study one module per month.

Monthly workshops: these are held for 1 day per month at District Education Centres and cover materials considered to be essential to the tasks to be completed (e.g. training in techniques of supervision of teaching, development of a school library, development of funding proposals), and to the basic concerns of principals.

School visits: each principal is assigned to a BTTC supervisor who visits monthly for a full day. The purpose of the visit is to provide guidance in the implementation of the programme and to observe progress over time.

One of the main features of the assessment is that principals are not required to sit a written examination. Instead, they are asked to develop a portfolio of activities, tasks and assignments that demonstrate how they apply their training to the development needs of their schools. Evaluation is based on performance on assignments and tasks given; supervisors' reports on progress observed over time; and an exit interview conducted by an official of the Ministry of Education, the programme coordinator and the supervisor. Principals have to use their portfolio (developed over the year) to display and illustrate their growth in areas covered. A Certificate in Leadership and Management is awarded and an increase in salary has been promised to those who successfully complete the programme. Some 88 principals were enrolled in the first cohort in 1996–97, and 58 in the second cohort in 1997–98.

Training Teachers through Distance Education

What can be asserted with some assurance is that, if the
course is successfully launched and carried through, it will
be a major triumph for all those who strived to create it.
(Van der Eyken, 1994)

Given the limited success of past efforts to improve teacher education in Belize, the Government sought other innovative strategies to address the major problems faced in the 1990s. As already noted, distance education was viewed as an attractive alternative for upgrading the content and pedagogical skills of some 700 untrained teachers in the primary system – and to provide upgrading for principals in instructional leadership and management. There were several advantages in trying this approach. It made it possible for many teachers who could not leave their families and communities to pursue training. Secondly, the programme would be accessible to teachers in all six districts. Thirdly, it reduced the costs of the replacement of teachers in training. Fourthly, the establishment of a structure for supporting training in the districts could serve as a basis for the development of a programme for the continuing professional development of teachers. Fifthly, it provided an opportunity for trainers to observe the immediate implementation of teaching strategies in schools.

Distance education is defined by Keegan (cited in Markowitz, 1990, p. 4) as having five elements: (a) the separation of teacher and learner; (b) the planning and preparation of materials under the influence of an educational organisation; (c) the use of technical media to unite teacher and learner; (d) the provision for two way communication; and (e) the absence of the learning group. Markowitz argues that 'fundamental to distance education is the fact that the student will seldom or never have personal contact with the instructor'. Perraton (1993) points out, however, that this conception of distance education is a misnomer, since the most effective distance education programmes include an element of face-to-face teaching.

The strategy that is being implemented in Belize reflects both Markowitz's perspective and Perraton's argument by combining four components: self study using materials prepared by the college; face-to-face summer sessions; monthly supervisory visits; and monthly 1-day workshops. The Belize programme is, therefore, more accurately referred

145

to as one of extramural studies that utilises distance learning methodologies and materials.

Adding an extramural arm to the college's existing provision created some of the greatest challenges ever faced by BTTC – especially given the small size of Belize and its limited human, material and financial resources. It also generated many valuable lessons for the Ministry of Education and for other small states attempting to implement such programmes.

It is to a critical review of these challenges, and the lessons to learn from the various responses, that we now turn.

Successes and Challenges in Distance Education for Teachers

Successes

Perraton (1993) offers suggestions for measuring the success of distance learning initiatives that can be applied to Belize. These include satisfying numerical goals, examining completion rates, comparing the examination results of intramural and distance students, and calculating cost factors.

Numerical Goals and Completion Rates

The Belizean project set out to train 700 primary school teachers who needed upgrading to a minimum of a Level 1 certificate. This was to be undertaken through the introduction of the Level 1 full-time and part-time programmes. Since 1992, when the project was launched, 747 teachers have been admitted into the Level 1 programme – 336 in the part-time extramural and 411 in the full-time programme. Some 266 remain enrolled in part-time study, and 347, or 75% of those admitted, have completed all Level 1 requirements. The remaining teachers have some courses outstanding. By 1996, 56% of teachers in the system were, therefore, professionally trained and the original numerical goals are now within reach.

The part-time extramural option completed its first full cycle in June 1997 and the results are very encouraging given the many teething troubles and setbacks that were experienced initially. Results from the Level 1 part-time programme show a completion rate of 60%, with 40 of the 67 who were in the first cohort completing all requirements in June 1997.

Examination Results

To demonstrate the impact of the distance education strategy, the performance of two groups of student teachers currently enrolled in

Level 2 were compared. One group of 29 student teachers was from the first cohort of the Level 1 part-time programme, who were enrolled in 1994, and the other group of 28 was from the full-time Level 1 programme, who were enrolled in that same year. The full-time students pursued their training over a 1½ year period, and the part-time students completed their training over a 2½ year period. Nineteen of the 29 students from the Level 1 part-time programme (66%) obtained grades of C+ or above on the recently completed student teaching exercise, which was moderated by the external examining body from the University of the West Indies. In comparison, 12 of the 28 (43%) of those from the full-time programme obtained grades in the same band. Students who were interviewed by the external examiners attributed their success to the continuous supervision they received in the distance mode and the opportunity they had to practise the new strategies they learned over the 2½ years of study.

A further comparison was made of student teachers' performance in the academic subject areas. Table III shows the results from the 1994 cohort of full-time and part-time distance students.

The entries in the column titled resit show the number of students who have had an opportunity to resit an examination and who have passed the course since the first sitting. The student teachers from the full-time programme had more opportunities to resit.

It is evident from Table III that the groups compared well, and that there were areas where both had difficulty. However, there is evidence that the method of training had a positive impact on those who pursued the part-time distance programme in the support provided through continuous supervision over the 2½ years. Student teachers from the full-time programme received supervision for only one semester in comparison.

Another major accomplishment of this component is the capacity-building achieved for the faculty in the development of distance learning materials and the management of distance learning programmes. After a series of staff development sessions for the teaching and supervision staff, 10 faculty members embraced the opportunity to write and publish. This experience has had a visible impact on the work they have produced since. They have also become more conscious of the need for clear and detailed assignments and tasks to be prepared for students.

In the distance programme, delivery of a course is no longer the sole responsibility of the course tutor. Assignments are carefully read and critiqued by supervisors before they are dispatched to students. This has been a challenge for course tutors who were accustomed to 'doing their own thing', but it has resulted in greater collegiality and much clearer and more relevant and realistic assignments. Marking of tests and assignments is also a team effort. The overall result of this collaborative effort is a faculty that is involved in the total delivery of the programme rather than the individual delivery of a course. This has helped to build team spirit that has resulted in the sharing of students' successes and a collaborative approach to solving problems.

Courses	Full-time ($n = 80$)				Part-time ($n = 67$)			
	Sat	Passed	Resit	%	Sat	Passed	Resit	%
English Language	80	80	1	100	66	64	0	97
Arts	80	79	21	99	67	56	31	84
Mathematics	79	77	7	97	68	67	5	98
Science	79	74	2	94	65	55	0	85
Social Studies	79	76	1	96	63	62	0	98
Belizean Studies	79	76	8	96	63	57	0	91
Classroom Organisation	78	78	2	100	69	67	5	97
Teaching Methods	80	76	1	95	68	67	5	99
Testing & Measurement	79	72	0	91	64	44	0	69
Child Development	79	68	21	86	66	59	5	89
Instructional Aids	79	79	0	100	68	68	0	100
Music	38	37	1	97	40	39	1	98
Art	56	55	0	85	51	51	0	100
Physical Education	67	67	0	100	42	42	0	100
Student Teaching L1	72	70	5	97	66	64	5	97
Total graduated	65 (81%)				40 (60%)			

Table III. Comparison of the performance of students in the Level 1 full-time and part-time programmes who were admitted in 1994. Source: BTTC records.

At the project mid-term review in 1995, the college's capacity to reach its goals was questioned and the evaluation team noted several concerns, among which were the late delivery of assignments, slow pace of module production, and absence of district support centres (BPED, 1995, p. 13). However, by the end of 1997, the college had completed all 84 modules in nine courses and three district centres had been established to support the training provided at the college, an accomplishment that many believed would not have been realised.

Cost Factors

It is widely held that externally-funded projects that do not make provisions for sustainability usually fail. Those involved in the development of this project understood the importance of field supervision for the distance programme. This led to a request for additional funds in the recurrent budget. The Ministry of Education had great foresight in responding positively to this request and increasing this line item by over 300% in the recurrent budget for the 1996 and 1997 fiscal years. Savings on the traditionally expected replacement costs for intramural trainees also helped to make this investment possible and to make the whole distance education initiative viable.

Although much has been accomplished, there remain many challenges. We now examine these in more detail.

Challenges

Attitudes to Change and the Accrediting Body

The first major challenge came when the college presented its new structure for approval from its accrediting body. A pilot of the Level 1 (full-time) programme was launched in 1990 and the first cohort of 40 teachers was admitted. A second cohort was admitted in 1991. During that time, BTTC was seeking approval for the changes that were being proposed for introduction under the project from 1992. The structure and content of the Level 1 full-time programme was to form the basis for the development of materials for the part-time version. Since BTTC has representation on the JBTE, it kept it fully informed as plans were being developed.

The initial reaction to the proposed changes suggested that there were some concerns. This plan departed from what was officially covered in the regulations. All the other training colleges under the JBTE were offering 3 continuous years of intramural training. Belize was the only country in the Board offering the Two Plus One Certificate. The major objection seemed not to be to the delivery of a programme by distance, but to the decision to split the training into two levels. It was feared that coverage of content would be more limited and that some teachers would opt not to pursue the second level of training and so would be 'short-changed'. When it was learnt that the Board was not considering the innovation favourably, there was initial scepticism among some Belizean educators and teachers about the proposed change. Some teachers felt that the new qualification would be regarded as substandard and that their training would not be counted if they wanted to pursue further studies in Belize or abroad. There were others who held the view that Belize did not need to be in the JBTE and argued that this was the long awaited opportunity to sever ties.

A few months before the BPEDP was launched, further discussions took place. The new Board Chairman affirmed its role as an accrediting body, but pointed out that one of its responsibilities was also to assist member states in the development of plans to address their individual needs. In July 1992, the college thus 'got the blessing' of the Board for the new structure. With the reprint of a new Manual, the Three Year Certificate with School Experience was formally introduced and in September 1992, the Level 1 full-time programme at BTTC was officially launched with accreditation. Two years later, in September 1994, the Level 1 part-time and the Level 2 programmes were implemented. As already noted, the Ministry of Education awards a certificate to those who successfully complete the first level of training. A salary upgrade is also given. The JBTE grants certificates to those who successfully complete the second level. These graduates also receive a salary upgrade. The increase in salary at the end of each phase of training provides some additional career incentives to the teachers. This has helped to minimise some of the negative criticisms that were levied against the reform at its inception, and has also helped to stem the rapid increase in the salaries budget of the Ministry that results from upgrading large numbers of teachers.

Once the programme was launched, there were new challenges. By necessity, new methods of assessment were introduced, especially in the distance mode. Teachers were given assignments that involved more practical application to the classroom. Many found the assignments to be more challenging and beneficial. Because these assignments are more practical, and because most teachers have difficulty with written English, course grades are sometimes higher than the grades on written examinations. Almost all the external examiners have commented on this in their reports. Faculty members have expressed the need for more openness and flexibility in the assessment of courses offered through the part-time distance option. Because external examiners are overseas, faculty members do not have the opportunity for one-on-one discussions about issues affecting their courses. These issues will be revisited later.

Attitudes to Change and the Faculty

A second major challenge relates to the attitudes of the BTTC faculty to change. The decision to reform teacher education came from the Government, the funding agency for the college. BTTC's role was to assist in determining what these changes should be. Although faculty members were kept well informed and were invited to make input in the planning process from time to time, some openly resisted and others viewed the proposed changes with scepticism. There was more resistance to the extramural programme than to the full-time model because of the extra workload demands and the uncertainty of the implications for job security. With reference to staff involvement in module production, one consultant advised that the college's plan to involve internal full-time staff in the external programme should be clarified and recommunicated to all concerned because the extramural was not initially seen as a priority. This adviser felt that the critical mass of internal college support needed to produce the required number of modules on time and at a respectable level of quality was not available.

With the introduction of an extramural component, the college became a dual mode institution so job descriptions had to be modified. Faculty members who were once full-time lecturers were required to do more supervision of student teachers in the field. There was the fear that some jobs would be lost – and indeed that happened. Moving to an extramural mode also took away a considerable amount of the autonomy, power and control that course tutors had in the full-time programme. They had control over content, over the method of assessment, and the marking of students' scripts. In the part-time mode, the delivery of the course is shared among district supervisors. Course tutors therefore have to ensure that modules are clear and that they adequately cover the content of the course; that assignments are set for the beginning of each course; that assignments are clear and unambiguous; and that mark schemes and answer keys are developed along with the assignments. These are presented to supervisors before they are issued to students to ensure common understanding of the requirements of the course. This is necessary if standards are to be maintained across the districts.

In the full-time programme, the tutor is responsible for and does all the marking of assignments and examinations. In the part-time mode, some assignments are marked either at the district level or centrally under the guidance of the course tutors. Final examinations are table marked, with the course tutor as table leader. Course tutors are also required to present workshops for colleagues who are supervising the extramural students and to visit the districts and conduct workshops for students as requested. This new role was seen as too demanding and some faculty members who were unwilling to travel resigned. Some of those who stayed clearly indicated a preference to remain with the full-time programme. Faculty members who were assigned to the districts were the least resistant to the changes because what was now required was not, for them, a significant departure from the past. Sessions in team-building and the management of change were conducted to try to address these problems, but more sessions are needed.

As noted earlier, resistance to change was due in part to the workload demands of the new job. The human resource demands of this innovation were beyond the basic capacity of the college. Classroom teachers were therefore recruited to serve as supervisors, and assistance from volunteer agencies in the United Kingdom and USA was sought. However, even with such help, the workload remains very demanding and faculty members find it difficult to manage the new programme and participate fully in other project activities such as the new curriculum development process.

Small countries like Belize, therefore, need to be especially wary of overloading the few people who are willing and able to make such changes possible. Belize's success can be partially attributed to a set of hardworking and dedicated faculty members. However, in attempting any future changes, it is argued here that planners must listen more to those involved in implementation and be more conscious of contextual factors and the demands of the change. Overburdening willing people can have the negative effect of lowering morale and reducing the impact of the intervention. Small state systems must be particularly aware of the 'absorptive capacity' of the country to incorporate and pursue complex change (Van der Eyken et al, 1995). This refers not only to the human resource capacity, but also to organisational, financial and material resources.

Moreover, if BTTC should attempt any future changes, it is argued that it must begin with more collaborative planning with those who will be involved in the change from an early stage. Roles and functions would need to be clearly defined as early as possible. Indeed, for any country taking on a transformative project of this size and nature, it is important that all stakeholders are well informed and that they are helped to understand and participate actively in the planning process.

Learning from the Belizean Experience

Planning and Implementing Distance Education in a Small State

Many of the problems that BTTC faced in the development and implementation of the revised teacher education programme could have been avoided if better training for the planners had been provided further in advance of implementation. More realistic planning and preparation could have taken place and more realistic timelines could have been set, especially as they affected the limited human resource capacity of the college. In small countries like Belize, the number of persons trained in specialised fields is usually quite limited. As a result, many employees take on multiple roles and have to perform multiple tasks (Bray, 1991). The BPEDP was launched in February 1992, but it was not until October 1992 that any training or exposure to the planning and management of distance education programmes was provided for the administration of BTTC. With the reform scheduled for implementation in September 1993, this should have been one of the first steps in planning. Although the planners were optimistic and eager to work, they lacked essential experience in distance education planning and management. At the end of a study tour to the United Kingdom that was arranged for the administrators in 1992, it became clear that the deadlines set could not be met. By early 1993, it was recognised that greater priority should be invested in developing the whole distance education system, in addition to the teaching and learning materials. Developing such a system required a common policy and practice for all districts, and the documentation of routines and procedures to a much greater extent than had been envisaged by BTTC at that time. This is an important principle for all engaged in such work.

Policy Options for Materials Development

If involvement in planning the overall distance education programme did not present enough challenges, the development of materials certainly did. Several options were considered for course development based on a theoretical framework proposed by Crossley & Murby (1994). These are: (a) adopt modules already written elsewhere; (b) identify pre-existing materials close enough to what was needed and adapt them to suit the Belizean context; (c) develop new materials in full; and (d) collaborate with external agencies in materials development where the capacity did not exist locally.

In this way, nine courses, totalling 84 modules, had been provided by 1998 and all four of these options were employed. This multiple/combined materials development strategy has been the key to Belize's success to date. No one model alone would have been a realistic option given the college's limited capacity for original materials development, and the absence of alternative human and material resources in a small state such as Belize. Thus, for example, BTTC sought permission to adapt the Commonwealth Secretariat's (1993) *Better Schools* resource materials for the whole Principals' Training Programme – with the addition of its own Belizean study guide. Four courses were adapted using a 'wrap around' strategy that produced original guidelines and assignments related directly to pre-existing textbooks chosen from those available on the commercial market. Most significantly, of the 84 modules produced, 55 were written in-country, some with the support of local consultancy input. These included the child development and language arts courses. Finally, because of the absence of local writers in subject areas such as science and mathematics, some external agencies were contracted to collaborate in original materials development.

Each of these models has its own strengths and weaknesses and much can be learned from the Belizean experience. Collaboration with external agencies elsewhere in the Caribbean, for example, generated unanticipated delays beyond the control of the college. The delivery of 21 science and mathematics modules was, thus, delayed by 1 year, causing much frustration and changes to implementation schedules. In the light of this experience, it is argued that inevitable communication and coordination problems should be built into production timelines and that all contracts should contain penalty clauses for failure to meet deadlines. Perhaps more fundamentally, the Belizean experience demonstrates that a small state can benefit greatly from the application of distance education strategies despite the inevitable problems and the absence of economies of scale (Bray & Packer, 1993). The cost-effectiveness rational is less influential in such contexts, but other savings can be made if professional training can be undertaken on-the-job; and distance education can help widen access to those in isolated locations and to potential candidates unable to travel away from home and community commitments. When materials can be adopted or adapted from systems with similar needs and conditions, then the potential benefits are widened and the distance education policy option becomes increasingly viable for small states. As is the case in Papua New Guinea (Crossley & Guy, 1990/91), once good quality distance materials have been produced, they can be used by staff teaching the same courses intramurally – and there is evidence that this unintended benefit improved the quality of such teaching at BTTC, further strengthening the teacher education reform overall.

Conclusion

The transformation of teacher education in Belize since the start of the BPEDP in 1992 has been dramatic and far-reaching. Much had been achieved through a predominantly distance education strategy that many thought to be inappropriate for a small state with limited human and material resources. To some extent, there is evidence that, in implementing multidimensional educational reform, too much was expected of key personnel; that unrealistic implementation deadlines were initially established and insufficient pre-implementation planning and training was carried out. On the other hand, the flexible management of the project, combined with the consistent efforts of many participants, have ensured considerable and sustainable success. While many of the specific lessons to be learned relating to teacher education have already been considered, a number of broader implications deserve mention in conclusion.

Involvement in the BPEDP has, at the broadest level, contributed significantly to the strengthening of Belizean planning and management capacity relating to teacher education and educational development in general. There is now, for example, a pool of local managers and writers trained and experienced in distance education strategies and materials development. A system of District Resource Centres has also been established which could, in future, serve as a basis for the continuing professional development of teachers nationwide. With the means to carry out future training at the district level, further savings on government expenditure are now possible, and more teachers, at all levels, can be reached and supported in the field. The Belizean experience also highlights the strategic importance of local participation in the planning process if realistic and sustainable development is to be achieved. Finally, BTTC's collaboration with local and external agencies in the development and implementation of extramural professional development programmes for teachers well demonstrates how, with the effective use of modern information and communications technology, distance education can be a most appropriate policy option even for small states such as Belize. This has been achieved in a way that has shown how small states can stay in tune with contemporary international developments, but simultaneously challenge the uncritical application of global models and assumptions. In so doing, the Belizean experience helps to demonstrate how increased local ownership and context sensitivity are essential if we are to achieve sustainable educational transformation that will meet the diverse needs of our rapidly globalising, but multicultural, world.

References

Belize Information Service (1997) Fact Sheet, Belize City.

Belize Ministry of Education (1992) *Education Statistical Digest*. Belize City: Planning Unit.

Belize Ministry of Education (1997) *Education Statistical Digest*. Belize City: Planning Unit.

Belize Primary Education Development Project (1995) Mid-term Review, Belize City.

Bray, M. (1991) *Making Small Practical*. London: Commonwealth Secretariat.

Bray, M. & Packer, S. (1993) *Education in Small States: concepts, challenges and strategies*. London: Pergamon Press.

Commonwealth Secretariat (1993) *Better Schools Resource Materials for School Heads*. London: Commonwealth Secretariat.

Crossley, M. & Guy, R. (Eds) (1990/91) Distance Education in Papua New Guinea, Special Issue of the *Papua New Guinea Journal of Education*, 26(2).

Crossley, M. & Murby, M. (1994) Textbook Provision and the Quality of the School Curriculum in Developing Countries: issues and policy options, *Comparative Education*, 34, pp. 99–114.

Evans, G. (1947) *Report of the British Guyana and British Honduras Settlement Commission*. Cmd 7533. London: HMSO.

Markowitz, H. (1990) *Distance Education: staff handbook*. The Guide Series. Urbana: University of Illinois.

Moyne (Chairman) (1938) *West Indies Royal Commission Report*. Cmd. 6697. London: HMSO.

Perraton, H. (1993) *Distance Education for Teachers*. London: Routledge.

Thompson, C. (1991) *Preschool and Primary Education in Belize.* Belize City: Society for the Promotion of Education and Research (SPEAR).

Van der Eyken, W. (1994) *Belize Bristol Link Programme – Final Evaluation Report.* Bristol: Centre for International Studies in Education, University of Bristol.

Van der Eyken, W., Goulden, D. & Crossley, M. (1995) Evaluating Education Reform in a Small State: a case study of Belize, Central America, *Evaluation: The International Journal of Theory, Research and Practice,* 1, pp. 33–44.

Verbakel, H. (1997) *Distance Education Project Report.* Belize City: Ministry of Education.

World Bank (1991) *Staff Appraisal Report for the Belize Primary Education Development Project.* Report No. 9485-Bel. Washington, DC: World Bank.

Education for All? Transforming Educational Provision for the Inclusion of Street Children in Brazil

LESLIE GROVES & DAVID JOHNSON

Introduction

This chapter discusses the effects of political transition upon the processes of educational transformation in Brazil. The central argument made in this chapter is that in Brazil, like in most countries which have experienced transitions from authoritarianism to democracy, educational transformation gives rise to multiple and often conflicting sets of goals.

Carnoy & Samoff (1990) examined the education policies of several states experiencing transition from colonial to socialist societies and concluded that these states embraced competing views for their national education systems. One set of priorities, readily identifiable in many policy documents, is the transformation of the education system to increase access to education for more of the country's population. The underlying ideological position in this case is the view that the purpose of education is to promote equality in social relations and to build national identity. Another set of priorities might be to develop the education system so that it is capable of developing human resource capacity necessary to increase economic production. The underlying ideological position here is modernisation and economic growth.

While there is no fundamental conflict between these views – it is possible to conceive of a society which seeks to raise the standard of living for all because in this lies the answers to social equality – it has become clear that in practice, in most countries experiencing transition, the focus on modernisation and economic growth often displaces priorities such as access for all (Carnoy & Samoff, 1990). More important is the fact that governments seem able to successfully promote, at community level, the acceptance of the role of education as an instrument for economic growth. According to Carnoy & Samoff (1990), where this happens, an ideology of individual competitiveness becomes widespread. Such an ideology is potentially divisive to the point where community members who utilise the public school system recognise that the fewer children who attend, the greater the opportunity for the success of their own children. This individualistic ideology is, however, a subtle one and involves a complex set of group psychological processes. More likely than not, it is played out between 'insider' and 'outsider' groups rather than at the level of the individual. Insider groups might comprise, for example, 'normal' children while outsider groups might include those with disabilities or severe learning disorders. In writing about street children in Brazil, Blunt (1994) gives a good illustration of this. He points out:

> *that there has been no public outcry of concern or indignation that the state does not enforce attendance of poor and working children is evidence that community members recognise the advantage for their children if the poorest children do not attend. (1994, p. 254)*

Thus, while the broad agenda for educational transformation might appear to be, and indeed is very often, progressive, there are often specific areas which are neglected or compromised. The central question for this chapter, therefore, is how do states in transition from authoritarianism to democracy reconcile the conflict between achieving social justice, equality and equity for all, but at the same time, achieve, through the education system, the basis for economic growth and prosperity? As we have argued earlier, these goals need not be contradictory, but the evidence shows that in practice, it is often the case that states delay transforming those aspects of education (such as education for children with severe learning difficulties or disabled children) that are likely to compete for resources with aspects of change likely to result in high economic returns.

It is our intention in this chapter to focus on a specific policy issue – that is, the inclusion of marginal groups, specifically street and working children – in the educational process in Brazil. It is also our intention to look more closely at the forces behind transformation; that is, the catalysts for change. In the case of Brazil, the transformation of national policy towards marginalised children and their inclusion in the process of education was inspired by a social movement which widened considerably during the years in which the country was governed by a military dictatorship. With the transition to democracy, the role of the social movement for the inclusion of street and working children continued, both in its advocacy for change in legislation, but also in its attempts to implement change. Our aim is to explore the innovations developed by this movement and to look at the role of government and international non-governmental organisations (NGOs) in broadening access for marginalised children.

The chapter is organised as follows. First, we will discuss the growing phenomena of urbanisation and street and working children. Second, we will look at policy towards street and working children and its transition through different phases of Brazil's socio-political history. Third, we will consider briefly those factors that mitigate against the inclusion of street and working children in education and then move on to discussing some policy initiatives and programmes in Brazil designed to overcome these constraints.

Street and Working Children – an urban phenomenon

Street children are a rapidly growing, unique urban population throughout the world. According to Keil & Viola (1997), there are more than 100 million children who live and seek to survive on the streets and who are excluded from schools. A variety of factors contribute to the exclusion of street children from schools, not least of which is the fact that existing forms of provision do not accommodate their needs. We shall return to this issue later.

It is perhaps useful first to consider briefly who 'street children' are and to develop a critical understanding of the underlying causes of the phenomenon of street children. 'Street children' is the generic term used to refer to children who use the street for their daily survival. Although there is no precise definition, the most widely accepted is that proposed by the International Catholic Child Bureau and adopted by the United Nations Children's Fund (UNICEF):

> Street children are those for whom the street (in the widest
> sense of the word, including unoccupied buildings, wastelands
> etc.) more than their family has become their real home, a
> situation in which there is no protection, supervision, or
> direction from responsible adults. (Fyfe, 1985)

The salience of this definition notwithstanding, its all-encompassing nature has often led to a misleading and distorted understanding of the reality these children confront. The term would appear to imply that these children constitute a homogeneous group, experiencing the same reality throughout the world (Stromquist, 1994). It is important, however, to understand that although these children may share a number of common characteristics, each child lives in a specific environment (Keeton & McConnell, 1994). The term 'street child' is therefore one which encompasses a number of subgroups. These are: children-of-the-street, who live on the street and are generally independent of their families; children-on-the-street, who use the street for work or other purposes and maintain regular contact with their families; and children-for-the-street, who are at risk of joining the street due to family breakdown or severe employment hardship (Blunt, 1994, p. 239).

According to Keil & Viola (1997), the phenomenon of street children is not new. Not only have children been used as slaves for centuries, they have also used public areas in order to survive. The problem has, however, been greatly magnified by the processes of urbanisation and industrialisation. Today, street children are essentially an urban phenomenon and over 90% are in the metropolitan areas of less developed countries, including Rio de Janeiro, Mexico City, Nairobi and Manila (Blunt, 1994). Unsurprisingly, more developed countries have fewer street children than less developed countries but numbers appear to be growing.

The rate of urbanisation in Brazil, as in many other developing countries, is increasing at an alarming rate, with far-reaching repercussions. The rapid growth in the urban population has created a demand for social services and resources which the Government has found difficult to meet. The consequence has been overcrowding, increased poverty, and social and cultural stress. Housing shortages and poor living conditions have consequently forced many nationals, including children, onto the street and the problem has been compounded by the global economic recession and debt servicing (Graham-Brown, 1991).

While it is clear to see how these factors give rise to a growing population of street and working children, it is important to recognise, however, that street children are not just passive victims of their circumstances but are active participants. They have the power of choice and for many, street life is a consciously selected alternative. This chapter does not attempt to offer a full discussion of the social, economic and political factors underlying the rising incidence of street children. It is perhaps worth pointing out that the plight of street children is an international issue, which has been greatly sensationalised by the Western media, and yet relatively neglected by academic literature. More recently, some studies have begun to theorise the issue and useful discussions of the underlying causes of street and working children are found in Oliveira et al (1992), Keeton & McConnell (1994), Vélis (1995) and Ngo Kim Cuc (1996), and Stromquist (1994).

Political Transitions, Social Movements and Street Children in Brazil

The main concern of this volume is the link between political transition and educational transformation. According to McLeish (1998), political transition is a primary catalyst for educational transformation. While, as some chapters in this volume show (see, for example, N'zimande & Mathieson), the link between transformation of the political system and that of the educational system in countries engaged in democratisation is undeniable (McLeish, 1998), democratic political goals can often be at odds with the way to achieve change in educational or social systems. A useful illustration of this point lies in the fact that between 1960 and 1970, when Brazil was ruled by a military regime, it consciously adopted conflicting macro-level and micro-level policies and practices. The military government passed two major laws to protect the welfare of street children. However, the laws gave the military and police wide powers to intervene in the lives of children and adolescents in 'irregular' circumstances, and in practice, the policy criminalised the gatherings of street children, effectively repressing informal learning and recreational activities (Dewees & Klees, 1995).

More important, most writings on educational transition do not focus on who the transformers are. Very often, such as in the case of South Africa and Brazil (see N'zimande & Mathieson, this volume), grass roots movements which were catalysts for transformation in the 'repression years' find themselves in growing conflict with the new emergent state. The degree of distance between the new state and the old progressive social movements often determines how successful educational transitions are.

In Brazil, Dewees & Klees (1995) draw attention to 'the unusual transformation of national policy towards children, brought about by a social movement which grew out of grassroots activism' (1995, p. 78). The emergence of the fight for the rights of children in Brazil was embedded in the struggle against military dictatorship. This led to 'the most progressive transformation of laws protecting children seen anywhere in the world' (Dewees & Klees, 1995, p. 78). The struggle culminated in the 1990s with the development and adoption in Brazil of the Child and Adolescent Statute, which brought about substantial changes in the way public and private institutions dealt with street and working children. However, a decade on, the implementation of the statute remains weak and the underlying causes of street and working children grow in intensity (Hewitt & Smith, 1999).

The question that must be asked, therefore, is why? Dewees & Klees (1995) ask whether the history and gains of the social movement in Brazil for the democratisation of child rights was 'progressive transformation or retrograde retrenchment?' What is it, then, that undermines the gains made by progressive organisations when the new state is formed? According to Dewees & Klees (1995), it would be naive to assume, that transformations based on democratic change are necessarily moving in one direction – forward. Change is often recursive. Thus, Dewees & Klees suggest that the problem of translating macro-level policy into micro-level action is not necessarily a problem of incompetent governments – rather, it is the extent to which governments are successful in protecting dominant interests.

Thus, in Brazil, despite years of gains made in transforming policy towards marginalised children, and the adoption of a human rights legislative framework, the transformation process stopped short of securing access and inclusion for street and working children on a wide scale.

There are still numerous factors that mitigate against the inclusion of street children. At the beginning of this chapter, we argued that one of the most important in this regard is the extent to which the 'bigger agenda' for transformation conflicts with an issue such as the inclusion of marginalised groups. There are several other factors, which are outlined here briefly.

Factors Mitigating against Inclusion

The city of Recife, capital of the north-eastern state of Pernambuco, is one of the poorest cities in Brazil, with nearly half the population living in poverty (Centro Luiz Freire, 1994). Recife's children constitute 40% of the total population (Centro Luiz Freire, 1994) and a large proportion of them use the streets on a regular basis and do not attend school despite the fact that Brazilian legislation guarantees free and compulsory education for all children between the ages of 7 and 14 (Federal Constitution, 1988, Chapter VII).

There are numerous difficulties and constraints to planning adequately for the education of street children. One of the primary reasons is the quality of the Brazilian education system itself. The system is characterised by exceptionally high proportions of children who fail, play truant or are never registered. A survey carried out in Recife revealed that 75% of pupils interviewed had repeated the year at least once (Prefeitura de Recife – Sintesis, 1996). The poor quality of the education system means that a number of children lose interest and confidence rapidly, preferring to spend their days on the street than in the classroom. Many children see the curriculum as uninteresting and too far removed from their own realities to be of any benefit (Boyden & Holden, 1991). The 'school of life', on the other hand, teaches them how to find food, defend themselves and have fun. Boyden & Holden conclude that teachers and other staff are partially responsible for the lack of interest shown by the children. Many teachers demonstrate a lack of motivation in working with street children and their training has not taught them how to work with this type of clientele. A more serious claim, made by street children themselves, is that they were discriminated against by their teachers. Thus, according to UNESCO (1995), a different type of pedagogy is clearly needed.

Poverty is the key reason behind the difficulties street and working children face in accessing basic education. The financial necessity of work makes it difficult for many of the children to attend school as working hours frequently clash with school hours. Many parents need their children's income and are therefore reluctant to permit them to attend school. The need for immediate survival prevails. One parent is reported as expressing a view of education as this: 'manual labour isn't rewarding ... you earn little and work a lot ... but first comes bread, then school' (Centro Luiz Freire, 1996, p. 33). For those parents who are willing to send their children to school, the indirect costs of education mean that often schooling remains a financial impossibility. Those who are fortunate enough to be able to attend for various reasons often find it impossible to remain. Many work at night for an income and are therefore too tired to succeed in class or are unable to attend regularly. Often the children themselves prefer to work as the benefits of education are seen as being too long term (Centro Luiz Freire, 1996).

The low self-esteem that many street children have of themselves and of their abilities is another barrier to those wanting to access schools. Years of abuse and discrimination have meant that many children have accepted the negative profile given to them by society (Dewees & Klees, 1995). Many of the children interviewed had no concept of the future, never knowing whether they would still be alive the following day; others were too ashamed of their poverty to enter into the classroom: 'How can you go to school when you are dirty, smelly, hungry and have no smart clothes?' asked Fabio, a 16 year-old who spent 6 years living on the streets.

It would seem, therefore, that the conventional education system excludes, and is rejected, by many street children. We ask in this chapter whether this notion of exclusion, borne out by a review of some of the literature, is correct? If so, what measures are being taken by both the Government and NGOs to address this problem? In an attempt to answer these and similar questions, one of the authors spent 3 months living and working with street children in Recife. During this time, the author/researcher obtained a large amount of data from key informants from 21 agencies, including the opinions of street children themselves. However, given the confines of this chapter, our discussion in the subsequent pages will be limited to some of the major responses to the three key criteria selected in order to assess the impact and success of each initiative. These were: (1) whether the education of street children was a specific or indirect policy objective; (2) how sensitive the initiative was to the children's needs and reality; and (3) whether it was achieving the objective of improving access to basic education for street children.

Innovations Aimed at Inclusion: findings

The growing attention of the international community to the plight of street children has resulted in some international development projects paying closer attention to the developmental needs of these children. In Brazil, a number of government measures have recently been introduced which have either supplemented or run parallel to the numerous non-governmental projects which have arisen over the years and which aim to increase the access of street children to school. These initiatives will be discussed in terms of their location at five levels: international, federal, state, municipal and NGO.

International Initiatives

Very little work has been done on an international level specifically in relation to improving access to basic education for street children, but Article 3 of the World Declaration on Education for All, which guarantees the rights of street and working children to an education, has served to focus the attention of international donor agencies on the problem. Thus, a number of international organisations have provided financial and technical support to general educational programmes in Recife. Two programmes are worth mentioning. The first is the World Bank's Projeto Nordeste, which has adopted a position to improve all schools in the north-east of Brazil. The view is that the improvements will lead to wider access. The second is the financial and technical support provided by the Save the Children Fund to programmes aimed at assisting street children.

Whilst these are clearly important initiatives to transform educational provision and to increase access for those not attending schools, there are no programmes specifically aimed at street children at this level. Overall, a specific framework for the education of street children is lacking.

Federal Government Initiatives

The research undertaken revealed that there is no specific federal government policy with regard to the education of street children. Instead, there have been a number of statutory initiatives designed to improve the overall position of children, which run parallel to the initiatives aimed at improving the Brazilian education system. Whilst it is hoped that these measures will provide the framework upon which to base the fight to improve access to basic education for street children (Ministry for Education and Sport, 1993, p. 12), it is still too soon to judge the effectiveness of these measures and the extent to which they will be implemented. Such measures are clearly an important step forward. However, as the failure of the Brazilian education system in attracting and sustaining the interest of many children, on the one hand, and the general neglect of these children, on the other, are clearly largely responsible for the rising numbers of children taking to the streets, such an improvement will be a long-term process. In the short term, it is still important that the federal government finds ways to ensure that this generation of street children obtains at least a basic level of education.

State Government of Pernambuco Initiatives

The state of Pernambuco has been relatively active with regard to improving conditions for street children, and emphasises the importance of improving access to education. The Centro Especial de Atendimento a Meninos (CEAME), a branch of the 'Fundação da Criança e do Adolescente' (FUNDAC), works specifically with street children. The CEAME is responsible for implementing the Projeto Mão Amiga (Helping Hand Project), a relatively new initiative set up in 1995 to work with children who have had the rights laid out in the Declaration on Education for All violated or denied. The project works in four stages, from street work to the final reintegration of the child into society, and it is hoped that at the end of the process the children will have 'mastered the instruments and knowledge necessary for learning, in accordance with Article 1 of the World Declaration on Education for All' (Projeto Mão Amiga, 1995, p. 1). The coordinator of the project, Sandra Monica, argues that it is important to work with the children before sending them to school as a child straight from the streets would never be able to adapt to the conventional school system. Education is an integral part of the programme.

The majority of the children found that the programme was sensitive to their needs and many were proud to be a part of it. The main criticism provided by street children who had participated in the project concerned the final stage. Many felt that they had been given the false hope that once they had completed the course they would be able to find employment. Unfortunately, only 7% have succeeded in gaining employment. The researcher was unable to obtain statistics as to the percentage of children who continued with their education.

Although improving access to basic education for street children is not a specific priority for the state of Pernambuco, the issue is being tackled within the framework of a more general rehabilitation programme. The policy would appear to be that by working with street children and attempting to reintegrate them into society, they will then be in a better position to attend the conventional school system.

Municipal Government of Recife Initiatives

On a municipal level, the education of street children is a specific policy for a number of initiatives. The 'Bolsa-Escola' programme addresses the issue of the opportunity costs of education in an interesting way. Families that keep their children in school are granted a monthly allowance of half a minimum salary or $64 per child. The aim is that this incentive scheme will enable working children to attend school without compromising the potential income they might otherwise have secured. This is clearly a major step forward with regard to the education of working children.

A number of municipal schools have chosen to work with street children as a specific group requiring education. The Escola Benicio Clementino da Rocha runs night classes for street children who are over 14 years of age in addition to teaching non-street children. At present, the school works with around one hundred street children. Although the curriculum is the same for all children, a different methodology is used when educating street children. The pupils clearly have different needs and talents to the average student. It has been observed, for example, that street children are particularly gifted when it comes to mathematics but have great difficulties when it comes to Portuguese classes. The teachers try to use the language of the children and adapt the subject matters to their lifestyle. Games and videos are used rather than traditional 'blackboard' methodology. Teachers are encouraged to attend workshops and seminars related to street children in order to further their understanding and training. The children receive sex and drugs education and are encouraged to develop their awareness of their rights and duties as Brazilian citizens. There are frequent outings, which help to maintain the child's interest and to give him or her the chance to experience different environments.

It is important to note that this initiative was inspired not by the government but by a teacher who worked in an NGO with street children. It remains, however, a municipal school although the municipality has so far refused to grant any extra assistance or extend the programme to other schools. The methodology used appears to be very successful. So far, around 20% of pupils have completed the programme from the first to the third module. Whilst this figure may appear low to the reader, it is in fact a significant achievement bearing in mind that the programme only started a few years ago and that it has received no government support. This initiative is clearly one that the municipal government could learn lessons from and attempt to extend the methodology to other schools. The provision of extra financial and technical resources could also make a lot of difference.

Another important development with regard to access to education for street children has been the implementation of the 'Educação Básica de Jovens e Adultos' (EBJA) programme by the Secretary for Education.

This programme has been introduced to respond to the demands of young adults and also older adults who were unable to attain a basic level of education as children. The municipal government hopes that this project will not only reduce illiteracy rates but will enable students to 'participate actively as citizens' (Prefeitura da Cidade do Recife, 1996, p. 15). The EBJA is clearly important with regard to the education of those street children who have reached the age of 14 and wish to receive an education. Such a measure only applies to those adolescents who have the necessary motivation. It does not tackle the problem, however, of those who are unable or unmotivated to attend school and therefore is not sensitive to the needs of this group. With regard to the attainment of the objectives, the researcher was unable to obtain the necessary statistics.

It is evident that there are a number of interesting initiatives which prioritise improving access to basic education for street children, but these are confined to those children over the age of 14 in the municipality of Recife. It would appear, however, that those children below this age group have been ignored. It is argued by the municipalities that it is unnecessary to set up programmes for these children as they are guaranteed a free and compulsory education by law. This would appear to be rather naive in view of the large numbers of street children under the age of 14 who are currently excluded from school.

Non-governmental Initiatives

The array of NGOs that work with street children in Recife is as impressive as it is diverse. Unfortunately, it would be impossible to attempt to discuss them all in this study and so, after reviewing the materials gathered, four initiatives have been chosen to demonstrate the different approaches used to address the problem of improving access to basic education for street children.

Comunidade dos Pequenos Profetas

The Comunidade dos Pequenos Profetas (CPP) was set up in 1983 and was the first project of its kind in Recife. The aim of this 'community' is to improve the lives of street children by providing them with a secure environment in which they can develop socially and obtain an education. The community currently runs three different and yet complementary activities. Through street work, the CPP accompanies street children in their own environment in order to gain their trust and to understand their needs. First aid is given where necessary as well as friendship and advice. Where appropriate, children are directed to one of two centres. The Granja Clarion is a farm outside of Recife where street

167

boys are given an alternative to the dangers of urban life. Once settled, all children are registered at one of four local schools. The youngest go to school in the afternoon whereas those over 14 attend night school. In the morning, the children receive '*reforço escolar*' or supplementary classes in the community's non-formal school. The children learn important work and social skills as well as receiving support from a psychologist and social worker. Contacts are established, where possible, with the children's parents. The second centre, the Nossa Casa project, is a house in the centre of Recife, which receives street girls during the day. The house has space for 15 girls, who are given a secure place where they can eat and wash. They also receive psychological support and are given a non-formal education. There are literacy and art classes as well as sex and drugs education.

Education is clearly a policy priority for the CPP. With regard to the project's sensitivity to the children's needs and reality, the vast majority of the children were happy and content. This was demonstrated by the fact that many children brought along their friends and brothers. When questioned with regard to the non-formal school, most felt that it was very important to have a supplement to their formal school. Concerning the attainment of the objectives, the majority of the children are motivated to attend school on a regular basis, as demonstrated by their attendance records. The majority of the children stay in the CPP until they find employment or return to their families.

Casa da Passagem

The Casa da Passagem is an NGO which has been working with street girls since 1989. The general aim of the project is to 'make the state and society understand the necessity to create services and to allocate resources for the comprehensive assistance of poor girls'. The specific aim is to give each girl the opportunity to see herself as a person and to build up her own survival strategies (Mendonça, 1997, p. 14). The Casa has a specific methodology with regard to education. Nearly all the girls are registered in the formal education system but the Casa provides a supplementary non-formal education. The girls are taught the value and importance of education and an emphasis is placed on teaching the girls to accept their situation and to find their own solutions. It is argued that the Casa's educative process facilitates the girls' integration into the formal education system. The girls are encouraged to educate others and frequently run their own workshops in schools and conferences. Girls who arrive from the streets spend their days in the first house where they are given clothes, are fed and are taught about hygiene and the Casa's methodology. They are given literacy classes as well as psychological support. When the girls are ready to move on, they go to the second house – the training centre. Here they are taught skills such as computing, sewing or cooking. The products made by the girls are sold in order to raise funds for the project. The Casa works closely with the mothers of the girls as well as the local communities in order to reduce the risks of further neglect and abandonment.

Again, education is a specific policy for this initiative. It would appear that the project is sensitive to the girls' needs as over 70% of the girls continue with the programme. The girls themselves reported to the researcher the fact that they thought very highly of the project. It was not possible to obtain specific statistics with regard to the employment or continuing education of the girls.

Cruzada de Ação Social

A third model of intervention is demonstrated in the work of the Cruzada de Ação Social (CAS), an NGO formed in 1955 to assist the underprivileged population of Pernambuco. With regard to the education of street children, the CAS runs 18 crèches for children at risk under the age of 6. Children over 4 years of age receive literacy classes in preparation for joining school. The crèches are seen as a preventative measure to ensure that these children do not go onto the streets. For older children, the CAS runs three training centres, which offer basic education classes as well as teaching the children a skill. The Centro Professionalizante do Joven (CPJ) works specifically with street children up to the age of 18. In 1996, the centre was attended by 290 children and youths. Children under 14 or those who have a very low level of education attend the CPJ school, which has been officially recognised and is considered to be a formal primary school but with a special pedagogic methodology. Teachers work within the children's reality, using themes which they can directly relate to, such as drugs or violence. Emphasis is placed on teaching the children about their rights as citizens and the importance of education for their future. The children are given transport vouchers and $20 a month to enable them to attend the school. If they do not attend, their grant is reduced. Once the children have reached the fourth grade they are registered within the conventional public school system. The CPJ then provides them with vocational training in areas such as bakery, broom-making and false teeth fabrication. Education is clearly a priority for the CPJ and attendance at school is strictly monitored.

Community Schools

Community schools have also been particularly effective in ensuring that street children have access to basic education. These schools have been set up by local communities who have been concerned by the failure of the public education system, and have become a popular alternative for many. It would appear that these schools are more adapted to the realities of their pupils as they work in very close contact with the families and use a pedagogic methodology which reflects the lifestyles of the children (Centro Luiz Freire, 1994, p. 21). Unfortunately, only 17% of these schools have been recognised by the Secretary of Education. The Centro de Comunicação is a community school located in the Planeta dos Macacos favela, which works with 120 children under the age of 7. The coordinator and founder, Josepha Sartena Araujo, argues that this preliminary education not only acts as a preventative measure to impede children from taking to the streets but also facilitates the children's ability to integrate when they are transferred to the public system at 7 years of age.

These four examples of non-governmental initiatives provide an interesting illustration of the different ways in which access to education for street children may be improved. It is interesting to note that not only do the various non-governmental initiatives employ different methodologies, but they also have differing relationships with the formal education system. The CPP and the Casa da Passagem give the children additional classes as a supplement to, rather than as an alternative to, the formal system. The CPJ school has received official recognition and has consequently been integrated into the formal system whereas the Centro de Comunicação provides an alternative to the formal system.

It is clear that there is a complex network of governmental and non-governmental initiatives in Recife, which work at different levels to improve access to education for different groups of street children. Children-of-the-streets, for example, are dealt with by projects such as the CPP or the Projeto Mão Amiga; children-on-the-streets are assisted by initiatives such as the Bolsa-Escola; whilst children-for-the-streets are supported by schools such as the Centro de Comunicação. There are clearly many lessons that can be drawn from the various methodologies employed by these initiatives in order to improve access to basic education for street children.

Street children clearly face special problems and have special needs. If it is to be effective, the education system must start to reflect this, especially in countries where such high proportions of the child population use the streets on a regular basis. One of the fundamental ways in which this can be done is to develop a curriculum which is relevant to the realities of these children rather than a reflection of middle-class needs (as emphasised by the Centro Professionalizante do Joven). One of the weaknesses of the conventional system is the emphasis on basic literacy and numeracy to the exclusion of other skills and values. Incorporating a focus on attitudes and values in addition to skills and knowledge would have obvious benefits to the education system as some non-formal projects illustrate. It is not only street and working children who need to understand and value themselves in relation to society, but all children. Thus, education should provide a base for critical analysis and independent thinking in order for the children to understand their situation and consequently fight to change it (Casa da Passagem). The curriculum should be further developed both to empower students economically by providing them with relevant skills (Meu Primeiro Emprego) and to allow them to participate fully in civic and political life (National Movement of Street Children). It is essential that street children are educated about their own rights if they are to be able to confront the challenges of life.

With regard to long-term solutions to the problem of ensuring that street children have access to a basic education, it is clearly important to tackle the problem at source. If children are taught the value and pleasures of receiving an education, they will be less tempted to take to the streets. It is therefore essential to transform the ways in which schools are run and in which teachers teach. It is also important that less of an emphasis is placed on enrolment rates and more on absenteeism, repetition and drop-out rates, which are a far more accurate reflection of the quality of an education system. The study on which this chapter is based also revealed the need for larger-scale survey research in order to establish most accurately what percentages of children who have taken part in these initiatives, continued with their education or found employment.

Conclusions

Contemporary Brazil is a paradox in many ways and in no way more so than with regard to children's rights and education. Despite progressive legislation and attention to these issues, the situation is worsening for many. Street children are largely excluded from the formal educative process and it would appear that in all the haste to improve the educational and human rights landscape in Brazil, the education of street children has largely become a forgotten issue. This study has provided important insights into the issue of the education of street.

The initiatives studied clearly provide important lessons for policy-makers, educators and programme designers. The programmes discussed here all appear to make a difference to the lives of street and working children. Unfortunately, their impact is limited due to a lack of resources, in some cases, and motivated staff, in others. The study points to the imbalance in initiatives taken by the state and those taken by community-based organisations. It is clearly fundamental that both the Government and society start to take responsibility for these children's lack of schooling. Reform of the Brazilian educational system is crucial, not only to grant street children one of their basic rights but also as a measure to prevent future generations of children from taking to the streets.

Education has now been accepted by most as a fundamental prerequisite for sustained economic growth and democratic participation. There is therefore no justification for not placing the education of street children high on the political agenda. The price of refusing an entire generation of emotionally and materially deprived children an education can only be high and may indeed prove to be one which society can ill-afford to pay.

References

Blunt, A. (1994) Street Children and their Education: a challenge to urban educators, in N. Stromquist (Ed.) *Education in Urban Areas.* London: Praeger.

Boyden, J. & Holden, P. (1991) *Children of the Cities.* London: Zed Books.

Carnoy, M. & Samoff, J. (1990) *Education and Social Transition in the Third World.* Princeton: Princeton University Press.

Centro Luiz Freire (1994) *Uma Estratégia de Sobrevivência Escolar na Região Metropolitana do Recife.* Olinda: Centro Luiz Freire.

Centro Luiz Freire (1996) *Educação, Trabalho e Pobreza em Pernambuco.* Olinda: Centro Luiz Freire.

Dewees, A. & Klees, S. (1995) Social Movements and the Transformation of National Policy: street and working children in Brazil, *Comparative Education Review*, 39, pp. 76–100.

Fundação da Criança e do Adolescente e Cruzada de Ação Social (May 1995) Pesquisa Meninos de Rua, Recife.

Fyfe, Á. (1985) All Work and No Play: child labor today, Trade Union Congress and UNICEF. New York: UNICEF.

Graham-Brown, S. (1991) *Education in the Developing World – conflict and crisis.* London: Longman.

Hewitt, T. & Smith, I. (1999) *Street Lives and Family Lives in Brazil: culture and global change.* London: Routledge.

IBGE (1994) Municipios Brasileiros Crianças e Suas Condições de Sobrevivencia – Censo Demografico 1991. Brasilia: IBGE.

Keeton, V. & McConnell, M. (1996) Street Children in Brazil: the policy issue, policy background and current policy and programs, http://lanic.utexas.edu/project/ppb/papers94–95/mconnel.html, 20 December 1996.

Keil, I. & Viola, S. (1997) Ensinar e Aprender: Notas de um processo de Intervenção Pedagógica com Crianças e Adolescentes en situação de rua, in R. Gonzalez (Ed.) *Educação e Direitos: Experiências e Desafios na Defesa de Crianças e Adolescentes*, pp. 25–38. Porto Alege: MNMMR.

Mendonca, A. (1997) *Passagem para o ser.* Recife: Bagaco.

Ministry for Education and Sport (1993) *Integral Care National Programme for Children and Adolescents in Brazil.* Brasilia: Ministry for Education and Sport.

Ngo Kim Cuc (1996) *Children of the Dust.* Bangkok: World Vision International.

Prefeitura da Cidade do Recife, (October 1996) *A Escola Reconhece o Cidadão.* Recife: Secretaria de Educação e Cultura.

Projeto Mao Amiga (1995) Information Leaflet.

Stromquist, N. (1994) *Education in Urban Areas: cross national dimensions.* London: Praeger.

UNESCO Staff (1995) *Working With Street Children.* Paris: UNESCO.

Vélis, J-P. (1995) *Blossoms in the Dust – street children in Africa.* Paris: UNESCO.

Globalisation, Education and the Colonial Transition of Two Remnants of Empire: a comparative analysis of Hong Kong and Macau

MARK BRAY

The links between education, colonialism and colonial transition have been the focus of an extensive literature (e.g. Altbach & Kelly, 1991; Watson, 1982; Arnove & Arnove, 1997; Bray, 1997). To some extent, the forces impelling both the rise and the fall of colonialism have been global in nature. The twentieth century was an era of decolonisation which gathered speed in the initial decades after World War II. While most colonial territories had achieved changes of sovereignty by the late 1960s, however, a few colonies remained at the end of the century. This chapter focuses on two of these remnants of empire. It argues that the nature of transition among the remnants has been, and for those that still await the process will be, significantly different from the nature of transition in the main body of empire. This applies in the field of education as much as in other domains of social and political development (Bray, 1994; Aldrich & Connell, 1998). The global forces of change have still been evident among the remnants, but have produced different patterns in different places and at different points in history.

The chapter focuses on two particular colonies that were among the remnants of empire. Hong Kong was a British colony until sovereignty reverted to the People's Republic of China (PRC) in 1997; and Macau was under Portuguese administration until undergoing a similar transition in 1999. Arnove (1999) has asserted a need to 'reframe' comparative education with a dialectic of the global and the local. By this, he means that, on the one hand, the workings of a global economy and the increasing interconnectedness of societies pose common problems for education systems around the world, and that on the other hand, regional, national and local responses vary. This chapter illustrates his point by showing first how Hong Kong and Macau are similar to but different from other parts of the world, and second how they are similar to but different from each other.

Enlarging on this methodological point, Hong Kong and Macau make a good pair for meaningful analysis because they have a great deal in common but also significant differences. The commonalities include the facts that they are both small in area, are both mainly inhabited by people of Chinese race, both have economies based on services and light industry, both have been colonies of European powers, and both went through a period of political transition towards reintegration with China at the end of the twentieth century. The differences include the fact that Hong Kong was a British colony while Macau was under Portuguese administration. Also, Hong Kong, though very small compared with mainland China, is much larger than Macau; and, of particular relevance to this chapter, their education systems have evolved in very different ways.

To provide a framework for analysis, the chapter begins with some background information on Hong Kong and Macau. It then addresses the broad literature on globalisation, education and colonial transition, before turning to the specific cases of these two territories. The chapter comments on the scale and nature of educational provision, again noting similarities and differences. This discussion permits commentary on ways in which analysis of patterns in the two territories contributes to broader conceptual understanding.

An Introduction to Hong Kong and Macau

Hong Kong

In a chronological sense, Hong Kong was the younger of the two colonies. However, discussion here commences with Hong Kong because it is larger, underwent post-colonial change of sovereignty slightly earlier, and in several respects set the model for Macau's colonial transition.

The territory of Hong Kong comprises the island of Hong Kong, a number of other islands, and part of the Chinese mainland. The island of Hong Kong was ceded to the British in 1842. A section of the Kowloon Peninsula was ceded in 1860 and the New Territories were acquired on a 99-year lease in 1898. The total land area is 1070 square kilometres.

Colonial policies passed through many phases during the 155 years of British administration, and it is difficult to summarise them in a few sentences. One overriding feature was that Hong Kong, like Macau, was seen primarily as a trading post rather than a territory for economic exploitation in its own right. In this respect, it differed from many other

British colonies. Hong Kong had a largely transient population, and most aspects of social policy in the early years were low key. There was no early intention to raise an intermediary class of English-trained natives as 'go-betweens' in the way that Raffles envisioned for Singapore and Macaulay championed for India (Jones, 1990, p. 142).

Nevertheless, early education policy differed from other aspects of social policy in being more active and interventionist. One aspect was in the provision of school grants, a policy which paralleled measures in Britain itself. As observed by Sweeting (1990, 1995), much of the history of education in Hong Kong has been a pattern of increasing government commitment and intervention.

Although it was probably not foreseen at the time, the 99-year lease on the New Territories taken out in 1898 sowed the seeds for the colony's demise. The lease expired in 1997, when the whole of Hong Kong (i.e. including Hong Kong Island, which had been ceded 'in perpetuity') was returned to China. The terms under which Chinese sovereignty resumed were established between the British and Chinese governments in 1984. Hong Kong became a Special Administrative Region (SAR), with its own government and laws.

Since 1997, Hong Kong has been governed under the formula of 'One Country, Two Systems', which permits Hong Kong to have a high degree of autonomy. In particular, while the rest of China remains officially socialist, Hong Kong remains officially capitalist. The SAR system, which has been put in place for at least 50 years, also permits Hong Kong to have its own currency, legal system and education system. With reference to education, the Basic Law (China, 1990, Article 146) states that:

> On the basis of the previous educational system, the
> Government of the Hong Kong Special Administrative Region
> shall, on its own, formulate policies on the development and
> improvement of education, including policies regarding the
> educational system and its administration, the language of
> instruction, the allocation of funds, the examination system,
> the system of academic awards and the recognition of
> educational qualifications.

The population of Hong Kong is approximately 7 million. Almost 98% are Chinese, for the majority of whom Cantonese is the mother tongue. Among the remainder, the largest groups are from the Philippines, Indonesia, the USA, Canada and the United Kingdom.

Economically, Hong Kong is well known for its recent achievement of high rates of growth. In 1997, Hong Kong was estimated to have a per capita Gross Domestic Product (GDP) of US $26,200 (Hong Kong, 1998, p. 416). Economic growth has greatly facilitated expansion of education.

Macau

As a distinct political entity, Macau is nearly 300 years older than Hong Kong. Portuguese traders secured from the Chinese authorities rights of settlement in 1557 (Afonso & Pereira, 1986, p. 34). Although the Portuguese were primarily interested in Macau for economic reasons, the territory also played a major religious and cultural role. The church established many schools, one of which was given university status in 1594. It operated until 1762, and taught theology, humanities, Greek, Latin, rhetoric and philosophy (Gomes dos Santos, 1968). Macau was a major conduit through which Western education and science entered China, Japan and Korea.

After the mid-seventeenth century, Macau's fortunes declined (Gunn, 1996). Portugal proved unable to hold her empire together, and competition for East Asian trade became increasingly intense. The foundation of Hong Kong in 1842 was a particularly serious blow, for its far superior port took over the strategic significance that Macau had previously enjoyed. Macau became little more than an inward-looking backwater.

After World War II, the Chinese Government wished to repossess the territory, but was unable to force the issue. For a time, policies were left at the level of official pronouncements. However, China's Cultural Revolution in 1966 led to violent riots in Macau and to vigorous anti-Portuguese propaganda. Unexpectedly, when the Portuguese announced that they intended to leave, the Communists altered their stance. The Chinese authorities were conscious of Macau's role as an outlet for external trade, and found it more useful to retain Macau as a foreign port than to repossess it (Shipp, 1997).

Eight years later, Portugal itself experienced a revolution. The new government had a very different view of world affairs, and immediately set about decolonising its African territories. In Asia, East Timor was unilaterally seized by Indonesia, and matters would perhaps have been simpler for Portugal if China had similarly taken Macau. However, the Chinese maintained their refusal to reassert sovereignty. Subsequently, in 1987, the Portuguese and Chinese governments agreed that Macau would revert to China in 1999. Like Hong Kong, Macau became a SAR for at least 50 years after the transition. Concerning education, the wording of the 1993 Basic Law (China, 1993, Article 121) is similar to the provision for Hong Kong.

The total land area of Macau is just 21 square kilometres. A population of approximately 440,000 gives a density of 21,000 persons per square kilometre. This far exceeds Hong Kong's 6,500 persons per square kilometre. As in Hong Kong, over 90% of the population is Chinese. Two significant minority groups are a small cadre of Portuguese and a mixed-race group known as the Macanese.

Official figures placed the 1997 GDP per capita at US $17,100 (Macau, 1998, p. 405). Manufacturing employed about 20% of the labour force, with restaurants, hotels and other services employing over half. Within the service sector, tourism and gambling were particularly significant.

Globalisation, Education and Colonial Transition

As I have indicated, the forces of decolonisation may be considered global in nature (Gallagher, 1982; Ansprenger, 1989; Lloyd, 1996; Betts, 1998), even though the transitions did not occur in all regions at the same points in time. Many Latin American nations, for example, moved from colonialism to sovereignty during the nineteenth century, whereas for most of Asia and Africa, decolonisation was a phenomenon of the twentieth century. Even within the twentieth century, colonial transition was evident in most parts of Asia before most parts of Africa, and again, African transitions were generally achieved before those in the Caribbean and South Pacific. The United Nations, which included in its 1945 founding charter a clause about self-governance, played a major role. One specific watershed was a 1960 United Nations declaration on the granting of independence to colonial countries and peoples (Chamberlain, 1998, pp. 24–26).

Because of this tide of change, at the end of the twentieth century very few colonies remained. Hong Kong was one of the largest remaining colonies as measured by economic strength and population size. After the changes of sovereignty of Hong Kong and Macau, the remaining colonies were all very small in population. They included such territories as Cayman Islands, French Polynesia, Gibraltar and Montserrat.

One necessary question for the present context is when colonial transitions may be said to begin and end. The answer is generally a matter for interpretation rather than indisputable fact. Concerning the specific cases of Hong Kong and Macau, most analysts see the 1984 Sino-British Agreement and the 1987 Sino-Portuguese Agreement as key stages near the commencement of the colonial transitions in those territories. Most analysts also see the changes of sovereignty in 1997 and 1999 as central points in the transition. However, when the transitions will be described as complete is a matter of conjecture. One lesson from the literature is that transitions take much longer than mere change of flags. This is especially evident in the education sector, since major variables include values and attitudes as well as bureaucratic structures.

Among the common features of all colonial transitions has been a need for reorientation of education systems. In particular, curricula need to be changed to reflect the new political circumstances. This usually requires change in syllabuses, textbooks, and perhaps, media of instruction. Many transitions from colonialism have also required expansion of education in order to make education systems less elitist and to provide manpower for localisation of civil services and other sectors.

In some respects, the remnants of empire, including Hong Kong and Macau, have faced rather different circumstances from territories in the main era of colonial transition. The major differences in circumstances for such remnants have commonly included the following.

- *Transition, but not to full sovereignty.* The majority of previous colonial transitions (though not all) were to sovereignty. This pattern was less dominant among the remnants of empire. In Hong Kong and Macau, the transition was to reintegration with their neighbour. In the Marshall Islands, Palau, and the Federated States of Micronesia, it was to statehood in free association (with the USA).
- *Attitude of the colonial powers.* Whereas many earlier colonial transitions were the result of political struggles and in some cases armed conflict, this was not generally the case for the remnants of empire. At the end of the century, the colonial powers in general accepted or even welcomed the changes of sovereignty.
- *Time frame.* Colonial transition in the 1990s operated on a much longer time frame than was the case for earlier transitions. Thus, the periods set between the signature of the Sino-British/Portuguese Declarations and the actual changes of sovereignty were over 12 years for both Hong Kong and Macau. Long durations also characterised negotiations over the Marshall Islands, Palau, the Federated States of Micronesia, New Caledonia, and Aruba. This may be contrasted with the hectic pace of colonial transition in India, Burma and Ceylon, for example, all of which gained independence within 3 years of the end of World War II. Decolonisation of Indonesia, Vietnam, Laos, Cambodia and Libya was not far behind, and the changes of sovereignty in French West Africa were entirely accomplished within 4 years.
- *Availability of skilled personnel.* Many of the newly sovereign states in the main era of colonial transition were acutely short of skilled personnel. For example, the Republic of the Congo (later called Zaire, and then again Congo) became independent in 1960 with just 16 African university graduates, and Zambia followed in 1964 with barely 100 African graduates. This picture was very different from that in Hong Kong and Macau. Even Singapore, which during the 1990s in many respects resembled Hong Kong (and to some extent Macau), was a very different place at the time that it attained self-government in 1959.

Each of these factors has implications for the education sector as well as for other domains. Among the points that will be enlarged upon in this chapter are that transition to integration with another state rather than to sovereignty required curricula and textbooks to emphasise the new, larger framework rather than to stress the identity of a newly-emergent nation state. The fact that the colonial powers broadly supported rather than resisted the transition facilitated planning, and the long duration of the transition gave time in which to do that planning. Finally, the plentiful availability of skilled personnel of all types greatly facilitated processes of hand-over, in so far as it had not already taken place, from expatriates to locals.

Education and Colonial Transition in Hong Kong

Aspects of Early Transition

Analysis of patterns in Hong Kong shows that some changes, which in most colonial societies were made only just before, or even after, the change of sovereignty, were made much earlier in Hong Kong. In some respects, therefore, education in Hong Kong was decolonised long before even the 1984 Sino-British declaration. Two examples are secondary school examinations, and schools for expatriate children. They are worth elaborating not only for the contrast with territories during the main era of decolonisation, but also for the contrast with Macau.

In most British colonies, the major external examinations for secondary schools were operated by the Universities of Cambridge, Oxford and/or London. Hong Kong, however, has a long history of examinations set and administered within the territory. Cambridge Local Examinations were introduced in 1886, and replaced by Oxford Local Examinations in 1889, but in 1937, a Hong Kong School Certificate examination was established by the Government's Education Department (Sweeting, 1990, pp. 212–213, 358). In 1977, the Government established a separate Hong Kong Examinations Authority (HKEA) to take over this role, together with the 'H' level examination which was being operated by the Chinese University of Hong Kong for secondary Form 6 students, and the A level examination which was being operated by the University of Hong Kong for Form 7 students (Sweeting, 1995, p. 64). Thus, examinations were taken out of the control of bodies in the colonial country many decades ago.

The second example of early structural change relates to schools for expatriate children. A major issue for the governments of many territories being decolonised concerned the future of schools serving the families of the colonisers. These schools operated in the colonial language, followed curricula from the colonising country, and were mainly staffed by teachers recruited from the colonising country. In Papua New Guinea, for example, 'A' [Australian] schools were in effect metropolitan institutions operating on Papua New Guinean soil, in contrast to 'T' [Territory] schools for local children (Smith, 1987, p. 271). Similar differentiation was evident in other colonies, sometimes with further classification for different races. In most cases, the schools for non-indigenous children were resourced much more generously than the schools for locals.

The Papua New Guinean mechanism for tackling this matter was to some extent typical of the model used in other settings. Two years after Papua New Guinea attained independence in 1975, the Government on the one hand permitted private schools to be founded for those who were prepared to pay for alternative curricula, and on the other hand, established an International Education Agency (IEA) to take over the existing government schools for expatriate children (Smith & Bray, 1985, pp. 120–121). The IEA schools were funded by the Government according to the same formula as local schools, but were permitted to charge fees in order to supplement their resources and employ expatriate teachers on higher salaries.

The Hong Kong Government adopted a similar strategy, but did so long before the closing years of the colonial era. In 1967, a body called the English Schools Foundation (ESF) was created to operate two schools for expatriate children following curricula comparable to ones commonly found in state schools in the United Kingdom (Miller, 1997). In 1979, the Government transferred to the ESF its own schools for expatriates, which followed a similar curriculum. This move permitted the Government to meet what it considered to be its obligations to the children of expatriate families while avoiding accusations of distorted priorities and excessive funding for a racial minority. Although the ESF schools are aided institutions funded by the Government on the same formula as aided schools for local children, they are permitted to charge fees, to follow curricula based on United Kingdom models, and to pay teachers at higher salary scales.

Educational Changes between 1984 and 1997

During the period between the Sino-British Declaration and the reversion of sovereignty, education in Hong Kong went through many further changes. As in other colonial transitions, they included changes in curriculum and media of instruction. Morris & Chan (1997) have pointed out that some of the innovations were more evident at the level of policy than classroom practice; but even with allowance for this fact, the changes were significant.

Among the new subjects in many schools were Putonghua, government and public affairs, and liberal studies. Putonghua became of obvious increased significance as the national language of the PRC; and government and public affairs helped students to understand political processes in Hong Kong, the PRC and other parts of the world (Morris, 1992, p. 129). Liberal studies explicitly included among its major aims the understanding of China and of Hong Kong's colonial transition. For example, one of its six modules aimed to help students 'to appreciate the special relationship that HK [Hong Kong] and China enjoy and the mutual advantages that flow from that relationship, and to understand better the contribution that HK is making, and can make, to China's modernisation' (Hong Kong Examinations Authority, 1994, p. 446).

Concerning existing subjects, significant changes were made in the syllabuses for history and social studies. In 1988, the secondary school history syllabus, which previously had covered China only up to 1949, was amended to permit study up to 1970. Morris (1992, p. 129) comments that the new syllabus provided pupils with 'a more politicised historical framework than was previously the case, and one more relevant to Hong Kong's future'. The social studies syllabus, which is taken by secondary students in Forms 1 to 3, was also adjusted to give much greater focus on China than before.

Textbooks were also rewritten to fit the new political times. All school textbooks in Hong Kong are published by commercial agencies rather than by the Government; but publishers are required to secure official approval before their books can be adopted for classroom use. In some cases, the vetting process has led to direct recommendation for changes in wording, and in other cases, publishers have scrutinised their own texts to ensure that they do not contain material likely to offend the screening panel. Most of the changes are made quietly, far from the public eye. However, in 1994, intervention by the Director of Education hit the media headlines and caused considerable controversy. The Director had announced censure of a paragraph in a new Chinese history textbook which contained an account of the incident in Beijing's Tiananmen Square on 4 June 1989 (Lee & Bray, 1995, p. 366). Ultimately, the Director withdrew his censure, and the controversy died down. However, the signal remained clear to publishers, who are likely to have further increased their own caution.

Important changes were also evident in civic education. In 1985, 1 year after the signing of the Sino-British Declaration, the Government issued a set of Guidelines on Civic Education in Schools (Civic Education Committee, 1985). The document was directly tied to initiatives to develop representative government, which were themselves part of the transitional arrangements initiated by the colonial authorities. Eleven years later, a revised set of guidelines (Hong Kong, 1996) made an explicit link between civic education and the political transition, suggesting, for example (p. 21), that:

> *the civic learner needs to know the cultural and political identity of Hong Kong as a Chinese community, as a British colony for a certain period, and as the HKSAR [Hong Kong Special Administrative Region] of China from July 1997. At a time of political transition, we need our citizens to actively adopt a new national identity, and to be participative and contributive to bring about smooth transitions, to sustain*

> *prosperity and stability and to further improve the Hong Kong*
> *society.*

The political transition also brought to the fore important questions about the medium of instruction (Pun, 1997; Adamson & Auyeung Lai, 1997). In 1990, 91.7% of secondary schools claimed to offer instruction through the medium of English, while the remainder taught in Cantonese (Lee, 1997, p. 166). The demand for English chiefly reflected the economic benefits that parents perceived their children to gain from having a command of the language, and the proportion of secondary schools claiming to operate in English had risen steadily from 57.9% in 1960.

However, many students had great difficulty learning through English, and a substantial proportion of schools that claimed to teach in English actually taught either in Cantonese or in mixed code. To address this situation, the Government sought ways to encourage schools, pupils and parents to shift from English-medium to Chinese-medium. To some extent, the rationale was pedagogical, but it was also political. Although the main moves were to Cantonese rather than Putonghua, the shift was seen as a move to at least one form of Chinese and away from the colonial language. In 1997, the Government's Education Department issued 'firm guidance' on the languages which schools would be permitted to use as media of instruction (Hong Kong, 1997; Poon, 1998). In addition, many schools ensured that Putonghua was taught as a subject in either the main or the supplementary curriculum. By 1994/95, about 40% of primary and secondary schools were offering Putonghua as an optional subject; and following the launch in 1996 of a new Putonghua curriculum for Primary Form 1 to Secondary Form 5, this proportion was expected to increase markedly (Kwok, 1996, p. 5).

Education and Colonial Transition in Macau

The first contrast between Macau and Hong Kong is in the nature of control of education during the pre-transitional period. Before 1987, the role of the Government in Macau's schools was much more limited than the role of the Government in Hong Kong. Macau had no aided sector, and the majority of schools were privately managed and permitted to operate with a high degree of autonomy. Similar comments apply to higher education. For two centuries after the 1762 closure of the university college mentioned earlier, Macau had no local institution for university education. In 1981, a local university was established; but for the first 7 years of its life what was then called the University of East Asia (later renamed the University of Macau) operated autonomously as a private institution.

The signature of the Sino-Portuguese Declaration in 1987 provided an impetus for a much expanded government role in Macau's education.

In 1988, a Committee for Educational Reform was established, and a major seminar was organised for public discussion in 1989. Policies on schools and higher education were released 2 years later (Macau, 1991a, 1991b). The policies indicated the Government's desire to move towards free primary education, to expand secondary and higher education, and to forge a much more coherent education system from the loosely-coupled collection of schools that existed at that point. The law on basic education was followed in 1993 by regulations for private education (Macau, 1993), and by laws on curriculum organisation for kindergarten, pre-primary and primary schools (Macau, 1994a) and for secondary schools (Macau, 1994b). This burst of government activity was itself one of the contrasts with Hong Kong. Since the Hong Kong Government already had considerable inputs and control over schools and universities in the territory, the Sino-British Declaration did not lead to a comparable increase in the volume of activity.

A second contrast was evident in public examinations. Whereas the Hong Kong Government had developed its own examination system remarkably early, the Macau Government had barely tackled the matter at all. Prior to 1990, when the University of Macau began to operate an entrance examination open to all schools, Macau had no territory-wide examination system. Even then, the nature of the examination framework was much less systematic than that in Hong Kong. Most secondary schools arranged for their pupils to sit examinations set in the PRC, Taiwan, Hong Kong, Portugal or England (Tang, 1999a, pp. 84–85).

The difference between Hong Kong and Macau was also evident in the place of schools for expatriate children from the colonial country. Whereas the Hong Kong Government could be described as ahead of the normal pattern in decolonising structures, the Macau Government had not reached an equivalent stage. Even in the late 1990s, Portuguese-language provision, which primarily catered for Portuguese expatriates and for the local Portuguese-speaking minority, was still a major component of the government sector of education. However, in 1998, the Macau Government implemented a plan to privatise the Portuguese-medium provision along a path which in some ways resembled Hong Kong's ESF and Papua New Guinea's IEA. Such action permitted the post-colonial authorities to concentrate their attention on the Chinese-speaking majority, and to avoid at least some disputes about the wide disparities in resources available to schools serving different races. Thus, the Macau Government was following a track which resembled that which the Hong Kong authorities had taken quite early and which other colonial territories took at or near the time of change of sovereignty.

Turning to the curriculum, because Macau has had a much less centralised framework than Hong Kong, changes in school subjects have been less direct (Lo, 1999; Tan, 1999; Tang, 1999b). In the mid-1990s, the Macau Government embarked on important curriculum projects which commenced with finding out the nature of curricula in the different schools (see, for example, Macau, 1994c). In 1995/96, provisional teaching syllabuses, which had been prepared by committees including members from both official and private schools and also from the University of Macau, were trialled in 15 schools. The Government also sponsored production of textbooks in some subjects.

However, curricula in private schools continued to a large extent to evolve according to decisions taken within the schools rather than as a result of direct government action. In so far as some schools use Hong Kong textbooks and syllabuses, their curricula changed to reflect reunification with China, but it was Hong Kong's reunification rather than Macau's reunification which was chiefly reflected. Other Macau schools adopted curricula from mainland China. In this aspect, at least these parts of Macau's educational provision were much closer to patterns in mainland China than were Hong Kong schools. The proportion of schools with direct links to China has always been much greater in Macau than in Hong Kong. Also much greater are the numbers of teachers in Macau who were trained and recruited from the mainland. In this respect, although the schedule for Macau's reunification was set at 2½ years after Hong Kong's, in some ways it was more advanced. Partly because Hong Kong had a larger and more sophisticated system of education, it was much more self-contained than were the school systems in Macau.

Developments in civic education in Macau may also be contrasted with those in Hong Kong. As early as 1987, the Macau Catholic Schools Association started to prepare a civic education textbook, which by 1990 had been adopted by most Catholic secondary schools (Law, 1992). A more nationalistic approach was adopted by the pro-Communist Macau Chinese Education Association, and in 1995, 2 years after publication of Macau's Basic Law, a textbook on the Basic Law was published for secondary schools. Although the preparatory work for the publication of this textbook was led by the Macau Chinese Education Association, key figures from Catholic and Protestant schools were also involved. The parallel with Hong Kong was in the nature of the activity, though in Hong Kong the government role was more direct and the process better resourced and more systematic. Also in parallel with Hong Kong, however, was a considerable gap between the aspirations of the reformers and what happened at the school level (Ng, 1997; Tse, 1999).

Macau also shows some differences in the languages taught in schools. As in Hong Kong, Putonghua is increasingly evident in Macau classrooms, but it is less the result of centralised action on the part of the Government. During the early 1990s, reformers in Macau also attempted to strengthen the place of Portuguese. In 1994, a plan drawn up by the Macau Government proposed that some grants to schools would only be provided if those schools agreed to include the Portuguese language on the curriculum (Yue, 1994). This plan aroused great opposition, and was subsequently abandoned. It is worth noting, however, as a perhaps unexpected feature of colonial transition. One interpretation of the move is that the Portuguese authorities, after 400 years of neglect of education for the majority Chinese, suddenly realised first that very few people in the territory could speak, read and write in Portuguese, and second that this was the last chance to change the situation and thereby strengthen the Portuguese influence in a part of the world which was of increasing economic importance. In Hong Kong, the colonial language (English) had been widely taught in schools for local children for a much longer period. Also different was that the majority of schools, far from rejecting the colonial language, welcomed it because of its uses for international communication. Indeed, the irony in Hong Kong was that the colonial government continually made pronouncements, albeit weakly implemented, which discouraged reliance on the colonial language and emphasised the value of Chinese.

Also worth contrasting is the extent to which the governments in the two territories found it necessary to promote Chinese as the medium of instruction in secondary schools. As noted earlier, in 1990 91.7% of Hong Kong secondary schools claimed to offer instruction through the medium of English, while the remainder taught in Cantonese. The Government felt uneasy about this, and for pedagogic as well as political reasons decided that no more than 15% of secondary students in the public system should be taught in English. Macau, by contrast, could not be said to have needed equivalent government pressure to persuade schools to teach in Chinese. As already noted, society was in general unenthusiastic about increased teaching of Portuguese in Macau schools; and the schools which used English as the medium of instruction were in a minority. In 1998/99, among the 47 schools which had secondary sections, 36 (76.6%) were officially recorded as using Chinese as the medium of instruction while only seven (14.9%) were recorded as using English and only three (6.4%) were recorded as using Portuguese. The remaining one school (2.1%) was a Luso-Chinese institution, which primarily taught in Chinese but also with Portuguese (Macau, 1999).

Models and Conceptual Understanding

Returning to the point made at the beginning of this chapter, valuable lessons can be learned from identification of similarities and differences, first between Hong Kong and Macau, and then between those two territories as a pair and other parts of the world which have undergone colonial transition. These lessons assist in conceptual understanding of the nature of colonial transition in different societies and at different points in time.

One instructive insight concerns the wide initial differences in the nature of educational provision in the two places. Despite the similarities of colonial rule, ethnicity and small size, the nature of schooling in the two territories has been markedly different. The primary reasons for this lie in the priorities of government policies and in the relative sizes of populations and economies in the two territories (Bray, 1992; Bray & Koo, 1999). Now, under the influence of the common destiny of reunification with China, the education systems of the two territories have in some ways begun to resemble each other more than before. However, differences remain, and are likely to continue to do so. This is again because of historical legacies, differences in the views of key decision-makers, and continued disparities in the sizes of populations and economies.

At the same time, Hong Kong and Macau have features in common which differ from those of other colonies which have undergone transition. As could be predicted, both territories have seen substantial reorientation of their education systems, but, in line with some other remnants of empire, major differences are evident from general patterns during the main era of colonial transition. Four points on this topic were made earlier and are worth reviewing here.

The first of these four points concerned the fact that transition was not to independence but to reintegration with China. Among the effects of this, in both Hong Kong and Macau, were that schools have placed increasing emphasis on the official language of the country which the two territories are joining, i.e. Putonghua. To some extent, particularly in Macau, this was the result of market forces and perhaps also a feeling of patriotism rather than government intervention, but the effect has been the same. In contrast, the majority of countries which moved to sovereign independence emphasised domestic languages. Also, textbooks in Hong Kong and civic education materials in both places have stressed identity with China rather than the identity of Hong Kong and Macau as separate entities. Again, this contrasts with other parts of the world, where transition required former colonies to stress their new identities as independent nations.

The second point concerned the attitude of the colonial powers. In neither Hong Kong nor Macau was it necessary for citizens to wage liberation struggles to force out colonial regimes. Indeed, rather to the contrary, many citizens, particularly in Hong Kong, viewed the end of the colonial era with regret. Whatever the views of the people, however, the governments of the United Kingdom and Portugal on the whole viewed the colonial transition with relief as the shedding of a relationship which was no longer considered appropriate at the end of the twentieth century. Hong Kong's change of sovereignty was accompanied by some bickering between the United Kingdom and PRC governments, but this did not change the basic premise that the change would certainly occur. The Portuguese Government was less confrontational, and even less questioning of the inevitability of transition. Ironically, the Portuguese Government expressed more interest in Macau during the twilight of the colonial period than it did in the preceding two centuries. Some analysts viewed the Portuguese policy with scepticism, but it also had its positive side in providing resources for education and momentum for reform.

The third point concerns the time frame for change. The fact that Hong Kong and Macau each had over 12 years to prepare for the change of sovereignty allowed considerably greater planning before the change of flags than was possible in most other colonial transitions. Thus, in the majority of transitions, the bulk of curriculum reform came after the changes of sovereignty rather than before. One may, of course, envisage continued curriculum reform in both Hong Kong and Macau; but the fact that so much had been accomplished in advance meant that subsequent changes were much less radical than they were in such places as India, Kenya, Mozambique and Vietnam.

The fourth point is about availability of skilled labour. This was so much accepted as part of the scenario of Hong Kong and Macau that it was largely taken for granted. However, comparative analysis exposes a very different picture in many colonies that underwent transition in the 1950s and 1960s. The cases of Congo and Zambia have already been remarked upon. Almost as acute were the manpower crises in Angola and the Central African Republic. Had Hong Kong and Macau undergone their colonial transition in the 1950s or 1960s, the pressures would not have been quite as severe as in these countries; but they would certainly have been very different from those that actually prevailed.

Conclusions

The colonial transitions of Hong Kong and Macau may be seen as part of the global processes of decolonisation which were evident in Latin America during the nineteenth century and which effected change in most of Asia, Africa, the Caribbean and the South Pacific during the twentieth century. In this respect, taking Hong Kong and Macau as a pair, major similarities are evident between patterns of change in the two colonies and in other parts of the world. However, this chapter has also exposed major differences in patterns. It has also shown major similarities and differences between Hong Kong and neighbouring Macau. These similarities and differences show the value of comparative education as a tool for enhancing understanding and for exposing features which might otherwise be overlooked. For academics, analysis of changes in the two territories helps strengthen conceptual schema and theoretical models. Such analysis can be part of the dialectic of the global and the local, which Arnove (1999) had in mind when advocating 'reframing' of the field of comparative education.

Returning to a point made at the outset, it is important to recognise continuities as well as changes. In some respects, education systems may be vehicles for resisting transition as well as for promoting it. Bureaucratic structures cannot be changed overnight; and even less easily can values and attitudes. Experience elsewhere indicates that legacies will remain in the education systems of Hong Kong and Macau long after the changes of sovereignty.

Moreover, comparative analysis exposes one particular irony which might easily pass unnoticed and which deserves comment. The irony arises from the roles of the mini-constitutions in the two territories. In both Hong Kong and Macau, colonial transition was negotiated with the rather unusual framework of a pair of Basic Laws which are guaranteed to operate for at least 50 years after the changes of sovereignty. Among the clauses in these Basic Laws is maintenance of the colonial languages, English in Hong Kong and Portuguese in Macau, as official languages.

To the people of Hong Kong, retention of English as an official language may seem quite natural and something which the post-colonial government would probably have wanted to do anyway because of the international uses of the language. Portuguese, however, is rather different in status. It seems much less likely that, in the absence of the Basic Law, the post-colonial government would have retained Portuguese as an official language for 50 years. The significance of the negotiated framework becomes even more obvious when Macau is compared with other parts of the world. Concerning Mozambique and Angola, for example, one cannot imagine a situation in which independence was achieved but only on condition that the colonial language was retained for another 50 years. Even less can one envisage such a situation in Goa, which was seized by India in 1961.

The final observation to be made here concerns operation of the arrangements for 'One Country, Two Systems'. This is an arena which many analysts considered to be of great importance but which also seemed to be unprecedented and untested. Yet, while in the political and constitutional sphere the type of arrangement envisaged for Hong Kong and Macau was unique, it was far from unique in education. England, for example, has a different education system from Scotland, Wales and Northern Ireland, and diversity is even more marked in Canada, where Alberta, for example, operates its education system mainly in English but Quebec does so mainly in French. With these long-standing examples from different parts of the world, it becomes easy, at least in education, to envisage operation of the principle of 'One Country, Two Systems'. The field of comparative education can thus provide reassurance as well as conceptual understanding.

Acknowledgement

This chapter draws on an article by the author and published in Macau, namely: M. Bray (1999) Education and Political Transition in Hong Kong and Macau: a comparative analysis, in R. Wilson (Ed.) *Macau and its Neighbours toward the 21st Century*. Macau: University of Macau. It also draws on M. Bray (1999) Education and Colonial Transition: the Hong Kong experience in comparative perspective, in M. Bray & W. O. Lee (Eds) *Education and Political Transition: implications of Hong Kong's change of sovereignty*, pp. 11–23. Hong Kong: Comparative Education Research Centre, The University of Hong Kong. The author thanks the publishers of those two books for permission to use the materials in revised form.

References

Adamson, B. & Auyeung Lai, W. (1997) Language and the Curriculum in Hong Kong: dilemmas of triglossia, in M. Bray & W. O. Lee (Eds) *Education and Political Transition: implications of Hong Kong's change of sovereignty*, pp. 87–100. Hong Kong: Comparative Education Research Centre, The University of Hong Kong.

Afonso, R. & Pereira, F. G. (1986) The Political Status and Government Institutions of Macao, *Hong Kong Law Journal*, 16, pp. 28–57.

Aldrich, R. & Connell, J. (1998) *The Last Colonies*. Cambridge: Cambridge University Press.

Altbach, P. G. & Kelly, G. P. (Eds) (1991) *Education and the Colonial Experience*, 2nd revised edn. New York: Advent Books.

Ansprenger, F. (1989) *The Dissolution of the Colonial Empires*. London: Routledge.

Arnove, R. F. (1999) Introduction – Reframing Comparative Education: the dialectic of the global and the local, in R. F. Arnove & C. A. Torres (Eds) *Comparative Education: the dialectic of the global and the local*, pp. 1–23. Lanham: Rowman & Littlefield.

Arnove, A. K. & Arnove, R. F. (1997) A Reassessment of Education, Language and Cultural Imperialism: British colonialism in India and Africa, in W. K. Cummings & N. F. McGinn (Eds) *International Handbook on Education and Development: preparing schools, students and nations for the twenty-first century*, pp. 87–101. Oxford: Pergamon Press.

Betts, R.F. (1998) *Decolonisation*. London: Routledge.

Bray, M. (1992) Colonialism, Scale and Politics: divergence and convergence of educational development in Hong Kong and Macau, *Comparative Education Review*, 36, pp. 322–342.

Bray, M. (1994) Decolonisation and Education: new paradigms for the remnants of empire, *Compare*, 24, pp. 37–51.

Bray, M. (1997) Education and Decolonisation: comparative perspectives on change and continuity, in W. K. Cummings & N. F. McGinn (Eds)

International Handbook on Education and Development: preparing schools, students and nations for the twenty-first century, pp. 103–118. Oxford: Pergamon Press.

Bray, M. & Koo, R. (Eds) (1999) *Education and Society in Hong Kong and Macau: comparative perspectives on continuity and change*. Hong Kong: Comparative Education Research Centre, The University of Hong Kong.

Chamberlain, M. E. (1998) *European Decolonisation in the Twentieth Century*. London: Longman.

China, People's Republic of (1990) *The Basic Law of the Hong Kong Special Administrative Region of the People's Republic of China*. Hong Kong: Consultative Committee for the Basic Law of the Hong Kong Special Administrative Region of the People's Republic of China.

China, People's Republic of (1993) *Lei Básica da Região Administrativa Especial de Macau de República Popular da China*. Macau: Conselho Consultivo da Lei Básica da Região Administrativa Especial de Macau de República Popular da China.

Civic Education Committee, Education Department (1985) *Guidelines on Civic Education in Schools*. Hong Kong: Government Printer.

Gallagher, J. (1982) *The Decline, Revival and Fall of the British Empire*. Cambridge: Cambridge University Press.

Gomes dos Santos, D. M. (1968) *Macau: Primeria Universidade Occidental do Extremo Oriente*. Lisboa: Academia Portuguesa da História.

Gunn, G. C. (1996) *Encountering Macau: a Portuguese city-state on the periphery of China, 1557–1999*. Boulder: Westview Press.

Hong Kong, Government of (1998) *Hong Kong: a new era*. Hong Kong: Information Services Department.

Hong Kong, Education Department (1996) *Guidelines on Civic Education in Schools*. Hong Kong: Government of Hong Kong, Education Department.

Hong Kong, Education Department (1997) *Arrangements for Firm Guidance on Secondary Schools Medium of Instruction: consultation document*. Hong Kong: Government of Hong Kong, Education Department.

Hong Kong Examinations Authority (1994) *Hong Kong Advanced Level Examination: regulations and syllabuses*. Hong Kong: Hong Kong Examinations Authority.

Jones, C. (1990) *Promoting Prosperity: the Hong Kong way of social policy*. Hong Kong: The Chinese University Press.

Kwok, S. (1996) Pioneering Putonghua, *South China Morning Post*, 23 April, p. 5.

Law Yuen Ming, I. (1992): Educação Cívica Escolar em Macau, in H. K. Wong (Ed.) *Educação Cívica em Macau*, pp. 64–74. Macau: Centro do Estudo de Macau, Universidade de Macau.

Lee, W. O. (1997) Social Class, Language and Achievement, in G. Postiglione & W. O. Lee (Eds) *Schooling in Hong Kong: organization, teaching and social context*, pp. 155–174. Hong Kong: Hong Kong University Press.

Lee, W. O. & Bray, M. (1995) Education: evolving patterns and challenges, in J. Y. S. Cheng & S. Lo (Eds) *From Colony to SAR: Hong Kong's challenges ahead*, pp. 357–378. Hong Kong: The Chinese University Press.

Lloyd, T. O. (1996) *The British Empire 1558–1995*. Oxford: Oxford University Press.

Lo Yiu Chun, J. (1999) Curriculum Reform, in M. Bray & R. Koo (Eds) *Education and Society in Hong Kong and Macau: comparative perspectives on continuity and change*, pp. 135–149. Hong Kong: Comparative Education Research Centre, The University of Hong Kong.

Macau, Governo de (1991a) Sistema Educativo de Macau. Lei no.11/91/M, Boletim Oficial de Macau, supplement to no. 34, pp. 393–403.

Macau, Governo de (1991b) Ensino Superior em Macau. Decreto-Lei no.11/91/M, Boletim Oficial de Macau, No. 5, pp. 435–446.

Macau, Governo de (1993) *Estatuto das Instituições Educativas Particulares. Decreto-Lei no.38/93/M*. Macau: Imprensa Oficial.

Macau, Governo de (1994a) *Decreto-Lei no.38/94/M*. Macau: Imprensa Oficial.

Macau, Governo de (1994b) *Decreto-Lei no.39/94/M*. Macau: Imprensa Oficial.

Macau, Governo de (1994c) *Características do Sistema de Ensino de Macau: Currículo*. Macau: Direcção dos Serviços de Educação e Juventude.

Macau, Governo de (1998) *Anuário Estatístico*. Macau: Direcção dos Serviços de Estatística e Censos.

Macau, Governo de (1999) http://www.dsej.gov.mo/statisti/edu/981126/SJ005p.htm.

Miller, N. (Ed.) (1997) *The English Schools Foundation: 30 years in Hong Kong*. Hong Kong: English Schools Foundation.

Morris, P. (1992) Preparing Pupils as Citizens of the Special Administrative Region of Hong Kong: an analysis of curriculum change and control during the transition period, in G. A. Postiglione, with J. Y. M. Leung (Eds) *Education and Society in Hong Kong: toward one country and two systems*, pp. 117–145. Hong Kong: Hong Kong University Press.

Morris, P. & Chan, K. K. (1997) The Hong Kong School Curriculum and the Political Transition: politicisation, contextualisation and symbolic action, in M. Bray & W. O. Lee (Eds) *Education and Political Transition: implications of Hong Kong's change of sovereignty*, pp. 101–118. Hong Kong: Comparative Education Research Centre, The University of Hong Kong.

Ng Sheung Ching, C. (1997) Secondary School Civic Education in Hong Kong and Macau: a comparative analysis, M.Ed. dissertation, University of Hong Kong.

Poon, A. Y. K. (1998) Bilingualism and Monolingualism: a shift in Hong Kong's language in education policy, in V. Berry & A. McNeill (Eds) *Policy and Practice in Language Education*, pp. 89–104. Hong Kong: Department of Curriculum Studies, The University of Hong Kong.

Pun Shuk Han (1997) Hegemonic Struggles in the Language Policy Development of Hong Kong, 1982–1994, in W. O. Lee & M. Bray (Eds) *Education and Political Transition: perspectives and dimensions in East Asia*, pp. 81–98. Hong Kong: Comparative Education Research Centre, The University of Hong Kong.

Shipp, S. (1997) *Macau, China: a political history of the Portuguese colony's transition to Chinese rule.* Jefferson: McFarland.

Smith, P. (1987) *Education and Colonial Control in Papua New Guinea: a documentary history.* Melbourne: Longman Cheshire.

Smith, P. & Bray, M. (1985) Educating an Elite: Papua New Guinean enrolment in international schools, in M. Bray & P. Smith (Eds) *Education and Social Stratification in Papua New Guinea*, pp. 115–145. Melbourne: Longman Cheshire.

Sweeting, A. (1990) *Education in Hong Kong Pre-1841 to 1941: fact and opinion.* Hong Kong: Hong Kong University Press.

Sweeting, A. (1995) Hong Kong, in P. Morris & A. Sweeting (Eds) *Education and Development in East Asia*, pp. 41–77. New York: Garland.

Tan, J. (1999) Secondary School History Curricula, in M. Bray & R. Koo (Eds) *Education and Society in Hong Kong and Macau: comparative perspectives on continuity and change*, pp. 171–194. Hong Kong: Comparative Education Research Centre, The University of Hong Kong.

Tang Kwok Chun (1999a) Stability and Change in School Mathematics: a socio-cultural case study of secondary mathematics in Macau, PhD thesis, The University of Hong Kong.

Tang Kwok Chun (1999b) Secondary School Mathematics Curricula, in M. Bray & R. Koo (Eds) *Education and Society in Hong Kong and Macau: comparative perspectives on continuity and change*, pp. 195–205. Hong Kong: Comparative Education Research Centre, The University of Hong Kong.

Tse Kwan Choi, T. (1999) Civic and Political Education, in M. Bray & R. Koo (Eds) *Education and Society in Hong Kong and Macau: comparative perspectives on continuity and change*, pp. 151–169. Hong Kong: Comparative Education Research Centre, The University of Hong Kong.

Watson, K. (1982) Colonialism and Educational Development, in K. Watson (Ed.) *Education in the Third World*, pp. 1–46. London: Croom Helm.

Yue, K. L. (1994) The Macau Controversy on Language of Instruction, *Yazhou Zhoukan*, 28 August, pp. 64–65 (in Chinese).

The Role of Donors in Educational Reconstruction and Transformation

MIKE KIERNAN

Introduction

The role of donor funding for development is apparently contradictory: while the volume of aid generally is decreasing, its influence is increasing.

The Development Assistance Committee of the Organisation for Economic Cooperation and Development (OECD), representing 21 of the world's richest countries, allowed its aid to fall to an average of 0.3% of gross national product (GNP), its lowest for more than 20 years. Despite being US $57 billion, this still remains, in real terms, less than the 1990 level.[1] Though there have been many declared statements of increased aid (and here one welcomes the new United Kingdom development aid policy), the global outlook is not very good. For example, the greatest single contributor, Japan, is in some economic difficulty. It is therefore unlikely that it will increase its contribution. Aid is also in danger of being redirected. Indeed, the underpinning of the South-east Asian economic 'tigers' by Western countries will consume billions which otherwise might have assisted Less Developed Countries (LDCs).

With regard to education, there is a considerable difference between intent and performance. Despite the optimistic statements at the Jomtien Education For All Conference and at the Social Summit in Copenhagen, aid to education accounts for about 5% of development assistance, and even less than 2% if we focus on basic education. While there have been many donor/agency statements of intent to increase funding to education in general, and to basic education in particular, it would appear that, despite dramatic changes by some bilaterals (USAID for example), the volume of aid to education has not, and is not likely to, increase significantly.

Ironically, the influence of international agencies in LDCs is increasing. There are three main reasons for this: (a) government money is consumed by recurrent expenditures, with salaries and allowances accounting for well over 90% of budgets, thus limiting governments' powers to direct the future of education; (b) donor money finances most development expenditures, thus increasing its power in critical areas such as quality inputs; and (c) much donor money is becoming increasingly dependent upon education policy reform; and since much of this reform is linked to macro-economic reforms imposed by the International Monetary Fund (IMF), it limits national governments' ownership of educational development.

Aid and its Impact on Education

In exploring the very complex area of the relationship between donor funding and education development we could start by asking the following questions.

- Has donor assistance in the past made any impact on education in developing countries?
- How does donor assistance influence the shaping of education provision?
- Can we see a new role for donors to education in the twenty-first century?

One can begin in the somewhat euphoric days of the 1960s and 1970s when there was a high level of optimism in Africa in particular as the winds of change began to blow away the shackles of colonial power. Most of the new leaders were themselves teachers and in their view education would provide the manpower to drive the institutions of the new states, and would provide the national unity which the colonial 'divide and rule' policy sought to prevent. Governments responded to the advocacy of donors ('one extra year of education will increase agricultural output by x tons') and education expenditure reached almost 30% of national revenue. Education for All, Universal Primary Education (UPE), Compulsory and Free Education, Education for Self-reliance, became the rallying calls for governments and donors alike. With hindsight – and we are all wiser now – we can reflect and see that we overestimated the transforming power of education. We demanded too much of education: skilled personnel, new citizens, national cohesion, increased productivity, etc. However, we have learned that education is not the panacea for all societal ills – it is one, but not the only, critical component in national development – and that it is the links between education and other societal issues (health, production, work, democracy) that are the determinants of national and social development.

This is not to say that education does not contribute to national development. A great deal was achieved in the 1960s and 1970s, for example. Africa educated a cadre of civil servants who took over the administration of their governments. Basic literacy spread and many had access to information and knowledge hitherto denied them. Millions gained access to primary education, some hundreds of thousands to secondary and some tens of thousands to university levels. But the transformation of society did not take place. Education became linked almost exclusively to public service employment and an increase in the number of years in school did not produce an increase in the tons of maize or tons of exports. Donors invested in heavy capital expenditure projects, which overstrained the capacity of the national governments in maintaining these. Projects of all kinds were initiated, pilot phases were pronounced overwhelming successes and were written up and presented at international conferences. But the projects could not be replicated nationally: the new ideas in many cases were not sufficiently internalised and even if they were, the Ministry of Finance could not sustain support in view of the increasing economic decline which started with the great oil crises of the later 1970s.

Today, it is estimated that almost 70% of educational institutions in Sub-Saharan Africa are in a serious state of disrepair. And this refers only to the physical aspects. If one were to talk about basic educational supplies (chalkboards, textbooks, reference libraries), the situation is much worse. One cannot then avoid the general conclusion – and I emphasise the generality of the remark – that given the state of education as we find it in lower income countries and LDCs today, donor funding has not had any great impact.

But why should it have had, it could be asked, when governments themselves were investing so much in education in the early years of nation building? Part of the answer lies in the enormity of the task faced by national governments: in many cases countries had to start almost from scratch. The economic decline, started by the oil crisis and compounded by the general world economic depression, ensured that no great leap forward could be made. Quantitative goals (which had a high political profile) took precedence, with subsequent qualitative loss. There was also a predominance of 'crash' programmes or national campaigns as if education could be injected in a number of specific doses. Students were thrown into schools as teachers with only 2 weeks' 'orientation'. While national authorities wanted to change curricula to reflect national culture and aspirations, the residue of the past (and its attractiveness to the new middle classes) helped ensure that the structure and main content of education remained firmly Western. Western, though, in a 1940s and 1950s context. While European education has transformed itself greatly over the past 30 years, there has not been a corresponding change in Africa. Rote-learning and copying from the chalkboard – common in Europe in the 1940s and a thing of the past today – is still alive and well in many schools in Africa today. Examinations, many restricted to recall skills and convergent thinking, still dominate the educational scene to an inordinate degree.

How Donors Influence Education Development

Addressing the question of how donors influence the direction of education is likewise complex. The major donor in the early phase has been the World Bank, which through the International Development Association (IDA) provided seemingly attractive credit to countries to expand and improve educational services. There were (and still are) what one can call 'dominant' ideologies pervading in the World Bank. In the first phase, there was a strong emphasis on tertiary education based both on manpower needs assessment and on the need to rapidly replace foreign civil servants. The next phase was in vocational and technical education to provide the skilled manpower necessary for industrial transformation. This spilled over into the vocationalising of secondary education: secondary schools had to have woodwork and metalwork workshops (and home economics for girls). This approach was eventually ousted by the 'discovery' that general secondary education was the best form of post-primary education provision. Bilateral donors, at this time, either followed suit or initiated small projects on the margins.

The move towards the Basic Needs philosophy (1970s) affected the way in which education was perceived. The purpose of education now became linked to better health, lower fertility, and community productivity; thus, the concept of Basic Education, that magical number of years (as few and inexpensive as possible) which would transform an individual into a useful member of society. This was an opportunity to address the scale of the problems involved (something which projects never can take into account) but the Basic Needs approach seems to have faded as the spectre of Structural Adjustment began to raise its demanding head.

Prior to the era of Structural Adjustment, we should inquire where the national governments were in all of this. In many cases, they were overwhelmed by the complexities of the situation and constrained by the low levels of national planning and implementation capacity. Without the national capacity to articulate needs, to develop strategic plans, and therefore to argue for donor complementarity to national programmes, governments generally acquiesced to donor demands. Good national staff were swept up as Donor Programme Officers or were employed by the increasing number of non-governmental organisations (NGOs [2]), further weakening potential capacity within ministries to engage with donor domination of the educational policy environment.

What was also occurring was the increasing 'gap' between the rhetoric of development and the reality at the micro-level of education. Tanzania, for example, led the African way in educational and social philosophy in the 1960s and 1970s. While Education for Self-reliance was founded on a basic education philosophy (long before donors discovered the concept), the very forces established to implement it – the national civil service and the emerging political elite – were continually undermining it. In the early 1990s, research revealed that 80% of social service funds in Tanzania benefited the richest quintile of society; 20% of the education budget was allocated to funding undergraduate students abroad, while the very cost-inefficient national university (a 1:3 staff–student ratio) had surplus places at undergraduate level. Power politics was the reality. In many cases, more money is spent on the education of the political, economic and social elites than on, for example, basic education (though excluding salaries).

The Impact of Structural Adjustment Programmes

Many, however, would claim that the main problems in the 1980s were entirely due to the Structural Adjustment Programmes (SAPs) insisted upon by the International Monetary Fund (IMF) and World Bank. The 1980s was the first full decade of IMF/World Bank sponsored SAPs. In essence, this meant that governments in the developing world had to initiate austerity measures chiefly through a reduction in government spending. Since most of government spending went towards maintaining a massive civil service (over 50% of which are teachers) and as any significant reduction in this would be political suicide, the austerity hit the quality of services. From my observations, children had to move over and sit four or five to a desk, share a textbook with 10/20 others, be taught by a teacher who would never receive a day's in-service training, and sit for examinations for a declining number of places in institutions of higher education. Some countries introduced user payment officially in the form of fees; most others allowed user payment in the form of private tuition fees (which was a *de facto* acceptance of the inability of the state to pay adequate teacher salaries). During the decade, there was some criticism of the SAPs – but it was more an appeal for structural adjustment with a human face than a rejection of the approach itself. What was happening in many countries was continuing hardship on the poor and continuing corruption at state level, largely induced, it must be admitted, by the catastrophic decline in the value of the salaries of public servants. It is clear that public servants cannot be expected to provide professional and committed service on a monthly salary which provides subsistence for 7–10 days per month. It is arguable that corruption in this situation becomes a means of survival.

Education and Poverty Alleviation

It was not surprising, then, that the World Bank's 1990 Annual Report is starkly titled: *Poverty*. This was followed by an operational directive entitled the 'Poverty Reduction Handbook', which outlined strategies for alleviating poverty. The best one can say is that at least a new reality was emerging. Poverty was not going to be eliminated (we hear the far echo of the 1960s: the elimination of 'poverty, ignorance and disease') – it was going to be alleviated. The new policy did lead to very good analytic work in identifying poverty-determining factors and their interrelatedness. At worst, however, many poverty alleviation programmes became a matter of throwing money at the problem, perpetuating the aid syndrome with its accompanying impact on corruption and mismanagement. As Tolstoy said, we will do anything for the poor – except get off their backs.

However, the report did bring to the forefront a basic, common-sense but underexploited idea: that labour is the only asset of the poor and that the efficient use of this labour is the main strategy to alleviate poverty. Thus, a rationale was re-established for educating the poor. (Note, however, that the idea of a basic human right is absent.) So-called 'safety net' programmes or 'social funds' were established to blunt the impact of SAPs, which would, however, continue to dominate macro-economic policy planning. A key concept is the involvement of the private sector in the provision of social services. Market forces were deemed to provide much more efficient services and since parents everywhere are willing to sacrifice for the provision of education for their children, why not let the private sector provide what they pay for anyway? The basic flaw in all of this, especially in Sub-Saharan Africa, is that the private market does not automatically emerge in the vacuum left by the withdrawal of the state, certainly not in the field of social services. And while the poor do pay for education, mostly in the form of opportunity costs, these are not so easily cashable to pay education and health fees. The World Bank itself is now beginning to realise the weakness of the global application of its doctrine and a more realistic tone is noticeable in its discussions these days.

Again, however, the input of national governments in relation to this is noticeably absent. Globalisation begins to play a major and dominant role in setting the educational agenda, often limiting government action in varying degrees and hence reducing national ownership. The following factors can be identified:

- the increasing strength of commercial forces (international financial markets) and supra-governmental bodies (like the European Community);
- the impact of information about the effectiveness of national policies is becoming increasing available, putting pressure on governments to

adopt policies which are seen to be successful elsewhere (e.g. privatisation);
- power passing upward (European Union); downward (regionalism) but not nation-focused;
- world financial markets set limits for both fiscal and monetary policy for nearly all countries;
- limited scope for domestic policies (international pressure for open access); and
- multinational demands (tax concessions) limit freedom of individual countries to extract tax and therefore fund their own national programmes.

The Role of Donors in the 1990s and towards the Twenty-first Century

Within this context, how can government/donor relationships thrive? In the late 1990s we notice:

- the increasing role of the IMF as a development agency;
- the increasing independent role of the major bilaterals;
- the change in strategy by the major bilaterals; and
- the decline of focus on traditional 'projects' and increasing support for 'sector investment support'.

The roles of the IMF and the World Bank/IDA are becoming increasingly closer, almost indistinguishable in the case of LDCs. The initial Bretton Woods mandate of the IMF – to promote exchange stability, to maintain orderly exchange arrangements among members and to avoid competitive exchange depreciation – has almost gone by the wayside. Today the IMF is seen more as a prop for a privatised international monetary system (cf. the South Asia crisis). With regard to LDCs and Less Industrialised Countries (LICs), the IMF is acting more like a development agency. The IMF/Structural Adjustment Loans (SALs), intended to redesign national economic policies, were followed by SECALs – Sector Adjustment Loans – and were used to support major reforms in national sector systems, including education. SECILs – Sector Investment Loans – were then provided to achieve new national policy objectives. IDA credits provide funds for more specific objectives within this policy framework.

The 1995 World Bank Policy on Education, as expressed in the document *Priorities and Strategies for Education*, outlines six key reform areas:

- a higher priority for education;
- paying greater attention to outcomes;
- public investment focused on Basic Education;
- attention to equity;
- household involvement; and

- autonomous institutions.

The major multilateral education donors/agencies, such as United Nations Development Programme (UNDP) and UNICEF are becoming less and less operational in the education field, focusing largely on advocacy work instead. It is interesting to note that UNESCO (once a dominant force in education in LDCs) is but a pale shadow of its former glory.

The major bilateral donors in the wake of SAPs are beginning to act more independently. The World Bank is no longer accepted as the 'lead' donor in education. Bilaterals carried out their own internal reviews and as they assessed their performance of the 1970s and 1980s, there was a general recognition of (a) the limitations of the traditional project approach, (b) the need for more concentrated, longer term support based on more sustainable strategies, and (c) the need to work within a reformed national policy framework. Denmark, for example, reduced the number of countries receiving aid from over 40 to just over 20 and in the case of each development partner (as the relationship was now called) there will be support (long-term) for three to four sectors only. The Danish International Development Agency's (DANIDA's) preferred modality of support is called SPS – Sector Programme Support. The World Bank calls its own modality SIP – Sector Investment Programmes. The six principles set out by P. Harrold and Associates (1995) [3] sum up the main characteristics of both approaches:

- support will be sector-wide in scope, covering all relevant policies, programmes and projects within the sector;
- support will be within a coherent sector policy framework;
- local stakeholders must be in charge of the programme;
- all donors must 'sign on' in a process led by government;
- implementation arrangements are made common to all donors; and
- long-term foreign technical assistance is to be minimised.

In later versions, institutional capacity was added but these remain today the main principles of the new approach. It should be added that these principles are still at an early stage of implementation. It has proven more difficult than expected to throw off the old 'project' mentality. But the very fact of greater concentration and of longer-term support modality meant that bilaterals now began to look seriously at such options as budget support, recurrent cost expenditure support, policy change enablement, etc. – options which did not even arise in the days of 'pure' project support. This approach also meant that the World Bank had to take the opinions of bilaterals more seriously, first, because in many cases the World Bank could better legitimise its operations if bilaterals were 'on board' as co- or parallel financiers, and secondly, the success of the SIP approach depends on a high degree of donor coordination and cooperation.

Underlying these principles is the concept of 'partnership', which Sweden and Norway are strongly advocating in recent years. These add, as DANIDA does, greater stress on the creation of a democratic culture and respect for civil rights. The Swedish International Development Agency (SIDA), accepting the forces of a market economy, seems – in my opinion – to be attempting to put a social democratic aspect on the pure neo-liberalism philosophy of 'the market' by talking about a 'social' as opposed to a 'captured' market economy. It is an attempt to maintain some kind of supply side dimension to demand side economics. It is difficult to see if this will turn out to be nothing more than an appealing packaging of a bitter pill.

The question to ask now is whether these principles are adequate to address the needs of societies in change as they enter the twenty-first century.

There is no doubt that the continued support to the process of democratisation, if it becomes manifested in real decentralisation and meaningful community participation, will help to break the power of the strong interest groups now controlling education in many developing countries today. In education, it comes down to the right of a parent not only to vote for a political candidate but to have a meaningful say in the operation of the local school. It means turning the heads of teachers towards parents and not only towards the Ministry. Unless parents are empowered to demand minimum qualitative performance from schools, no amount of central or donor-induced reforms will work.

The change from projects to sector programme support will increase the power of government, if it has a clearly defined national strategy and if that strategy has broad national support. Better coordination of donor inputs will reduce the power of individual donors and focus government and donors alike on national priority issues and programmes. The central issue is agreement between donor and government on the key structural policy issues; not just agreement in order to obtain loans and grants, but more a shared vision.

The main weakness of this approach is the inability of many governments to take the necessary tough decisions to bring about greater effectiveness and efficiency in the system and to allocate more funds to basic education. This weakness is partly, ironically enough, an outcome of the democratic process, at least in its multiparty variation. Governments are afraid to proclaim unpopular programmes, as the opposition can so easily make political ground on the disquiet that would follow. Given the fragility of many of the new multiparty democracies, this is a real threat.

External Technical Assistance

What is the role of external technical assistance in this new scenario? It is well documented that technical assistance has not been effective over the past 30 years. It is accused of being overly expensive, of preventing or delaying national capacity building, of serving the interest of donors more than that of recipient countries and of downright inefficiency. A lot of this is true, but how many governments have helped create the environment in which external technical assistance could be effective? Governments have allowed Project Implementation Units to proliferate; counterpart staff who could benefit from technology and skills transfer were either not made available or frequently changed; national staff, who often received training abroad as part of the technical assistance package, returned to working environments which not only did not provide an opportunity to use the new skills gained, but in many cases, actively discouraged change. Technical assistance was not seen holistically but as the 'necessary evil' of an aid package.

Today there is more attention to national capacity-building but this is doomed to failure unless something is done to reform the civil service in two critical areas: (a) salaries, which must be competitive with the private sector, and (b) professional competence, based on an independent civil service commission and free of political nepotism.

External technical assistance is being rethought: a reduction of traditional long-term advisers, the strengthening of various forms of institutional linkages, and the use of more focused, short-term consultancy services. The problem with all of this is that it is equally likely to fail unless there is a strong and decisive national environment to 'embrace' these inputs; 'embracing' meaning to set the technical assistance in a maximum mode of efficiency (consultants borrowing your watch to tell you the time), with clear objectives and an efficient monitoring and evaluation system. One must also address the issue of cost – external technical assistance, in whatever form, is expensive. The use of new technologies – email, the Internet, etc. – can be harnessed to provide a great deal of technical assistance. The information is there; the question is how it can be used to effect change. The external adviser often had the role of being more acceptable than a national officer purely because he or she was foreign, seen, ironically, to be representing no vested interests.

Conclusions

This somewhat general overview of the aid to education situation does, however, lead us to some tentative conclusions.

- National governments will have to give a higher priority to education, not just as a percentage of national revenue (which can be comparatively small) but through ensuring the provision of minimum quality basic education and enhancing the environment for access to further education. This means some form of cost-sharing for secondary and higher education. Government priority to education must be seen not only in the context of overall macro-economic reform but in the context of strong political commitment to education. Commitment to education must not only be heard, it must be read from the National Budget. It must be higher than the Defence or Prisons budgets.

- Efficiency measures must be taken to increase the effectiveness of existing funding. When a 7-year cycle takes over 12 or more years to complete (due to factors such as repetition, drop-out and academic failure), we can see that efficiency improvement can release existing funds to providing access to greater numbers.

- Donors and governments must reach agreement on priority national programmes. Governments must allow all stakeholders to have a meaningful say in the determining of national education policies, and limit the influence of powerful lobby groups. Donors must take into account the political difficulties involved in adopting policy change. It is not just necessary to build up national capacity within government and the Ministry of Education; it is equally important to assist in building up a better understanding of educational choice among national stakeholders.

- Presuming real agreement is reached, in the form of a National Strategic Plan, or Master Plan or whatever, donors must then make a coordinated, long-term investment based on agreed targets under the general categories of (a) equitable access, (b) improved quality, based on improved relevant curricula, and improved monitoring and assessment systems and (c) improved management, based on effective decentralisation and democratic community empowerment. By keeping to these overarching goals, it is possible to demystify education so that 'our' jargon of internal and external efficiencies, cost–benefit analyses, etc., becomes translated to common terminology which all share-holders feel comfortable with.

- External Technical Assistance should be negotiated as an integral part of the overall support programme. It should have clearly stated objectives and time limits. It should be negotiated within a clear Human Resource Development strategy for the Ministry of Education itself.

- Monitoring and Evaluation should be carried out sector-wise. Those donors supporting primary education should, under the leadership of the Ministry of Education, carry out joint annual reviews. Donors and government are then using the same criteria and the focus is on national targets, not specific donor goals.

- There should be a clear 'end-of-aid' goal. This could be 10 or even 20 years in the future but it should be declared, otherwise all our talk about sustainability is only lip service. In this way, aid can be seen as complementary to national funding, not, as is often the case today, substituting for needed funding. By setting deadlines for the systematic reduction of aid, one forces the issues of effectiveness to the forefront.

Donor-educators must be a bit more realistic with regard to expectations. Education is the basis for any kind of meaningful development but the situation is not one of pure causality: it is not a case of 'the more education the more development'. Ministries of Finance, National Economic Councils and National Population Councils have to be brought into active education planning. There must be more interaction with civic society organisations (and I do not mean the regular NGO set-up). It is necessary to establish the synergies whereby education plays a critical, but complementary role. For example, in many societies, funding simple micro-nutrient supplement school programmes could give a better return to learning than pre-service training. This is, of course, only for the short term, but an ignoring of this makes much of our long-term planning unrealisable.

Donor-educators, working in the developing world, have to learn the complexity of development. Research should focus, naturally, on what happens in the classroom, but it should not ignore that the students in the classrooms often come from illiterate homes, very often come to schools malnourished, and all too often leave those schools either too early or without having gained any of the basic skills that can be used to take them out of the vicious circle of poverty.

Thus, perhaps the transition and reconstruction we should focus on is that of the transition from poverty to dignity and the reconstruction of systems to enable this transition.

Notes

[1] Figures quoted in this chapter are generally from secondary sources, mainly ICVA/EUROCTEP 'The Reality of Aid 1996' (Earthscan, 1996). Much of the education figures comes from the paper by C. Colclough (1997) Aid to Basic Education in Africa (Oslo: Ministry of Foreign Affairs). There is considerable variance between much of the data from various sources. Also, the figures quoted in most cases refer to Sub-Saharan Africa, not to the developing world as a whole.

[2] There are reported to be 57,000 NGOs in South Africa alone; over 200,000 in Bangladesh.

[3] P. Harrold (1995) *The Broad Sector Approach to Investment Lending: sector investment programmes*. Washington, DC: World Bank.

Transforming Education through Donor-funded Projects: how do we measure success?

HARVEY SMITH

Aid-funded Support for Education

As education specialists, we tend to judge projects in the field of education from the perspective of their educational value – whether we consider them to be educationally sound, whether they have what we would consider to be a positive impact on education systems. Those who have been involved in implementing such projects, thanks to contracts directly or indirectly with an aid donor, have also got used to what the donor is likely to consider as a successful outcome to the project, and this necessarily influences the way we manage the project or manage our contribution to it. When we speak of project success, we may simply mean that the donor is satisfied with the outcomes, or that we as implementers have successfully satisfied the donor. If, however, we are concerned with the rather larger question of whether aid-funded support for education is delivered in a way that is 'conducive to success' – and how its delivery might be improved in the future – we need to look more carefully at what is meant by success. What follows is an attempt to look at this concept in a broader way and to see what implications this might have for the future conduct of aid-funded support for education. This draws on my own recent research into perceptions of success in the management of aid-funded projects and is based on surveys of the literature on aid, change and project management (Smith, 1998).

Aid-funded support for education in developing countries is of four main types: broad sectoral or budget support, not tied to specific projects; capital funding, for example, for construction of schools; training and exchange schemes, which pay for places on higher education and training courses; and projects, which aim to make specific improvements in subsectors such as teacher training or curriculum development and/or to strengthen educational subsystems and management processes, and which may also include elements of the other three types. The level of priority attached to each of these has varied and will no doubt continue to do so. Budget support, for example, is now becoming more attractive as countries are encouraged by the World Bank or European Union to establish Education Sector Development Programmes. Nevertheless, there is no reason to suggest that any of these means of delivering aid will disappear completely in the twenty-first century. This chapter focuses on the provision of aid-funded support for education by means of projects. It is largely but by no means exclusively concerned with British government-funded projects aimed at improving education in developing countries.

For present purposes, by projects, I mean one-off undertakings intended to bring about a specific change or changes in an education system, within certain limits. In common with some other donors, Britain's Department for International Development (DFID) and its predecessor, the Overseas Development Agency (ODA), have used a fairly rigid project approach, with the key document being the logical framework. As this framework highlights inputs and outputs and pays little attention to processes and strategies, it is often perceived as being 'product-oriented'. Although ODA and DFID have talked of a move towards a 'process approach' to projects, their interpretation of this still requires a fully completed logical framework. In the past, the logical framework has been a document which has been seen largely as a tool for the donor and has been drawn up by the donor. In recent years this has changed, with the introduction of more participatory approaches to project design and an insistence by ODA/DFID that other stakeholders play a part in the design process. On the other hand, as my own recent experience of an education project design using a participatory approach showed, it may be only personnel of the central ministry who are able to participate – school directors, teachers and students, also important stakeholders, may not be.

Project Success

There is a general perception that large numbers of such aid-funded projects 'fail' (e.g. Cusworth & Franks, 1993, p. 11; London, 1993, p. 265; Turner, 1993, p. 499). This implies firstly that there is a general understanding of what success and failure mean when applied to projects, and secondly, that there is general agreement among stakeholders about whether the outcomes of any particular project are positive or negative – in other words, there is an implication that success can be measured objectively rather than being a matter of personal judgement.

Taking the issue of the meaning of success and failure first, we are confronted by an ambiguity. Success can mean both achieving what it was intended to achieve, and turning out well, having a favourable outcome. To call a project successful can therefore mean either that it appeared to achieve what it was intended to achieve, in other words it met its objectives, or that it turned out well, in other words, produced a beneficial outcome. These are by no means identical, and some projects may achieve their objectives but not have any great impact on the community, while others may not achieve their objectives but nevertheless have a beneficial impact – possibly even greater than was foreseen by the original design.

The second issue is the assumption that there can be general agreement about the positive or negative nature of the outcomes of a project. There are a large number of stakeholders in any project, but it seems to be generally only the donors' perceptions of success that are taken into consideration. One can assume – and I will return to this – that various players on the recipient side and even within the implementing team may have different perceptions, but unfortunately there appears to have been very little research into the perceptions of these other stakeholders, and the literature on aid projects has left me with the impression that, in general, what the donor perceives as success is assumed to be what everyone perceives as success.

Most of the research into educational projects has been concerned with case studies of individual projects. While it has been possible to draw generalised conclusions from some of these – for example, Leach's (1990) study of relationships between expatriates and counterparts in projects in Sudan, four of which were education or training projects – others are less generalisable. In order to develop a broader framework for investigating what might be meant by the success or failure of projects, I propose that we start with what is understood by the concept of an aid-funded education project, rather than by looking at what projects themselves do or do not do.

In essence, an aid-funded education project is self-defining. As a project, it is an undertaking designed to meet a specific objective or objectives within time and cost limits – although the objectives may not be only what appear as outputs in the logical framework. As it is aid-funded, it is concerned with meeting the aims of aid, whatever these may be. It is obviously concerned with meeting certain educational objectives – but it is more than just an undertaking within the field of education, as it is intended to bring about some change in the way education is delivered. It is therefore also, very importantly, concerned with change.

Viewed in this way, we can say that aid-funded education projects have four perspectives or dimensions. As education specialists, we focus on the education dimension, but it is equally legitimate to look at these undertakings from the points of view of aid, change and project management. Just as education specialists do not always agree, the perceptions of those who look at projects from the points of view of aid management, project management and change management may also be very different. In the anticipation that there may be lessons to be learnt from an examination of these perceptions and of the differences between them, I will look at some of the issues raised by the literature on aid, change and project management.

Perceptions from Aid Management

Within the field of aid and development there are a number of differing theoretical approaches. Those who see 'underdevelopment' as being a result of dependence on and dominance by capitalist countries may perceive aid as largely maintaining the dominance/dependence relationship. Successful aid would promote freedom from such dominance. As an example, a project which had as an outcome the reinforcing of English as the medium of instruction – even where the national government's policy to have English as the medium was apparently based on sound educational grounds – might then be seen as hindering successful development. A different theoretical basis for aid views developing countries as having a traditional, overpopulated sector and a modern sector, with development depending on the modern sector absorbing surplus labour from the traditional sector – in which case the role of aid is to strengthen the modern sector's capacity to absorb labour from the traditional sector. An education project which had as an outcome the strengthening of the modern sector would then be perceived as successful in developmental terms, while one which strengthened the traditional sector might be seen as failing – consequently, a project outcome which reinforced the role of English in schools might be seen as positive. More recent approaches to aid and development suggest that there are common patterns of socio-economic development, largely concerned with alleviating poverty, and that the right mix of internal policies and external support helps these patterns to develop. An English language teaching project may then be seen as failing if its outcomes do not overtly contribute to patterns of poverty alleviation.

Aid has never been seen as solely philanthropic and there are motives other than merely helping the poor, and from the aid perspective, projects may be seen as having both primary and secondary objectives. If development is seen as change resulting in improved standard of living and/or quality of life, an education project which meets this objective will have been successful to that extent. However, the previous British Government stated explicitly that aid was not only for this purpose but was also intended to strengthen the United Kingdom's commercial and political relations (Foreign and Commonwealth Office, 1994, p. 51) (the new Department for

International Development is not as explicit). By these criteria, a fully successful British aid project would therefore also have to meet the secondary objectives for British aid, and result in strengthened commercial and political relations for Britain.

As has been noted already, the principal focus of the literature on aid is the donor, and the emphasis is often on the donor's internal concerns. Examples of perceptions of success from the point of view of the other parties in the aid relationship are scarce. Taking success as the achievement of what was intended, usually the only explicit statement of what was intended is that set out in the project framework by the donor drawn up in consultation, to a greater or lesser extent, with the recipient government. But the real intentions of the host institution, the beneficiaries of the project, the staff of the project (local or expatriate), and even of the implementing agency, are not usually recorded.

Yet it can be expected that success may be judged by different criteria by different stakeholders. From my own experience, projects often cause considerable disruption to the institutions in which they are based, and one success criterion for the director of the host institution may well be whether the project causes the minimum disruption to normal activities, and possibly the minimum cost in other ways. Staff may see workloads increase – or may benefit from the project through increased income. Success may then also be judged on whether it increases the burdens staff on the recipient side have to bear, or whether it provides direct benefits. Such benefits may not be simply financial, but may include increased power or prestige. It is also the case that some on the recipient side are not blessed with the luxury which the donor has of being able to look several years ahead, as short-term problems are more than enough to deal with. In such cases, a success criterion may be the extent to which the project helps solve the pressing short-term problems as well as moving towards long-term change.

Even within the one dimension of aid management, then, there are apparently conflicting perceptions. If the outcome of a project is the strengthening of English as the medium of instruction – and such projects have absorbed a significant part of Britain's funding of education projects over the last three decades – this may be perceived as either a favourable outcome if it promotes the modern sector and encourages employment, or as an unfavourable outcome if it promotes dependence and does not directly help eliminate poverty. There are significant secondary objectives for aid – which may even conflict with the primary objective of development. Project outcomes may be perceived differently by different stakeholders in the aid relationship.

Perceptions from Change Management

As with aid, there are different theoretical approaches to the issue of planned change, largely treated as synonymous with 'innovation' in the education literature. Traditionally, projects would appear to be in line with the theoretical approach which suggests that development tends towards equilibrium, and that planned change is a process of unfreezing, moving and then refreezing. A project which achieves this is, to this extent, perceived as successful. But the opposing evolutionary theory of change suggests that development tends towards disequilibrium, in which case the project which has left things 'frozen' is not perceived to be as successful as one which enables further change to take place. This is an argument that we have seen in discussion of the term 'sustainability', which is interpreted by some as meaning that the activities or systems established by the project continue after the project, but by others as meaning that there is a capacity to further develop and improve the systems and activities after the project has finished.

A further concern is the level at which change is targeted. Behaviourist or individualist approaches see change as an individual's response to the environment, so that changes in external stimuli lead to changes in individual behaviour. A group dynamics approach sees change as being the result of group pressure to conform, so that there needs to be a change of group norms or values to change individual behaviour. Systems theorists would target the level of the organisation, seeing change in subsystems as having a knock-on effect, which brings about change in individuals. The adherent of group or systems theories of change may perceive a teacher training project which has trained 100 teachers, even where this was the stated objective of the project, as incomplete or unsustainable if there have been no accompanying changes in group norms or in the subsystems of the education system. The shift over the years in donor priorities, from training individuals to strengthening institutions, also means that perspectives have changed. But one obvious problem is that the end of a project is often too early to judge what sort of change – if any – has taken place and at which level that change is likely to be sustained.

Taking the meaning of success as achieving what was intended, from the point of view of change management another concern – and one which is overlooked by the logical framework – is whether the intention is in fact total adoption of the change. Kelly (1980, p. 69), writing of curriculum development projects, identifies four types of aims, only one of which is to see the proposed change implemented fully:

> *(a) adoptive aims intend that teachers will adopt an innovation and implement it faithfully;*

(b) adaptive aims intend that teachers will adapt some aspects of an innovation to their current practice – a compromise between the ideals and the realities of the teachers' situation;

(c) innovative aims intend that the dissemination of an innovation will stimulate further innovation and foster professional development; and

(d) instrumental aims encourage the achievement of change by indirect means e.g. changing examinations in order to encourage changes in a course.

From experience, I suspect that members of project implementing teams may often be pursuing aims which lead to less-than-total adoption but without necessarily being able to articulate this in the way Kelly has done.

One success criterion from the perspective of change management is ownership. But we need to ask, ownership by whom? The fact that senior staff of the Ministry of Education are in favour of a project and have been closely involved in its design does not mean that there will be a sense of ownership by others in the education system. We have seen problems with projects which have this support from above, but where school directors do not have the same sense of ownership and interpret the intended change as merely a burden. Similarly, starting from the other end, there are examples of projects where teachers are very willing to change their behaviour in the classroom but where this is blocked because school directors have been inadequately involved in the change from an early stage.

A further issue concerns the way perceptions change over time. What is seen as an innovation or a favourable change at the beginning of a project may no longer seem so at the end. Stakeholders change their perceptions over time as priorities and fashions change. Valadez & Bamberger (1994, p. 184) refer to a 1985 USAID report which showed that a number of projects were judged to be less than fully successful because of problems of sustainability, even though at the time the projects were designed, sustainability was not considered to be one of the keys to success.

From the perspective of change management, then, it is also the case that there are conflicting perceptions, These are based largely on issues such as whether the change brought about by an aid-funded project should 'refreeze' the situation or leave it 'unfrozen'; whether change should take place in individual behaviour, in group behaviour or in systems; whether total adoption of an innovation was really the intention; and whether the intended change has been targeted at the right people.

Perceptions from Project Management

The literature on project management shows a remarkable tendency to be concerned with structure, stages and techniques – the characteristics of the classical or traditional management approach which in other branches of management appear to have been superseded some years ago. Other areas of management have been influenced over the last decades by a human relations or behavioural approach, with its focus on people and motivation, by systems theory, and more recently by contingency theory, which argues that there is no one best management structure or system but that effective structures and systems are contingent on the situation, not least on aspects of the environment. The project management literature, on the other hand, is concerned with project structure, sees projects as a series of stages to be followed, and focuses on techniques such as critical path analysis, which should most efficiently achieve the project objectives. Perceptions of success from the perspective of project management therefore reflect these concerns.

In the project management literature, projects are defined by their objectives and by their so-called 'constraints' of time, cost and quality (or specification). A project is traditionally seen as fully successful only if it achieves its objectives on time, within budget and to the desired quality. However, research into success criteria for projects (aid-funded as well as non-aid-funded) shows that there are other factors taken into account by sponsors, clients, ultimate users and project teams, and vast lists of success criteria have been developed (e.g. Baker et al, 1983a, 1983b; Morris & Hough, 1987; Turner, 1993). The implication is that, although there are still broadly the two approaches to success and failure in the project management literature – whether the effects intended have been achieved and whether the project has been implemented on time, to budget and to standard – there is little common ground in the actual perceptions of success of the stakeholders.

One issue that is raised in the literature is whether a project has met real needs. Although this refers in part to the design of a project and whether its purpose was justified, it is often linked to the importance of the environment. This may mean the physical environment – as projects are unlikely to be perceived as successful if they do not take account of issues of landscape, climate, physical resources and so on – but more usually refers to the extent to which the project is appropriate to the political, economic, social and cultural environment. However well the project design takes such factors into account, the environment is dynamic and 'failure to respond' may well be the verdict on the project team which concentrates too hard on achieving the intended objectives. Often linked to the environment is the issue of unintended side effects: whether these are perceived as positive or negative also affects perceptions of overall project success.

It is the perspective of project management, then, which highlights the more formal elements of project success. The traditional project management approach is that the project is successful if it achieves its objectives on time, within budget and to the required standard – although the literature also shows that those involved in project management in fact apply other criteria, not least of which is appropriateness to the environment.

Common and Conflicting Criteria

As discussed, success can mean both achieving objectives and having a favourable outcome. For each of these three dimensions or perspectives, we can identify what appear from the literature to be the objectives of aid-funded education projects and what would be considered to be a favourable outcome. We can then see to what extent these coincide or are in conflict. I turn first to success as achieving objectives.

From the point of view of the management of aid, there are primary and secondary objectives. The primary objective is undoubtedly development, however this is defined. The secondary objective differs for different stakeholders. For the donor, this may be – as was stated explicitly by the British Government – strengthening commercial and political relations; for the recipient, this may be to obtain external support for the education sector so that more internal resources can be allocated to other sectors, such as defence.

From the point of view of the management of change, we can also identify primary and secondary objectives. The primary objective is to bring about some change in the behaviour of an individual, a group or an organisation. The secondary objective is that such change should be sustained.

From the point of view of project management, projects exist to bring about their own specific objectives. Primarily, success relates to whether these specific objectives have been achieved. Secondarily, success relates to whether these objectives have been achieved on time, within budget and to an agreed standard.

Thus, success, in the sense of achieving what was intended, becomes the achievement of project outputs within time, cost and quality limits, resulting in sustained change in behaviour in the target group, contributing to development and to some political, commercial, financial or other benefit for the donor and recipient. In principle, there is no reason why these should not coincide, provided that the constraints imposed by one objective do not impede the achievement of another. For example, the time and cost limits must be adequate to allow for developing sustained change in behaviour of the target group; the intended change in behaviour must be such as will lead to socio-economic development; the cost limits must not preclude the possibility of commercial benefit to the donor or financial benefit to the recipient; and so on. In practice, given that all project designs must include a degree of compromise, they may conflict.

If we now look at success in terms of favourable outcome, the situation becomes less clear. This depends in part on one's theoretical approach to aid, to change and to project management, even when that is 'felt' rather than clearly articulated, in part on one's role in the project (representative of donor, representative of recipient government, member of project team, counterpart, beneficiary, etc.), and in part on timing, as the extent to which an outcome is favourable may be judged differently at the end of the project and some years later. A favourable outcome in terms of aid may mean a significant impact on socio-economic development, especially as it relates to poverty, or an impact which is appropriate to the local situation (for example, in terms of technology), or the political or other benefits which the project brings about within the host institution. In terms of change, a favourable outcome may mean that the change is appropriate to the society or culture, that it has impacted positively on systems (such as bureaucracy), that it has not resulted in financial or workload burdens. In terms of project management, a favourable outcome may mean that the real needs were well identified and have been adequately met, that the objectives have resulted in sustainable benefits, that there were no unintended negative side effects, or even that there were some unintended positive side effects.

It will be seen from this that this definition of success presents a situation which is more complex and more likely to produce conflicting criteria. Successful achievement of objectives may not result in a favourable outcome, and what may be seen as a favourable outcome from one perspective may look different from another. Project outputs, although fully delivered, may not result in significant impact on the recipient country. There may be change in behaviour, but this may not be appropriate to the local environment and may lead to political difficulties. Political or other benefits which the host institution would perceive as a criterion for successful aid may be incompatible with meeting real needs. Unintended side effects may impede rather than promote development.

Conclusions

Although there seems to have been a general perception that many or even most projects fail, if we are unclear what we mean by success and failure then this perception has little value, and the project approach may be seen as far more negative than is justified. The first obvious implication of what has been said in this chapter is that we need to be very cautious in using the words 'success' and 'failure'. The terms are ambiguous in that they can refer either to the achievement of what was intended or to the extent to which something turned out favourably. In both cases, there may be disagreements, depending on one's perspective.

Secondly, the perspective is too often solely that of the donor. There is no reason why the donor's perspective should be more relevant than the recipient's or the beneficiaries', and there is a need to involve other stakeholders more fully in identifying project success criteria. Although donors have made moves towards including representatives of the recipient government or host institution in project evaluation teams, the terms of reference for the evaluation may well still be those of the donor. The following are specific but overlapping action points which might improve this situation:

- more research into identifying perceptions of project success from the recipient side and into how these can be articulated and made public;
- a greater effort within projects to facilitate the voicing of such perceptions, including providing training in monitoring and evaluation issues regardless of the purpose of the project; and
- more studies of impact carried out by and/or reflecting the views of a range of stakeholders, with such studies being written into (and costed as part of) projects.

Thirdly, we need to be aware that there are different perspectives on aid-funded education projects – I have suggested that in addition to education there are the perspectives of aid, change and project management – and that these produce potential differences in attitude to success and failure. All these perspectives need to be considered when projects are evaluated. They also need to be considered at the project design stage, when internal monitoring and evaluation procedures are established, and appraisals of project designs should also consider whether there is compatibility between the issues raised by viewing the project from the perspectives of each of these dimensions.

Finally, there may in fact be little value in talking about 'project success' or 'project failure'. Our concern should be with which aspects of a project have been perceived as successful and which as failing, and why. If we are to learn from these perceptions in order to meet future challenges, many more project evaluations and impact studies need to be made available. Such studies must justify the criteria by which success and failure are judged, and focus on issues which will result in positive impact on the conduct of future projects.

References

Baker, B. N., Fisher, D. & Murphy, D. C. (1983a) Project Management in the Public Sector: success and failure patterns compared to private sector projects, in D. I. Cleland & W. R. King (Eds) *Project Management Handbook*, pp. 686–699. New York: Van Nostrand Reinhold.

Baker, B. N., Murphy, D. C. & Fisher, D. (1983b) Factors Affecting Project Success, in D. I. Cleland & W. R. King (Eds) *Project Management Handbook*, pp. 669–685. New York: Van Nostrand Reinhold.

Cusworth, J. W. & Franks, T. R. (Eds) (1993) *Managing Projects in Developing Countries*. Harlow: Longman.

Foreign and Commonwealth Office (1994) *Foreign & Commonwealth Office Including Overseas Development Administration: the Government's expenditure plans 1994–95 to 1996–97*. London: HMSO, Cm 2502.

Kelly, P. (1980) From Innovation to Adaptability: the changing perspective of curriculum development, in M. Galton (Ed.) *Curriculum Change: the lessons of a decade*, pp. 65–80. Leicester: Leicester University Press.

Leach, F. (1990) Counterpart Relationships on Technical Co-operation Projects: a Sudanese study, D.Phil. thesis, University of Sussex.

London, N. A. (1993) Why Education Projects in Developing Countries Fail: a case study, *International Journal of Educational Development*, 13, pp. 265–275.

Morris, P. W. G. & Hough, G. H. (1987) *The Anatomy of Major Projects: a study of the reality of project management*. Chichester: Wiley.

Smith, H. N. J. (1998) Perceptions of Success in the Management of Aid-funded English Language Teaching Projects, Ph.D. thesis, University of Reading.

Turner, J. R. (1993) *The Handbook of Project-based Management*. London: McGraw-Hill.

Valadez, J. & Bamberger, M. (1994) *Monitoring and Evaluating Social Programs in Developing Countries*. Washington, DC: World Bank.

Transforming Education: participatory approaches for community empowerment

TERRY ALLSOP[1]

Introduction

Joining the Department for International Development (DFID) some 3 years ago, or the Overseas Development Agency (ODA) as it then was, I was clearly an innocent! I had never used the acronyms PRA (Participatory Rural Appraisal), RRA (Rapid Rural Appraisal) or PLA (Participatory Learning and Action); within weeks, I became very fluent and have never looked back. What now worries me occasionally is the dreaded question which my former philosopher colleague John Wilson used always to ask – 'What do you mean by ...?' What I hope to do in this chapter is to explore my own thinking and action over this period, based on work in three African countries – Egypt, Ghana and Nigeria – three very different settings for three very different kinds of approach to DFID work aimed at improving access, equity and quality within basic education, all of which claim to use participatory approaches at some point of the programme activity. And then it seems important that we try to tease out some general implications for our work, be it as donors or academics or whatever.

Meanings and Methods

Just to remind ourselves, an Institute of Development Studies (IDS) Policy Briefing (1996) characterises PRA as 'a family of approaches, methods and behaviours that enable people to express and analyse the realities of their lives and conditions, to plan themselves what action to take, and to monitor and evaluate the results'. Above all, it is perceived as an approach which should give equal status to the 'voices' of all those engaged in the development process, mitigating against the overwhelming advantages held by those who, for example, hold government office or who speak the English language fluently. It has become most clearly identified, for many, with a set of methods which allow local people, usually working in groups, to express and share information visually, through, for example, maps, flow diagrams, seasonal calendars, matrices or grids.

Robert Chambers, in his book *Whose Reality Counts?* (1997), expresses his own anxieties about the growth of interest in PRA, for example:

> *PRA has become an instant fad, demanded by donors in projects and introduced to programmes of NGOs and government departments. It has been made to go to scale too fast. Label has spread without substance. Quality has suffered from the very top–down centralised system which PRA seeks to modify and reverse. The old paradigm has co-opted and contorted the new. The behavioural, professional and institutional implications of PRA have not been understood, or if understood, not internalised. (ch. 10, p. 211)*

As students of educational change, it should hardly surprise us that existing institutions and structures seek to render new approaches less potent by taking them to themselves. Chambers sees dangers to PRA in at least three major areas: top–down fashion and spread; behaviour, attitudes and training; and field practice and ethics. These, in my view, are the areas in which any approach that was perceived to be innovatory would expect to be exposed to false prophets. Perhaps, therefore, we should avoid theology for a while, avoid specialist language, and try to draw understandings from three cases.

Three Cases

Egypt: a literacy project

Illiteracy in Egypt is a huge problem, with recent census figures suggesting around 17.4 million acknowledged illiterates in the adult population, with numbers undoubtedly growing annually as the stretched and modestly performing school system struggles to cope with the growing population of young people. Predictably, the highest proportion of illiterates may be found among women and in the least economically developed governorates (administrative regions), but also within the megalopolis of Cairo and the Nile Delta cities. Responsibility for addressing the problem rests with the General Authority for Literacy and Adult Education (GALAE), an agency which reports to the Minister of Education but which works outside the Ministry and with a separate budget. GALAE is managed at senior level entirely by retired military personnel, who bring a particular management style whilst engaging and heeding good professional advice on matters educational. Their priority, within their mandate, is to establish and maintain literacy classes throughout Egypt, and to achieve high levels of success in the basic tests of literacy and numeracy for which they are responsible. DFID began working with GALAE in what is called the Adult Literacy Training Project (ALTP). The project is helping GALAE to address a number of themes relating to the quality of its operation, for example, in:

- assisting with training of supervisors and key trainers;
- production of teacher training materials;
- production of a handbook for GALAE managers;
- enhanced media presentation; and
- introducing a social/community development dimension to GALAE's work.

The project works through a largely Egyptian team, with one resident United Kingdom adviser, supported by Egyptian and United Kingdom consultants. As well as work with GALAE at the centre in Cairo, fieldwork is focused in two governorates, Qena in Upper Egypt and Menoufia in the delta.

Introducing a social/community development dimension to the literacy programme is the aspect we should concentrate on now, as it has been generated by the Egyptian Social Development adviser to the project, with a significant participatory approach. In each of the two governorates, the project established a small team of field coordinators, based in the local GALAE office, whose task was to engage with 'project' villages in social/community development within the context of literacy work. (Note that 'villages' in Egypt lack a homogeneous image – in the delta they may well be 'towns' with populations of 30,000 with a strong industrial economic base, in Upper Egypt they are more classical rural communities on a much smaller scale.) The coordinators were all female, young social science graduates with a variety of employment backgrounds but no prior experience of literacy work. The GALAE office made appointments of counterparts to work with the coordinators. Both the project's adviser and her coordinator colleagues would probably say they were using PRA approaches; I would prefer to think of them as participatory with PRA affinities. They certainly worked in a very different way from the main GALAE approach. Box 1 attempts to summarise the effects of the participatory process, within GALAE's own organisation and within the literacy programme in the field.

What conclusions may we draw from this experience? Three suggest themselves:

- that developing participatory approaches on a small scale within an agency like GALAE may have a number of unanticipated outcomes relating to the management and institutional behaviour of the agency itself, some positive, some negative;

- that early assessments need to be made of the viability of the approach if it is to be considered for mainstreaming within the work of the agency. There are significant resource issues for the agency, itself already stretched for finance, after the end of the life of the project; and
- that it is too early to make clear evaluative statements about the participatory approach here, as the data are not yet available which shows the literacy achievements of the 'project' villages. Even when available, it will be virtually impossible to show a causal connection with the participatory approach.

Box 1

Early effects

1. Tensions between project coordinators and GALAE staff/counterparts caused by salary differentials, availability of transport, etc.
2. Tensions caused by the project coordinators appearing to be promoting a 'superior' approach to the mainstream of GALAE activity.
3. Early enthusiasm within 'project' villages sparked by participatory approaches introduced by the project coordinators. Many new classes started with volunteer teachers, with community leaders taking a strong lead.

Later effects

1. Integrated working of coordinators and counterparts in both 'project' villages and other sites, as the participatory approach became mainstreamed within GALAE practice. Further integration following United Kingdom study tour by coordinators and counterparts.
2. GALAE monitoring and evaluation procedures modified to allow assessment of outcomes of participatory approaches, to be used at first only in 'project' villages.
3. GALAE head office considering setting up a social/community development unit within its own managerial structure.

One other area of the ALTP work has adopted PRA nomenclature. The project commissioned research by the Cairo-based Centre for Development Studies (CDS) into the post-basic literacy aspirations of those graduating from the literacy programme (CDS, 1997). CDS promotes itself as a centre specialising in the use of PRA techniques. The researchers certainly used a broadly participatory approach, but the study was a good example of researchers using a battery of techniques familiar to all educational researchers working within a qualitative tradition. It was successful in eliciting views from the potential post-literacy student population, which will be very useful to GALAE in planning its future work. The launch of the report, at a seminar in Cairo, triggered more debate about methodology than about the results of the study. Many of the Egyptian academic researchers present were unfamiliar with PRA/qualitative research methodologies as they operate almost entirely with a quantitative, experimental paradigm.

Nigeria: a community education programme

The macro-political climate of Nigeria in the second half of the 1990s may appear to be extremely unfavourably placed for any innovative work in basic education. In its work, DFID is committed to working only with the local, or district, level of government, which thus provides boundaries for the scale of operation of any programme. Additionally, the very large primary school sector suffers from chronic underfunding, with very little incentive for teachers to perform in other than a minimalist mode.

These preconditions actually allowed us to describe a set of boundary conditions within which we would work to develop a potentially useful programme. These included:

- work intensively in a small number of locations;
- focus on enhancement of quality of both primary schooling and adult education;
- use participatory approaches in programme planning;
- use an action research approach throughout the life of the programme, testing key hypotheses relating to describing minimum inputs and responses for sustaining quality education; and
- using Nigerian resources, both human and material, wherever possible.

It is important to note that this programme has been designed to work within the framework of the government-provided primary education system. It is not, as is occurring in a number of African locations, creating what is coming to be called 'non-formal primary schooling', often with the engagement of indigenous or international non-governmental organisations (NGOs). These are important, frequently creative, initiatives which allow quite radical formulations of what is meant by primary schooling. But the programme described here still works within the educational-political belief that national government should be able to commit sufficient of the national resources so as to ensure a certain quality and quantity of primary education for all its citizens. We recognise that this is a fragile belief in many countries in sub-Saharan Africa.

Box 2 shows the complex and lengthy process of design undertaken over several years, for a programme of total value £2.1 million only. The detailed preparation has taken place in only four communities within each of the Local Government Areas (LGA), so even after the start-up of the programme, a great deal of similar preparative work will be undertaken as other communities are brought on-stream. The cost of preparation was high, approximately 10% of the total programme budget. I have needed to argue, when pressed by DFID managers, that the process of educational change actually began in the communities when the participatory preparation process began, and that the distinction between preparation and programme funds is increasingly inappropriate and irrelevant.

Box 2

Nigeria Community Education Programme

Sequence of development:

1993 – Joint ODA/Federal Government of Nigeria mission – support for basic education – move away from secondary/tertiary commitments.
1994 (March) – Further mission agrees to concentrate on poverty-focused, community-based assistance to primary schooling, adult literacy and nomadic communities.
1995 (April) – First participatory rural appraisal mission to four communities. Four separate PRA reports produced.
1995 (September) – In-country workshop, with ODA advisers, to review findings.
1995 (October) – Feedback and validation of reports in communities.
1995 (November) – Project design workshop in Kaduna – 90 participants including consultants, ODA advisers, community members, other stakeholders.
[At this time increased difficulty in working as a bilateral agency in Nigeria]
1995 (end November) – Draft proposals to ODA.
1995 (end December) – Project proposals to ODA West & North Africa Department for appraisal (bid for £2.14 million).
1996 (April) – ODA approval given.
1996 (April–November) – Complex negotiations prior to Nigerian agreement to programme.
1996 (June) – Communities revisited.
1997 (January/February) – Project managers recruited and trained.
1997 (April) – Project start-up workshops.
1997 (December) – First monitoring visits by ODA advisers.

What we now have is a community-based programme, where action plans are devised at local level, submitted to a project management committee for approval, and implemented with the guidance of a locally-recruited project manager. Funds are released on a quarterly basis against these action plans by the Lagos-based programme manager, the only staff member not recruited locally, with careful accounting procedures. The range of allowable expenditures will be subject to only two significant criteria – that they are 'affordable' within a realistically supported recurrent expenditure framework, and that they can be shown to be likely to contribute to quality enhancement in primary schooling or adult education.

Well, coming up for 1 year into the life of the programme, was all the effort worthwhile? What reflections can we offer on the participatory approach? At least the following.

- The two communities in each of the four project areas which participated in the preparation activities have high expectations of the return on their investment of time and commitment. They are extremely articulate in expressing these expectations. Some, after all, have already done their bit by building adult literacy centres and other facilities. The response time of the programme has not been, in my view, consistent with these expectations, perhaps inevitably as we are looking for the development of systems which can be replicated across perhaps 50 communities in an LGA. This has to be a crucial issue in the fragile relationship between donor and recipient community.
- The two communities do not necessarily see that others within the LGA should receive benefits of the same order of magnitude.
- Taking forward the participatory approach into other communities is proving very interesting. Training workshops are priming facilitators to work in a phased process which will eventually reach all the communities. Interesting questions of methodology arise in relation to replication: does every community have to work through all the steps in the process; is it sufficient for the facilitator to identify similarities and differences to previous examples; can we afford the time and human resource inputs?

Ghana – reform of basic education

For two decades following independence, Ghana was noted as a country with an education system which produced high quality outputs, albeit for a minority of young people. There followed a decade of economic crisis when standards in schools plummeted and many members of the teaching force either left to pursue other economic activity, or went to teach in neighbouring West African countries. From 1987, the Government of Ghana attempted to institute important structural and other changes in the education system, focusing particularly on those traditional planks of reform – reshaping of the school structure to a 6–3–4 system, developing new curricula and textbooks, building new schools. These were all necessary inputs, certainly, but by 1995, the reform was widely perceived to have failed, both in relation to standards achieved (very large numbers of students were leaving primary school unable to read and write) and in relation to enrolment (in rural areas many children, particularly girls, remained out of school, and drop-out rates from primary school were high in most areas). It is worth recording that this phase of reform was almost entirely centrally driven, by the Ministry of Education, and to a considerable degree, by donor agency agendas.

From 1995, the Government of Ghana resolved to make a second attempt at significant reform, the legal instrument being the creation of legislation for a programme leading by 2005 to Free, Compulsory, Universal, Basic Education for all Ghanaian children – the so-called FCUBE programme, which has received endorsement at the highest level in Ghana. Prior to the official launch of FCUBE in mid-1996, both Government and donors collaborated in preparatory studies across all aspects of the sector, led by the World Bank. Most bilateral donors, along with the World Bank and European Union, have become involved. This time around, the language of all those involved in the reform has a distinctively participatory flavour, which appears to recognise the earlier lack of engagement of key stakeholders. Three examples, working from different starting points within the system, may give a flavour.

(a) There is a new determination within the leadership of the Ministry of Education that the key unit in the reform shall be the district (of which there are 110 in Ghana, typically holding responsibility for around 200 primary and junior secondary schools). New approaches to financial and resource management are being tested, in order to provide district level professionals with the necessary resources to effect change. Newly formed District Education Oversight Committees, not just formed from the ranks of education professionals, will have quality assurance functions, as will the School Management Committees, which will have much broader community membership and wider powers than the existing PTAs. It is much too early to know whether these increased local participatory structures will provide additional dynamic for the reform process.

(b) Within the central Ministry of Education/Ghana Education Service, some experimentation is taking place with the use of participatory techniques to engage more fully both districts and communities in key elements of the reform. An interesting example is the approach being taken by the Girls' Education Unit (GEU) within the Ghana Education Service. They are about to utilise what they are calling PLA (Participatory Learning in Action) approaches in trial communities in two districts to: help communities identify the constraints to girls' successful participation in basic schooling; identify the existing resources for overcoming constraints; and develop and implement an action plan mobilising these resources.

(c) Arising from earlier donor activity in primary education renewal, specifically the Primary School Development Project supported by the World Bank, there was considerable concern that communities were not participating in schooling affairs in any meaningful way, this in the context of very poor learning outcomes and high levels of teacher indiscipline. A mechanism to stimulate community interest and action was thus proposed and came to be called the Schooling Improvement Fund (SIF). The challenge was to design a community-based strategy that would couple limited incentives with effective animation to improve the education environment. In this way, it was hoped that communities could be energised and effectively empowered to take initiatives to improve education delivery and to begin to make legitimate demands on the education system. In three pilot districts, community animation has been undertaken by a Ghanaian NGO, Centre for the Development of People (CEDEP), involving all local stakeholders in the production of a schooling improvement plan. After only 1 year of operation, it is too early to make substantive assessments, but a number of interesting points have emerged. The role of the education professionals can be dominant at the level of the individual school, but the district-level professionals have not exerted particular pressures. What is very striking is that neither education professionals nor community members have generally shown much awareness of the kinds of changes which would make for enhanced quality of learning, which is the whole point of the exercise. For example, funding requests have been dominated by infrastructure and extra-curricular items, rather than those inputs which would improve the classroom environment for both teachers and learners. It is simply not clear at this stage whether the SIF approach will provide lasting benefits, and there are clearly questions to be asked about sustainability.

Implications

Although the 1997 DFID White Paper does not talk of participatory approaches directly, they presumably provide an essential underpinning to any partnership which claims to address the needs of those in a society who live in poverty. What I hope is clear from the three examples we have discussed, is that the principle of adopting a participatory approach is pertinent to a wide range of contexts, from the small-scale local project, to the national sector-wide programme. What also seems to follow is that each environment for support is unique, and that purveyors of recipe-like approaches should be treated with the utmost caution. What we need is a heuristic methodology which, with each context, takes us back to fundamental questions of the 'why' and 'what' type rather than the 'how' questions of technique. And we shall need many more practitioners, in ministries, NGOs and community organisations, who can work with the necessary methodologies; donor agencies should support quality training for these groups. What, on the other hand, we seem to know little about is how far it is possible to go in engaging community organisations in low-income countries in the necessary reshaping of basic schools in order to escape from the prevailing low standards of pupil achievement. Ironically, we shall not find much evidence from the study of more developed school systems.

Note

[1] The views expressed in this chapter are those of the author alone.

References

Chambers, R. (1997) *Whose Reality Counts? Putting the First Last*. London: IT Publications.

Centre for Development Studies (1997) The Post-literacy Aspirations of Adult Learners, Centre for Development Studies/Overseas Development Agency, Mimeo.

Department for International Development (DFID) (1997) *Eliminating World Poverty: a challenge for the twenty-first century*. London: DFID.

IDS Policy Briefing (1996) *The Power of Participation: PRA and policy*. Brighton: Institute of Development Studies.

Notes on Contributors

Terry Allsop is a Senior Education Adviser with the United Kingdom Department for International Development (DFID). At the time of writing this chapter, he combined work in West and North Africa with responsibility for DFID's educational research portfolio. He is now based in Harare, with regional responsibilities in Central Africa. Prior to joining DFID in 1995, he had spent many years as a science teacher educator, first in Uganda, then in the Universities of Hong Kong and Oxford, and also as a science/technology adviser and science teacher.

Mark Bray is Director of the Comparative Education Research Centre at the University of Hong Kong. He previously taught in secondary schools in Kenya and Nigeria, and at the Universities of Edinburgh, Papua New Guinea and London. Since 1994, he has been Assistant Secretary General of the World Council of Comparative Education Societies, and during the period 1998–2000, he was President of the Comparative Education Society of Hong Kong. He has published extensively in the field of comparative education.

Michael Crossley is a Reader in the Graduate School of Education at the University of Bristol, where he is Director for MPhil/PhD Studies. Dr Crossley was previously Associate Dean (Planning) in the Faculty of Education at the University of Papua New Guinea and has taught in England, Australia and Papua New Guinea. He was Editor of the *Papua New Guinea Journal of Education* from 1985 to 1990; and is currently a member of the Editorial Board for *Comparative Education* and an Executive Editor for the *International Journal of Educational Development*. He is a Founding Series Editor for the *Bristol Papers in Education*; and has recently published (with Graham Vulliamy) *Qualitative Educational Research in Developing Countries* (New York: Garland, 1997); and (with Keith Holmes) *Educational Development in the Small States of the Commonwealth: retrospect and prospect* (London: Commonwealth Secretariat, 1999). Current research interests include evaluation partnerships in Kenya, research capacity in small states and methodological and theoretical studies on the future of the field of comparative and international education.

Danuta Elsner is a freelance consultant on educational management. She has been involved in several Polish and European projects on school and educational improvement. From 1994 to 1995 she was Chairperson of the European Network for Improving Research and Development in Educational Management. Dr Elsner is the author/co-author of over 130 publications, among them 10 books. She currently lectures in Educational and School Management in a number of Polish higher educational institutions.

Leslie Groves is currently undertaking a PhD at the Department of Social Anthropology, University of Edinburgh. A keen child rights advocate, she has been actively involved with young people and children since 1992. She has worked with various national and international non-governmental organisations as well as with the Department for International Development (DFID). Her primary research interests have centred on the education and social development of street and working children in Brazil, Vietnam and Tanzania.

Petros Hailemariam is Director General of the Department of Research and Human Resources Development of the Ministry of Education in Eritrea. Prior to independence in 1991, he served as Director of the Revolution School (1982–84); as Assistant Head of the Department of Education, of the EPLF (1984–87) and as Tutor of the Cadres School, Department of National Guidance (1987–91). Since independence, he has been 'Editor-in-Chief' of *Haddas Eritrea* [New Eritrea] (1993–95) and then Director General, Department of Print Media and News Agency, Ministry of Information (1995–97).

Jacques Hallak is Director of the International Institute for Educational Planning and the International Bureau of Education (UNESCO). Since 1994, he has been Assistant Director-General for UNESCO. He is the author, or co-author, of numerous books and articles on educational costs and finance, human resource development, educational research and planning capacity, and comparative perspectives on policies for educational change and development.

David Johnson is a psychologist and senior lecturer in the Graduate School of Education, University of Bristol. Dr Johnson has made an active contribution to the processes of political transition and educational transformation in South Africa and has been involved in educational change in many African, Asian and Latin American countries. Between 1991 and 1996, Dr Johnson mounted a large programme, based at the University of Bristol, which sought to increase the institutional capacity of educational management, planning and research in South Africa. He has also been involved in innovative projects aimed at achieving educational change in countries such as Pakistan, Belize, The Gambia and Malawi. Dr Johnson is joint coordinator of the Graduate School's CLIO Centre for International and

Comparative Studies and director of a number of research projects in literacy and learning.

Mike Kiernan has been working in developing countries since 1967, mostly in Africa, but also in Asia. He is currently working as Education Sector Adviser to the Ministry of Education, Malawi, in the area of educational planning, but has worked in teacher education, curriculum development, basic education and quality assurance. Mike Kiernan has worked with the Department for International Development, the World Bank, UNESCO and UNICEF, but mostly with Danish International Development Assistance (Danida). When not abroad, he is resident in Denmark, though he is said to be still unmistakably Irish.

Talvi Märja is an elected Member of the Estonian Parliament and has served for many years as Professor of Adult Education and as Chair of Andragogy at the Pedagogical University in Tallinn. Professor Märja, who is well known in educational circles in central and eastern Europe, has participated in numerous international conferences on adult education. She has also been very instrumental in the preparation and implementation of the Estonian Adult Education Act of 1993.

Susan Mathieson has been education researcher for the African National Congress's Parliamentary Research Department in South Africa since 1996. She was formerly working at the Centre for University Education Development at the University of Natal. She has an MA in Post-colonial Literary Theory from the University of Natal and a joint honours in Sociology and Law from the University of Warwick.

Teame Mebrahtu lectures in education and development at the University of Bristol, and is the coordinator of this area of study at the MEd level within the Graduate School of Education. He is the Director of the Bristol–Eritrea Partnership Project, which designs and implements summer in-service programmes for over 200 primary school heads, supervisors and district education officers in Asmara, Eritrea. During the last 18 years, he has served as Programme Tutor to postgraduate students from overseas, as Admissions Tutor and as Coordinator of the personal tutor scheme. Nationally, he has served as an Executive Committee Member of the United Kingdom Council for Overseas Students' Affairs (UKCOSA), World University Service, UK (WUS) and Christian Aid. His research and teaching interests include development theories, educational management and administration, and policy in developing countries relating to higher education, teacher education, multicultural education and the educational needs of refugees and ethnic minorities. He has written extensively on these topics and has made entries to the *International Encyclopaedia of Higher Education* and the *International Encyclopaedia of Education*. His interests in the global dimension of education and in the role of higher education in national and global development have led him to organise various international conferences, to undertake related consultancies and to be invited as a keynote speaker in international fora.

Blade N'zimande was, at the time of writing this chapter, an MP for the African National Congress and Chair of the Education Portfolio Committee in the National Assembly in the South African Parliament. He has a PhD in Industrial and Labour Studies from the Department of Sociology at the University of Natal. Prior to becoming an MP, he was Director of the Education Policy Unit at the University of Natal from 1985 to 1989. He is currently Secretary General of the South African Communist Party.

Harvey Smith has worked on aid-funded education projects and consultancies for over 20 years, including periods as lecturer, adviser, consultant and project director in institutions and ministries of education in Barbados, Cambodia, Egypt, Mali, Sri Lanka and Zambia. His PhD was on the management of aid-funded English teaching projects in developing countries. Since 1997, he has been Senior Education Adviser at CfBT Education Services.

Bernhard Streitwieser is a PhD candidate at Teachers' College, Columbia University, New York City, USA. His research interests concern educational transformations in the new Federal States of Germany, school reform, and teacher training. His publications deal with the ongoing teacher adjustment process in former East Germany.

Cynthia Thompson is currently the Principal of Belize Teachers' College in Belize City. Ms Thompson directed the implementation of the Teacher Education Component of the Belize Primary Education Development Project, which is designed to reform primary education in Belize. In her capacity as Principal and in her work with the project, Ms Thompson has been involved in the planning, development and implementation of reform efforts nationwide.

Larissa Jõgi is Assistant Professor of Adult Education in the Department of Andragogy, Tallinn Pedagogical University, Estonia. Between 1990 and 1999, Dr Jõgi has participated in 35 international conferences and seminars, chaired eight sessions, and has written 19 reports. During the last 5 years she has been involved in several adult education projects including the PHARE Distance Education Project in the Baltic countries. Her main research interests revolve around the sociological aspects of the development of adult education and adults as learners.

Keith Watson is Professor of Comparative and International Education and Director of the Centre for International Studies in Education, Management and Training at the University of Reading. He is Chair of the UK Forum on International Education and Training and Editor in Chief of the *International Journal of Educational Development*. He is the author of *Key Issues in Education* (Croom Helm, 1985), *Educational*

Development in Thailand (Heinemann, 1980) and editor of the four-volume series *Educational Dilemmas: debate and diversity* (Cassell, 1997), and *Doing Comparative Educational Research* (Symposium Books, 2000). He has written over 100 research papers and his main areas of research are in language policies, education in developing countries, with special reference to South-East Asia and Southern Africa, and educational administration and policy-making.

Oxford Studies in Comparative Education

Series Editor: David Phillips, University of Oxford

Forthcoming 2000
Education in Germany Since Unification
Edited by David Phillips
ISBN 1 873927 73 8

Published recently
Education Systems of the United Kingdom
Edited by David Phillips
ISBN 1 873927 73 8

Comparing Standards Internationally:
research and practice in mathematics and beyond
Edited by Barbara Jaworski & David Phillips
ISBN 1 873927 68 1

Processes of Transition in Education Systems
Edited by Elizabeth A. McLeish & David Phillips
ISBN 1 873927 48 7

Education for Reconstruction: the regeneration
of educational capacity following national upheaval
Nina Arnhold, Julia Bekker, Natasha Kersh,
Elizabeth A. McLeish & David Phillips
ISBN 1 873927 43 6

Education and Privatisation in Eastern Europe and the Baltic Republics
Edited by Paul Beresford-Hill
ISBN 1 873927 38 X

Education and Change in the Pacific Rim: meeting the challenges
Edited by Keith Sullivan
ISBN 1 873927 33 9

For full contents of these titles and others in
this series see www.symposium-books.co.uk

SYMPOSIUM BOOKS, PO BOX 65, WALLINGFORD
OXFORD OX10 0YG, UNITED KINGDOM
Voice: +44 (0) 1491-838 056 Fax: +44 (0) 1491-834 968 orders@symposium-books.co.uk

NEW FROM SYMPOSIUM BOOKS

Learning from Comparing: new directions in comparative educational research
Volume 1. Contexts, Classrooms and Outcomes
Edited by ROBIN ALEXANDER,
PATRICIA BROADFOOT & DAVID PHILLIPS
ISBN 1 873927 58 4 (1999)
Volume 2. Policy, Professionals and Development
Edited by ROBIN ALEXANDER,
MARILYN OSBORN & DAVID PHILLIPS
ISBN 1 873927 63 0 (2000)

Globalisation, Educational Transformation and Societies in Transition
Edited by TEAME MEBRAHTU, MICHAEL CROSSLEY
& DAVID JOHNSON
ISBN 1 873927 78 5 (2000)

Doing Comparative Education Research: issues and problems
Edited by KEITH WATSON
ISBN 1 873927 83 5 (due 2001)

Monographs in International Education
Operation Blackboard: policy implementation in Indian elementary education
CAROLINE DYER
ISBN 1 873927 88 6 (2000)

Modularisation of Vocational Education in Europe: NVQs and GNVQs as a model for the reform of initial training provisions in Germany?
HUBERT ERTL
ISBN 1 873927 98 3 (2000)

Reschooling and the Global Future: politics, economics and the English experience
JAMES PORTER
ISBN 1 873927 53 3 (1999)

For the full contents of all Symposium books, their prices and
an order form, please see www.symposium-books.co.uk

SYMPOSIUM BOOKS PO BOX 65 WALLINGFORD OXFORD OX10 0YG UNITED KINGDOM
Voice: +44 (0) 1491-838 056 Fax: +44 (0) 1491-834 968 orders@symposium-books.co.uk